Peoples and Places

Peoples and Places

How Geography Impacts Missions Strategy

MATTHEW HIRT

Foreword by Daniel L. Akin

WIPF & STOCK · Eugene, Oregon

PEOPLES AND PLACES
How Geography Impacts Missions Strategy

Copyright © 2022 Matthew Hirt. All rights reserved. Except for brief quotations in critical publications or reviews, no part of this book may be reproduced in any manner without prior written permission from the publisher. Write: Permissions, Wipf and Stock Publishers, 199 W. 8th Ave., Suite 3, Eugene, OR 97401.

Wipf & Stock
An Imprint of Wipf and Stock Publishers
199 W. 8th Ave., Suite 3
Eugene, OR 97401

www.wipfandstock.com

PAPERBACK ISBN: 978-1-6667-3334-1
HARDCOVER ISBN: 978-1-6667-2790-6
EBOOK ISBN: 978-1-6667-2791-3

05/25/22

Unless otherwise indicated, all Scripture quotations are from The Holy Bible, English Standard Version® (ESV®), copyright © 2001 by Crossway, a publishing ministry of Good News Publishers. Used by permission. All rights reserved.

Biblia Hebraica Stuttgartensia, edited by Karl Elliger and Wilhelm Rudolph; 5th rev. ed., edited by Adrian Schenker, © 1977 and 1997 Deutsche Bibelgesellschaft, Stuttgart. Used by permission.

The Greek New Testament, 5th rev. ed., edited by Barbara Aland, Kurt Aland, Karavidopoulos Iōan. D, Carlo Maria Martini, Bruce M Metzger, and Holger Strutwolf, © 2017 Deutsche Bibelgesellschaft, Stuttgart. Used by permission.

To my favorite ministry partner,

My loving wife, best friend, and travel buddy,

Heather L. Hirt

Contents

Foreword by Daniel L. Akin | ix
Acknowledgments | xiii
Abbreviations | xv

1 Make Disciples of Peoples *in* Places | 1
2 A Biblical Theology of Land in Relation to National Identity | 15
3 A Biblical Case Study for Implementing Contextual Geography in Missions Strategy: Paul's Use of ΚΥΚΛΩ in Romans 15:19 | 62
4 What Is a People Group? | 103
5 Emics and Etics: A Proposal for Discovering Emic Geography and Developing Contextual Missions Strategy | 144
6 Conclusion | 184

Bibliography | 199
Subject Index | 221
Ancient Document Index | 227

Foreword

LAST WORDS ARE MEANT to be lasting words. They are meant to make an impact. They are meant to leave an impression and make a difference. As Jesus was preparing to ascend back into heaven following his three year sojourn on this Earth as "heaven's missionary," there are a number of things he could have given as his final instructions. He could have told us to love one another, giving attention to our moral life. He could have urged us to obey the commands of God, giving attention to our ethical life. He could have warned us about false teaching, giving attention to our doctrinal life. All of these are critically important and worthy of our careful attention and devotion. And yet, Jesus chose to focus on our missional life with his parting words: "Go and make disciples of all nations" (Matt 28:19). Our King has told us to go and to go to the nations, the *ethne*. We go and we make disciples, devoted followers of Jesus, because that is what our King told us to do.

In his book *What in the World Is God Doing?*, Allen Fleece is exactly right: "This is the decision we do not make, because it has already been made. Whether we spend our lives for the purpose of reaching all men with the gospel is not optional. Christ has commanded every Christian to do just this. Now, there are many different ways of accomplishing this one purpose—but regardless of the particular work God has for each of us to do, the one aim of us all in doing our particular job for the Lord must be the evangelization of the whole world."

Each of us as followers of the crucified Galilean have been commissioned and commanded by our sovereign King to go and evangelize the whole world. Every single person of the seven-plus billion people on planet Earth is to be the object of our evangelizing passion. Every single person of the thousands of people groups in the world is to be the focus of our mission strategies. Every single person of the far too many unreached people groups is to be the assignment of the people of God. And every single person of the almost three thousand unengaged people groups (no gospel presence at all) must not be left out of our pleas to the Father to "send forth laborers into his harvest" (Matt 9:37–38). The gospel of Jesus Christ is for all nations. It is for all peoples.

But there is an important question we must raise: "Exactly what does our Lord mean when he tells us to make disciples of the *ethne*?" Further, it is wise to ask, "How does the whole of Scripture define or explain the idea of *ethne* or nations?" In recent decades it has been popular to think of the *ethne* primarily in terms that are ethnolinguistic, focusing almost exclusively on language and sociocultural similarities. Each of these categories are certainly important but they do not tell the whole story. In fact, these markers pay little or no attention to bibilical-theological categories. This is an issue that desperately needs to be addressed.

Matthew and Heather Hirt are dear friends of my wife, Charlotte, and me. They are both graduates of Southeastern Baptist Theological Seminary in Wake Forest, North Carolina, and at the time of my writing this foreword (December 2021) are serving with the International Mission Board of the Southern Baptist Convention in Nigeria. Further, they are both gifted thinker, as this book, *Peoples and Places: How Geography Impacts Missions Strategy*, by Matthew makes very clear. Matthew opened my eyes to a vital component in reaching the nations with the gospel I had neglected: the importance of geography and national (nations) identity. In this book Matthew Hirt makes a persuasive argument that when we craft our missions strategy, we must learn to think *within* the world of a people group as well as from the *outside* (where we inevitably must start). We also must remember three important biblical-theological truths: 1) God created the lands and the people (nations) who live in them; 2) the "land" often functions in the Bible as a substitute for the people who live in that land; and 3) a nation's identity is profoundly formed and shaped by its relationship to the land they occupy.

This is an essential work for future missiology. This book fills an important gap too often missing in missiological thinking and strategy. It is an honor and joy to commend its widest reading as the church faithfully seeks to fulfill the final marching orders of King Jesus.

Daniel L. Akin
President
Southeastern Baptist Theological Seminary
Wake Forest, North Carolina

Acknowledgments

I GIVES THANKS FIRST to my Lord and Savior, Jesus Christ. He saved me from being an atheist antagonistic to Christian faith and has called me to serve him to the ends of the Earth.

Thanks to George Robinson for being a mentor, a friend, and a faithful partner in the Great Commission. I am indebted to you for a single question over a cup of coffee over a decade ago that resulted in this book.

Thanks to Ricky Persons. You have been a wonderful pastor and ministry mentor. I have learned much from you, and I sincerely miss our hallway conversations over whatever was on our minds that day—whether it was a hard passage we were preparing to preach, a particularly profound insight, or simply sharing a funny story with one another.

Thanks to the SEBTS library staff, who scanned and emailed countless journal articles and book portions both while I was not on campus and during the COVID-19 pandemic.

Thanks to my chat group: Anna Daub, Keelan Cook, and Christy Thornton. There is no way I could have made it through this without all of you. Sharing our ideas with one another has made me a better scholar. Our conversations about the significant events of the day and our humorous comments have added a lot of fun to this wild journey we are on together.

Lastly, I could never have accomplished what I have without my creative and beautiful wife, Heather Hirt. You endured stacks of books and journal articles scattered around the house, random sticky notes, chapter outlines written on bathroom mirrors with dry-erase markers, and probably a lot of other things that I can't remember. Your encouragement when I was frustrated or exhausted has been the most valuable blessing. You are my favorite ministry partner and I look forward to making disciples with you wherever the Lord may lead us.

Abbreviations

AAS	*Acta Apostolicae Sedis*
AB	Anchor Bible
ABD	*Anchor Bible Dictionary*
ANF	Ante-Nicene Fathers
ApOTC	Apollos Old Testament Commentary
BDAG	Bauer, Walter, Frederick William Danker, ,W. F. Arndt, and F. W. Gingrich, eds., *A Greek-English Lexicon of the New Testament and Other Early Christian Literature*, 3rd ed. (Chicago: University of Chicago Press, 2000)
BDB	Brown, Francis, S. R. Driver, and Charles A. Briggs, *A Hebrew and English Lexicon of the Old Testament* (Peabody, MA: Hendrickson, 1997)
BECNT	Baker Exegetical Commentary on the New Testament
BNP	*Brill's New Pauly: Encyclopedia of the Ancient World*, edited by Hubert Cancik, Helmuth Schneider, and Christine F. Salazar, 20 vols. (Leiden: Brill, 2002–2010)
BSac	*Bibliotheca Sacra*
CEB	Common English Bible

CSB	Christians Standard Bible
EBC	Expositor's Bible Commentary
ESV	English Standard Version
HALOT	*The Hebrew and Aramaic Lexicon of the Old Testament*, by Ludwid Koehler and Walter Baumgartner, edited by Walter Baumgartner and Johann Jakob Stamm, translated by M. E. J. Richardson, rev. ed. (Leiden: Brill, 1994)
IJFM	*International Journal of Frontier Missions*
IMB	International Mission Board of the Southern Baptist Convention
JBL	*Journal of Biblical Literature*
JJS	*Journal of Jewish Studies*
KJV	King James Version
LCL	Loeb Classical Library
LEB	Lexham English Bible
LOP1	Lausanne Movement, "The Pasadena Consultation: Homogeneous Unit Principle," Lausanne Occasional Paper 1 (1977)
LSJ	H. G. Liddell, R. Scott, and H. S. Jones, *A Greek-English Lexicon*, 9th ed. (Oxford: Clarendon, 1996)
LXX	Septuagint
NASB	New American Standard Bible
NAC	New American Commentary
NICNT	New International Commentary on the New Testament
NICOT	New International Commentary on the Old Testament
NIDNTTE	*New International Dictionary of New Testament Theology and Exegesis*, edited by Moisés Silva (Grand Rapids: Zondervan, 2014)
NIDOTTE	*New International Dictionary of Old Testament Theology and Exegesis*, edited by Willem A. VanGemeren (Grand Rapids: Zondervan, 1997)
NIGTC	New International Greek Testament Commentary

NIV	New International Version
NKJV	New King James Version
NPNF¹	*Nicene and Post-Nicene Fathers*, series 1
NRSV	New Revised Standard Version
NSBT	New Studies in Biblical Theology
NTS	*New Testament Studies*
RSV	Revised Standard Version
RTR	*Reformed Theological Review*
TDNT	*Theological Dictionary of the New Testament*, Edited by G. Kittel and G. Friedrich, translated by G. W. Bromiley, 10 vols. (Grand Rapids, 1964–1976)
TDOT	*Theological Dictionary of the Old Testament*, edited by G. J. Botterweck and H. Ringgren, translated by J. T. Willis, G. W. Bromiley, and D. E. Green, 9 vols. (Grand Rapids, 1974–)
TJ	*Trinity Journal*
TynBul	*Tyndale Bulletin*
WBC	Word Biblical Commentary
WUNT	Wissenschaftliche Untersuchungen zum Neuen Testament
ZAW	*Zeitschrift für die alttestamentliche Wissenschaft*
ZNW	*Zeitschrift für die neutestamentliche Wissenschaft und die Kunde der älteren Kirche*

1

Make Disciples of Peoples *in* Places

JESUS COMMANDS HIS FOLLOWERS to make disciples of all "nations" (ἔθνη). A persistent question in contemporary missiology is: Who are the ἔθνη? It has been assumed and accepted in the last few decades that ἔθνη refers to ethnolinguistic people groups. The argument is made primarily on anthropological grounds rather than on a scriptural and theological foundation. Scriptural evidence exhibits a broader definition of the ἔθνη, however. The Bible indicates that several factors are taken into consideration when defining the ἔθνη. While language and family/ethnicity are included among the characteristics, geography is also an important aspect of how the Bible classifies the various ἔθνη (Gen 10:1–32; Deut 32:8; 1 Chr 14:17; Isa 37:18; Jer 12:17; Ezek 5:6; Luke 24:47; Acts 1:8; Rom 15:19; Rev 21–22).

One of the first questions asked when meeting someone in many places in the world is: "Where are you from?" It is difficult to separate humanity completely from its geographical location. When contemporary people group research defines ἔθνη primarily or exclusively in ethnolinguistic terms with little or no attention given to geography, it overlooks a critical component of how humanity defines itself. Geography as a facet of human identity must be reincorporated into a scriptural understanding of the nations.

While geography must be considered when distinguishing people groups, one must ask, "Whose geography?" Geographical terms and the importance associated with geographical features are usually culturally informed. What may appear to be an insignificant landmark to an outsider may appear as an inviolable barrier to an insider. For evidence, one need look no further than the often-invisible borders that demark geopolitical entities. Concepts of what are important and unimportant geographical divisions cannot be imported from the outside (etic) but must be considered from the perspective of the people groups themselves (emic). Contextualized geography is geography taken from the emic perspective for the purpose of understanding significant cultural distinctives leading to the development of a localized missions strategy.

This book will attempt to show that a scriptural missions strategy must take into account a biblical-theological definition of the nations that includes geography as a major category, and, more specifically, should take into consideration local contextual views of geographical boundaries.

Importance of the Topic

A "nation" is notoriously difficult to define. Walter Bagehot cleverly observed, "We know what [a nation] is when you do not ask us, but we cannot very quickly explain it or define it."[1] However difficult, defining the term is essential for developing missions strategy. First, Jesus commands his disciples to make disciples of all the ἔθνη, commonly translated as "nations."[2] This means that being obedient to Christ requires understanding the term ἔθνη on scriptural and theological grounds. Second, the way that one defines ἔθνη impacts what is emphasized in missions strategy. When ἔθνη was understood as geopolitical nation-states, missions strategy tended to focus on establishing national Christian councils.[3] When the definition shifted, the strategy shifted accordingly. Instead of establishing church councils that operated within geopolitical borders,

---

1. Bagehot, *Physics and Politics*, 20–21. Despite the fact that Bagehot's quote is rather old, his reflection is still relevant today in that many people neglect to define what a "nation" is, choosing to assume that there is an agreed-upon definition that they are using.

2. BDAG, "ἔθνος," 276.

3. Wrogemann, *Theologies of Mission*, 61. Wrogemann explains that the Western-imposed arbitrary territorial boundaries established in colonial regions resulted in Western missions efforts to focus on establishing groups of churches that were connected under the banner of these national church councils.

missions strategists began focusing more on planting churches among ethnolinguistic people groups.

Ἔθνος was a complex term in the first century, possessing a broad semantic range that makes the word difficult to translate.[4] Definitions of ἔθνος from the middle of the twentieth century were far from uniform, but almost all of them neglected a geographic component.[5] Donald McGavran defined a "people" (later a "homogeneous unit") as "a social organism which, by virtue of the fact that its members intermarry very largely within its own confines, becomes a separate race in their minds."[6] McGavran's definition is strictly sociological and explicitly related to intermarriage. Later iterations of McGavran's definition are broadened to include other aspects including geography, but the overwhelming emphasis still remains on sociological divisions.[7] While sociology may certainly impact geography, it must be determined whether geography can also impact sociological and anthropological divisions.

The first definition of a homogeneous unit adopted by the Lausanne Committee for World Evangelization at the Pasadena Consultation builds on McGavran's early definition indicating that "a [homogeneous unit] is 'a section of society in which all members have some characteristic in common . . .' To be more precise, the common bond may be geographical, ethnic, linguistic, social, educational, vocational, or economic, or a combination of several of these and other factors."[8] The definition of a "people group" accepted at the Chicago Consultation by the Strategy Working Group of the Lausanne Committee for World Evangelization minimized, but did not definitively eliminate, geography as a defining characteristic. Dayton conveys that a people group is "A significantly large sociological grouping of individuals who perceive themselves to

---

4. See page 153 of this book for a brief discussion on the various ways that ἔθνος is translated.

5. This may possibly be due to the potential confusion between geography and geopolitical units. Further research would be required to determine whether this is causation or correlation.

6. McGavran, *Bridges of God*, 9.

7. McGavran explicitly relates geography to sociological distinctions. He maintains, "Where people live, their geographical location, is an obvious part of the social structure and greatly affects church growth. Throughout Hindu India, the depressed-class ward has been separated from the rest of the village by physical distance—often a hundred yards or more." This is an example of sociology impacting geography, but not the reverse. McGavran, *Understanding Church Growth* (3rd ed.), 157.

8. LOP1.

have a common affinity for one another. From the viewpoint of evangelization this is the largest possible group within which the gospel can spread without encountering barriers of understanding or acceptance."[9] This definition was intended to set the trajectory for missions strategy going forward. However, while maintaining the "people group" term and even affirming similar definitions, the function and use of "people group" changed relatively quickly, further pressing geographical considerations into the background.[10]

Ralph Winter, who began the discussion about hidden peoples at Lausanne in 1974, seemingly downplayed geographic categories. His Lausanne address focused more on the number of languages than any other culturally defining category.[11] Winter discussed geography in the broadest terms possible and primarily to demonstrate that the previous geopolitical models resulted in significant population segments being overlooked (i.e., hidden peoples).[12] Winter did include a place for geography within his concept of "unimax people groups," but it was limited to cases where ethnolinguistic people groups were geographically isolated. Winter did, however, leave open the possibility of other factors besides language playing a significant role in people group identity.[13]

The ethnolinguistic designation has become the primary or sole definition, but neither the specific process by which that definition is

9. Dayton, "Reaching the Unreached Peoples," 32–33.

10. John Robb references the Lausanne Committee's definition, but reveals where the emphasis is when he explains, "These cultural, linguistic and other similarities are the basis upon which people communicate, interact and influence one another's values and way of life." He further shifts terminology referring to "ethnolinguistic peoples" in India and Los Angeles. He does not completely reject the significance of geography, but he intentionally diminishes its importance in favor of ethnic and linguistic factors. Robb, *Focus!*, 8–11. Kent Parks similarly overlooks the role of geography in the original people group definition when he asserts that "a people group may have a variety of defining factors which might include ethno-linguistic or ethno-cultural/religious elements, and may legitimately have unique elements (such as caste factors in India) but it will consist of various strata." Parks, "What Happened?"

11. Winter, "Highest Priority," 213–25.

12. Winter speaks in broad geographical categories such as the Western world, Africa, and Asia. In a few instances, he addresses individual countries such as Nigeria, India, and Pakistan. Winter, "Highest Priority," 228–34.

13. Winter explains, "Religion, class distinctions, education, political and ideological convictions, historical enmity between clans or tribes, customs and behaviors, etc., all have potential to develop strong sociocultural boundaries within ethnolinguistic clusters of unimax peoples." Winter and Koch, "Finishing the Task," 19.

determined nor the method by which people groups are differentiated is entirely clear. Jim Slack presented to the 2003 Joint ISFM/EFMA meeting that the τὰ ἔθνη are exclusively ethnolinguistic people groups.[14] He states that "the 'ta ethne' in the Old Testament, the New Testament, and specifically in the Great Commission are the ethnolinguistic people groups then and now."[15] In the course of providing evidence for his position, he specifically rejects geography as a defining characteristic of the ἔθνη. Additionally, the International Mission Board of the Southern Baptist Convention (IMB) places the linguistic category as the primary defining characteristic and subsumes all other factors under the less-defined category of ethnicity. Jenkins asserts, "A 'people group' is an ethnolinguistic group with a common self-identity that is shared by the various members . . . Language is a primary and dominant identifying factor of a people group. But there are other factors that determine or are associated with ethnicity."[16] The only mention of geography is when the same ethnolinguistic people group lives in multiple geopolitical locations. The IMB shifted from geographic regions to affinity groups which focused more on ethnic relationships rather than geographic locations.[17] Reducing the biblical ἔθνη to single primary factor is a significant departure from the original definition of a people group and runs counter to biblical evidence. The IMB has begun to make some efforts to address geography by describing their priority as "Reaching unreached people groups and places with the Gospel."[18]

The 4k Project, a missions strategy that is still in its infancy, does incorporate geography, but it does so in an arbitrary manner. Boehme explains, "The goal of Project 4K is to engage millions of Christians worldwide in adopting an Omega Zone of the world for concentrated prayer, personal visits, mission teams, financial support, and long-term

---

14. Slack, "'*Ta Ethne*' Ethnolinguistic People Group Focus."

15. Slack, "'*Ta Ethne*' Ethnolinguistic People Group Focus."

16. Jenkins further explains that the other factors involved associated with ethnicity are "self-name and a *sense of common identity* of individuals identified with the group. A *common history, customs, family and clan identities*, as well as marriage rules and practices, age-grades and other obligation covenants, and inheritance patterns and rules are some of the common ethnic factors defining or distinguishing a people." Jenkins, "What Is a People Group?"

17. Rankin, "International Mission Board Report" (2010), 174.

18. IMB, *Foundations*, 40–41.

ministry."[19] The project divides the world into four thousand "Omega Zones" and then categorizes them based on the A, B, or C classification from the World Christian Database. However, the geographical divisions simply utilize existing geopolitical boundaries. The attempt to incorporate geography and divide the missions task into "bite-sized pieces" is laudable, but its exclusive use of etic geography combined with the traditional ethnolinguistic approach does not significantly differ from other current models.[20]

Several recent blog and journal articles also indicate that many are reconsidering the concept of people groups especially in relation to the concept of geography.[21] Carlson and Clark express, "The most significant issue with defining *panta ta ethne* as 'ethnolinguistic people groups' is simple: to do so adopts a modern anthropological definition over a biblical-theological one."[22] Similarly, Williams and Moss argue, "Much contemporary missiological theory assumes a modern social-scientific definition for ἔθνη ... This line of thinking results in casting world missions primarily in terms of engaging socioculturally differentiated 'people groups.' Yet one could well question the legitimacy of interpreting the Great Commission through the controlling lens of modern anthropology."[23] While many authors have contributed to the discussion, few have offered any solution.

Why Geography?

Geography is an important aspect of the biblical definition of the nations. First, the biblical origin of the nations included geography as a significant category by which the nations were divided. Genesis 10:5, 20, and 31 stress that the descendants of Noah were divided according to their nations (גוֹי),

---

19. Boehme, *Fourth Wave*, 145.

20. The training material for the 4k Project explains, "An Omega Zone is really just a geographic area that already exists, for example: state, province, county, district, etc." *4K Workbook*. While these geographic distinctions may represent emic boundaries in some instances, the methodology employed does not seem to consider any distinction between emic and etic geographic boundaries.

21. Pratt, "Here's What We Mean"; Platt, "Rethinking Unreached Peoples"; Roderick and Gordy, "Every People Group," 71–82; Carlson and Clark, "3 Words That Changed Missions Strategy."

22. Carlson and Clark, "3 Words That Changed Missions Strategy."

23. Williams and Moss, "Focus on 'All Nations,'" 131–32.

families (מִשְׁפְּחֹת), languages (לְשֹׁנֹת), and lands (אַרְצֹת). The descendants of Noah, constituting what would later be referred to as the ἔθνη, were complex in their divisions. While language was certainly one of the factors, it was certainly not the only defining, or even primary, characteristic.

Missions, as depicted in the New Testament, does not neglect any of these categories, but it does tend to focus extensively on geography. Paul makes frequent geographic references in his letters.[24] While Paul used ethnic designations in Rom 1:16 (Ἰουδαῖος and Ἕλλην), he used geographic designations to describe the extent of his missionary activity in Rom 15:19 ("ἀπὸ Ἰερουσαλὴμ καὶ κύκλῳ μέχρι τοῦ Ἰλλυρικοῦ"). Roland Allen observes that Paul constantly speaks of the Roman provinces regarding his missionary endeavors.[25] Eckhard Schnabel similarly argues, "The basic strategy of Paul was simple: he wanted to proclaim the message of Jesus Christ to Jews and Gentiles in obedience to a divine commission, particularly in *areas* in which it had not been proclaimed before."[26] Schnabel specifies "areas" in contrast to Allen's "provinces," allowing for a broader understanding of geography. Provinces were strictly Roman geopolitical divisions, but other areas such as Arabia/Nabatea were distinct geographic entities but not Roman provinces.[27] Since geography is a significant category in the scriptural definition of the nations and in the early mission of the church, the matter of contextualization needs to be taken into consideration.

Geography is not isolated from other cultural factors. While geographic features can be empirically observed, the way that geography is understood arises within a cultural context. J. B. Harley urges, "Any appreciation of the historical importance of maps depends upon a clear conception of their nature, of the factors that have shaped their making and transmission, and of their role within human societies."[28] In order to develop a scriptural missions strategy that accounts for geography, local geographical factors must be taken into consideration. Concepts of what are important and unimportant geographical divisions cannot be

---

24. Rom 15:19; 1 Cor 16:1; 2 Cor 1:1; 9:2; 11:9; Gal 4:25; Eph 1:1; Phil 1:1; 4:14; Col 1:1; 4:15; 1 Thess 1:7–8; 2:1; 3:1; 1 Tim 1:3; 2 Tim 1:15, 17–18; 3:11; 4:10, 12, 20; Titus 1:5; 3:12

25. R. Allen, *Missionary Methods*, 14.

26. Schnabel, *Early Christian Mission*, 2:1299. Emphasis added.

27. Schnabel, *Early Christian Mission*, 2:1299–1300. Nabatea was annexed by Emperor Trajan around 111. Griffin, "Nerva to Hadrian," 123.

28. Harley, "Map and the Development," 1.

imported from the outside (etic) but must be considered from the perspective of the people groups themselves (emic).

If geography is culturally informed, as much as maps are visual representations of geography, then a missions strategy must develop methods of contextualizing strategy according to local geographical views. Dean Flemming defines contextualization as "the dynamic and comprehensive process by which the gospel is incarnated within a concrete historical or cultural situation. This happens in such a way that the gospel both comes to authentic expression in the local context and at the same time prophetically transforms the context."[29] In order to incarnate the gospel within a specific culture, all aspects of the culture must be carefully considered. Robert David Sack asserts, "We humans are geographical beings transforming the earth and making it into a home, and that transformed world affects who we are. Our geographical nature shapes our world and our selves. Being geographical is inescapable—we do not have to be conscious of it. Yet, realizing that we are geographical increases the effectiveness of our actions, the clarity of our awareness, and the inclusiveness and generosity of our moral concerns."[30] In order to develop a missions strategy that has a scriptural foundation, is theologically relevant, and can be applied transculturally, geography (but not necessarily geopolitical entities) must be recovered as a major factor in distinguishing people groups.

Limitations and Delimitations

In this book, I am arguing that a biblical-theological approach must take into account geography and specifically local contextual or emic views of geography. My perspective is that of a North American Caucasian male with considerable cross-cultural experience in various parts of North America, South Asia, and Sub-Saharan Africa. My perspective, or any single perspective, requires intentionally identifying one's own point of view in order to work toward an emic understanding of geography and national identity. It is assumed that an emic understanding can be discovered to some degree, although imperfectly since one can never fully overcome the barrier of approaching a context as an outsider.

I am an evangelical Christian who believes that the Bible is the inerrant and infallible Word of God. I affirm the sufficiency of Scripture,

---

29. Flemming, *Contextualization in the New Testament*, 19.
30. Sack, *Homo Geographicus*, 1.

and, therefore, that repentance and faith in Jesus Christ is the only way that people can be reconciled to God.[31] All people in all places and at all times need to have the gospel verbally communicated to them (either spoken or in writing). As a result, missions is an essential aspect of Christianity and developing missions practices founded on Scripture is one of the most important tasks for missiologists. Additionally, missions is not merely a New Testament subject. Bavinck observes, "It is in itself striking how often the Old Testament discusses the future of [the nations] and interests itself in the salvation that will one day be their lot."[32] This book will take into account the full scope of Scripture. However, I will refrain from addressing matters of historicity and redaction criticism. Addressing some textual criticism will be necessary in a few instances but will not be done extensively for every passage discussed.

This book narrowly focuses on the role that geography plays in definitions of people groups and nations as it relates to missions strategy and understanding how various nations self-identify. Additionally, the study will be limited to interacting with Western-trained missiological views. This study will not interact with other categories such as "unreached people groups" or "unengaged unreached people groups" except where necessary to interact with authors who make relevant points or arguments that have bearing on my argument. Furthermore, a biblical theology of the nations certainly includes factors beyond geography, including ethnic, linguistic, political, and religious. I will strictly argue that geography is an essential component of national identity without disregarding or diminishing the complex, multifaceted concept of the "nations."

The social sciences play an important role in the later part of my argument, but the I assume the priority of biblical theology over social sciences. Social sciences may be utilized as tools to better understand or to implement methods once biblical-theological categories and definitions have been established. I will interact with various sociological definitions and views of the nations but will do so only after biblical-theological categories and definitions have been established.

---

31. Mark Dever defines the sufficiency of Scripture as "the idea that the Scriptures sufficiently reveal everything God's people need for salvation, perfect trust, and perfect obedience." Dever, "Church," 635.

32. Bavinck, *Introduction to the Science of Missions*, 11. Wright also argues that "A strong theology of the mission of God provides a fruitful hermeneutical framework within which to read the whole Bible." C. Wright, *Mission of God*, 26.

The terms "emic" and "etic" were first used by Kenneth Pike with very specific definitions.[33] However, the concepts have since been used in varied fields with varying definitions for various purposes. In some instances, people have reversed the definitions.[34] I will be relying on Pike's definitions for "emic" and "etic." I am aware of the considerable literature addressing various topics such as psychology, education, medicine, anthropology, management, and many others, but Pike's definition was primarily seeking to speak into a missions context regarding Bible translation. Since he coined the terms and provided an extensive explanation of his definitions, I will interact with Pike's argument and others as they interact directly with Pike.[35]

This book is a theoretical proposal and does not prescribe a specific course of action or method for implementing this proposal. Various applications may be derived, and I do suggest some specific methods for discovering emic geography. However, missionaries must do the hard work of discovering local contextual factors. I have no intention to call for or establish a uniform method or means of implementation in all contexts.

Definitions of Key Terms

The definition of "people group" offered by the Lausanne Committee is generally accepted by missiologists. The Lausanne Committee defines a "people group" as "a significantly large sociological grouping of individuals who perceive themselves to have a common affinity for one another. From the viewpoint of evangelization, this is the largest possible group within which the gospel can spread without encountering barriers of understanding or acceptance."[36] The Lausanne definition will form the foundation for the definition I propose with some modifications.

First, the Lausanne definition is based exclusively on sociological groupings and does not explicitly seek to include biblical-theological categories. The definition proposed here emphasizes biblical-theological categories but remains open to drawing on sociological tools to assist in

---

33. Pike, *Language in Relation*, 37. See definitions below.

34. Headland, "Introduction," 20–21.

35. For list of various disciples and a list of some sources, see Headland, "Introduction," 16–24.

36. Dayton, "Reaching the Unreached Peoples," 32–33.

clarifying or distinguishing people groups once the biblical-theological categories have been established. Second, the proposed definition removes the terminology "significantly large" because the phrase is ambiguous and its meaning can vary among people groups. Since there is no upper or lower population limit required for a group perception of a separate national identity, it seems best to eliminate this phrase from the definition for concision and precision. Third, in addressing barriers to the gospel spreading, barriers of transmission must be considered in addition to barriers of understanding or acceptance. Barriers of transmission have some overlap with barriers of understanding or acceptance such as linguistic barriers, cultural barriers, and ethnic prejudice. However, the barrier of transmission may also include a geographic barrier where considerable physical or monetary exertion is required in order to transmit the gospel to a separate people group.

I will contend for the following definition: *A people group is a grouping of individuals who perceive themselves to have a common affinity for one another based on categories with a biblical-theological foundation, which may include language, ethnicity, geography, religion, political factors, or any combination of these factors. From the viewpoint of evangelization, this is the largest possible group within which the gospel can spread without encountering barriers of understanding, acceptance, or transmission.*

What counts as a legitimate geographic boundary will vary between different people groups. The global West tends to hold high regard for invisible, but very real, boundaries between states and countries. These invisible boundaries may or may not be accompanied by topographical features such as a river or a ridge. In other contexts, the geographical boundaries may also be invisible or visible, and the type and the penetrability of those borders will also vary.[37] Geography is a biblical-theological category that must be taken into account when developing missions strategy, but the specifics of the geographic boundaries must be discovered by missionaries in each specific context.

George Peters distinguished between "mission" and "missions." He defines "mission" as "the total biblical assignment of the church of Jesus Christ. It is a comprehensive term including the upward, inward and outward ministries of the church. It is the church as 'sent' (a pilgrim

---

37. A. Smith, *National Identity*, 22–23; Crider, "Mapping," 51–66. Anthony Smith identifies the broad categories of "boundaries" and "centers." Crider lists specific examples of geographic features, such as paths, nodes, districts, edges, landmarks, and high places.

stranger, witness, prophet, servant, as salt, as light, etc.) in this world."[38] Peters argues that "missions" is a specialized term. He indicates, "By it I mean the sending forth of authorized persons beyond the borders of the New Testament church and her immediate gospel influence to proclaim the gospel of Jesus Christ in gospel-destitute areas, to win converts from other faiths or non-faiths to Jesus Christ, and to establish functioning, multiplying local congregations who will bear the fruit of Christianity in that community and to that country."[39] I am focusing on missions in this book and will only address the broader mission of the church as necessary to clearly define or differentiate the scope and object of missions.

Strategy is an essential aspect of missions. No matter what term one chooses to use—whether it is "missionary method," "means for the conversion of the heathens," or simply a "plan for carrying out missions"—the missionary task must be executed in some way.[40] I will use the term "missions strategy" to describe the process of taking planned action to fulfill the missionary task. The definition of "missions strategy" is adopted from Terry and Payne, who propound, "Mission strategy is the overall process describing what we believe the Lord would have us accomplish to make disciples of all nations."[41] This definition places emphasis on both discovering the missionary task from a biblical-theological perspective and making disciples of all nations.

One of the responsibilities of a missionary is to discover, to the best of their ability, the barriers for the spread of the gospel as they are understood from an emic perspective rather than an etic perspective. Pike indicates, "The emic viewpoint results from studying behavior as from inside the system."[42] Similarly, he defines, "The etic viewpoint studies behavior as from outside of a particular system, as an essential initial approach to an alien system."[43] Neither a missionary nor anyone else will

38. Peters, *Biblical Theology of Missions*, 11.
39. Peters, *Biblical Theology of Missions*, 11.
40. R. Allen, *Missionary Methods*; Carey, *Enquiry*.
41. Terry and Payne, *Developing a Strategy for Missions*, 5.
42. Pike, *Language in Relation*, 37. See also Geertz, "From the Native's Point of View," 28. Geertz prefers the terms "experience-near" rather than "emic" and "experience-distant" rather that "etic." However, Mostowlansky and Rota explain, "In the scientific study of religions, the contrast between emic and etic has since been associated with Clifford Geertz's name." Mostowlansky and Rota, "Matter of Perspective?," 324.
43. Pike, *Language in Relation*, 37. See also Geertz, "From the Native's Point of View," 28.

ever perfectly grasp the emic perspective as a cultural outsider. However, Geertz explains,

> To grasp concepts which, for another people, are [emic], and to do so well enough to place them in illuminating connection with those [etic] concepts that theorists have fashioned to capture the general features of social life is clearly a task at least as delicate, if a bit less magical, as putting oneself into someone else's skin. The trick is not to achieve some inner correspondence of spirit with your informants . . . The trick is to figure out what . . . they think they are up to.[44]

While a missionary or missiological researcher cannot perfectly comprehend the various barriers to the spread of the gospel, some knowledge can be ascertained through various methods in order to gain a working knowledge. Additionally, understanding why a geographic barrier is significant may not always be necessary. Knowing that a geographic barrier exists may be sufficient in many instances.

Research Methodology

I will employ an interdisciplinary approach that lies within the broader category of qualitative analysis. My approach is drawn primarily from Enoch Wan's missiological research method, which includes the following criteria: scripturally sound, theologically supported, analytically coherent, relevantly contextual, and strategically practical.[45] Special emphasis will be given to contemporary and relatively recent historical writings on missions strategy in comparison and contrast to a scriptural-theological definition of the nations especially as that definition relates to geography.

Chapter 1 states the purpose and relevance of the study and establishes the limitations and delimitations of this study. Furthermore, the current chapter introduces and defines key terms related to people groups and recent developments in people group thinking.

Chapter 2 will establish the scriptural soundness of my argument by systematically examining key passages of Scripture related to the "nations" with special emphasis on demonstrating a close connection between geography and national identity. The main points and key passages will be: (1) God created the land and the nations to live in them (Gen

---

44. Geertz, "From the Native's Point of View," 29.
45. Wan, "Inter-Disciplinary and Integrative Missiological Research."

2:4–11; 10:5, 20, 31; Deut 32:8; Acts 17:26). (2) The land often functions as a substitute for the people who live in the land (Exodus 7–11; 1 Chr 14:17; 2 Chr 7:14; 17:20; 20:29; 36:3; Isa 8:9; 14:26; 37:18; 45:22; Ezek 5:5–6; 12:15; 20:23; 22:15; 29:12; 30:26; 36:19, 24). (3) The concepts of nation and land are linked in Scripture in such a way that the endowment, possession, and removal of land has profound effects (Gen 12:1–3; Deut 19:1–2; Jer 12:17; Luke 24:47; Acts 1:8).

Chapter 3 will demonstrate that my thesis is theologically supported by undertaking a biblical case study based on Rom 15:19 in which Paul uses a contextual-geographical approach to describe his missionary endeavors. This chapter will exclusively focus on the phrase "and from Jerusalem around to Illyricum."

Chapter 4 will survey the previous definitions of "people groups" and the development of missions strategy based on those definitions. As mentioned above, I will strictly focus on definitions of "people groups" rather than analyzing definitions of related terms (e.g., "unreached people groups," "unengaged unreached people groups," etc.), except where necessary to offer a fair explanation and evaluation of the strategies. Chapter 4 will demonstrate the contextual relevance of this study.

Chapter 5 will examine the distinction between emic and etic analysis and survey various sociological paradigms as they seek to define the nations. Then the scriptural, theological, and sociological conclusions will be integrated in order to develop a methodology for discovering emic geography and incorporating contextual geography into people group identity and missions strategy. This chapter will exhibit the analytical coherence of the argument presented in this book.

Chapter 6 will offer concluding thoughts on the study, reflecting on how contextual geography advances the conversation, providing questions for further research, and considering how incorporating contextual geography is strategically practical for missionaries in various contexts.

2

A Biblical Theology of Land in Relation to National Identity

Introduction

The connection between humanity and the land can be traced back to creation. The relationship forms a thread that runs through all of Scripture.[1] This chapter will develop a biblical theology of geography with reference to national identity. First, an intricate connection exists between people and the land in creation, both in the origin of humanity and as the nations dispersed over the earth. Second, various Scripture uses land and nations in a metonymy of subject where either a general concept of land or a specific land with geographical boundaries serves as a substitute for a specific nation. Third, this chapter will explore the impact that endowing and removing land has on national identity. Far from exhausting every example, this chapter will address key examples in each category which could then be applied more broadly.

People and the Land in Creation

When God created man (אָדָם) from the dust of the earth (אֲדָמָה), a bond was formed (Gen 2:4–17). The connection between the people and the

---

1. Beale, *Temple and the Church's Mission*.

land extended beyond the origin of humanity. When God divided the people into nations, he scattered them across the earth (Gen 10:1–31). Further, when the nations were scattered, God established geographical boundaries for them (Deut 32:8). While the relationship between people and the land underwent some revision during the intertestamental period in the book of Jubilees, Paul reaffirms the divinely established connection between humanity and the land and between nations and geographical boundaries (Acts 17:26).

אָדָם and אֲדָמָה: Genesis 2:4–17

The linguistic and thematic link between humanity and the land is found in the earliest chapters of Genesis. In the midst of the opening two chapters, which depict the creation of man and woman in God's image as the apex (Gen 1:27; 2:7), a considerable amount of space is dedicated to describing the formation of the land in general and especially Eden and its garden. These cannot be simply or easily dismissed. Rather, as von Rad relates, "Nothing is here by chance; everything must be considered carefully, deliberately, and precisely."[2] Sailhamer further explains, "Two primary themes dominate the Creation account: the land and the blessing . . . The preparation of the land and the divine blessing are important to the author of Genesis (and the Pentateuch) because these two themes form the basis of his treatment of the patriarchal narratives and the Sinai covenant."[3] The author of the Pentateuch intends to draw a strong connection between humanity and the land and is demonstrated particularly in Genesis 2:4–17.[4]

The linguistic connection between אָדָם and אֲדָמָה is broadly documented. Von Rad observes that "God 'forms' [man] from the ground; the bond of life between man and earth given by creation is expressed with

---

2. Rad, *Genesis*, 47.
3. Sailhamer, *Pentateuch as Narrative*, 81–82.
4. While some critical scholars believe the creation accounts of Genesis 1 and 2 to originate from two different authors (P and J, respectively), and that J has modified existing stories, Wenham forcefully argues, "Attractive though such hypotheses are, they must, in the absence of any sources where the stories occur independently, remain conjectural and it would certainly be unwise to base an exegesis of these chapters on guesses as to how the writer has modified his putative sources. The present form of the material is the surest guide to his intentions." Wenham, *Genesis 1–15*, 52. Cf. Speiser, *Genesis*, 19; Rad, *Genesis*, 74–82; Westermann, *Genesis 1–11*, 189.

particular cogency by the use of the Hebrew words *'ādām* and *'ᵃdāmā*."⁵ The linguistic connection between humanity and the land is developed further by Hamilton, who remarks, "*'ādām* was created from the *'ᵃdāmā* (2:7). *'ādām* must work the *'ᵃdāmā* (3:23). One day *'ādām* will return to the *'ᵃdāmā* (3:19). And all of *'ādām*'s relationships to the *'ᵃdāmā* are determined by Yahweh. Accordingly, the best English equivalent of *'ādām* may be 'earthling' or 'earth person.'"⁶ Further, אֲדָמָה as the source of אָדָם reveals something of God's intended nature for humanity. Rather than using the broader term for land (אֶרֶץ), the author of Genesis uses אֲדָמָה, which refers primarily to cultivated or arable land.⁷ This was the land from which אָדָם would gather a harvest and the land that he would "work" (עבד) and "keep" (שׁמר).⁸ אָדָם was created to obey the Lord to bring in the harvest from the אֲדָמָה. Sarna contends, "Agriculture is considered to be the original vocation of man, whose bond to the earth is an essential part of his being."⁹ The essential being of אָדָם cannot be identified apart from

---

5. Rad, *Genesis*, 77. Hamilton attempts to draw the connection further insisting that the words suggest "a connection between man's reddish brown skin and the reddish brown soil of the earth." Hamilton, "אָדָם," *NIDOTTE*, 1:264. This connection is possible but relies upon Akkadian etymology rather than its use in biblical Hebrew. See also Maass, "אָדָם," *TDOT*, 1:78–79; *HALOT*, 1:14; Keil, *Pentateuch*, 50.

6. Hamilton, "אָדָם," *NIDOTTE*, 1:264.

7. Plöger, "אֲדָמָה," *TDOT*, 1:90–91; Grisanti, "אֲדָמָה," *NIDOTTE*, 1:270; *HALOT*, 1:15.

8. The concept of gathering a harvest also connects back to the command of Gen 1:28: "Be fruitful and multiply and fill the earth [אֶרֶץ] and subdue it." The man and woman were commanded to be fruitful by reproducing biologically, but they were also to "subdue" (כבשׁ) the land, that is, to turn אֶרֶץ into אֲדָמָה. As the man and woman biologically multiply, the result is that they would also multiply worshipers as they "work" and "keep" the land in obedience to the Lord. Sailhamer offers an alternative translation to for עבד and שׁמר, suggesting that "a more suitable and grammatically sound translation . . . is 'to worship and obey.'" Sailhamer, "Genesis," 79. See also Beale, *Temple and the Church's Mission*, 67. Robinson explores the idea of viewing the relationship between God and אָדָם as one of discipleship in which the multiplication of the man would be to fill the earth with God's image. Akin et al., *40 Questions about the Great Commission*, 207–17. This seems to be an appropriate conclusion and one that aligns with the concept of being a harvest-gathering creation. One may further see a correlation between worship and man's origin and nature in God's instruction to build the altar out of אֲדָמָה in Exod 20:24. While it is outside the scope of this book, Jesus's use of harvest imagery in Luke 10:2 when he sends of the 70 (or 72) disciples, potentially corresponding to the 70/72 nations of the Table of Nations in Genesis 10, may point back to the implicit harvest relationship between אָדָם and אֲדָמָה. Beale, *Temple and the Church's Mission*, 201.

9. Sarna, *Genesis*, 17. See also Brueggemann, *Genesis*, 46; Plöger, "אֲדָמָה," *TDOT*, 1:91.

אֲדָמָה. The Lord is the ultimate giver of life and identity (Gen 1:26; 2:7), but God made humans from the humus, and that connection cannot be easily ignored.

Not only was אָדָם made from אֲדָמָה but אָדָם was also placed in the אֲדָמָה. This might seem obvious, since people had to be placed in a physical location, but considerable space is dedicated to describing Eden and the garden in Genesis 2. Immediately after forming אָדָם, God plants a garden in Eden, where he places the man (Gen 2:8). The garden consisted of various trees that were good for food and pleasing to look at (Gen 2:9). The details of the garden are followed by describing the broader world around the garden with rivers and land containing precious metals and stones. Von Rad perceives, "This strangely profound section strives without doubt to sketch the real geographical world. It projects an extremely archaic map of the world, although, it is true, this is only with regard to the waters of the inhabited world."[10] Dempster further observes that "The design of Genesis 2 showcases the centrality of the garden and its associated river, as the creation of man and of woman bracket its description."[11] As subsequent generations of humanity begin to spread out over the earth and nations begin to form, the connection between the land and nations becomes an integral aspect of their identity.

The Origin of the Nations: Genesis 10:5, 20, 31

On the surface, Genesis 10, often referred to as the Table of Nations, is a genealogy of the post-flood descendants of Noah and his sons. However, this list of families (מִשְׁפָּחֹת) is the background for God's command to Abram to leave his land and that all the families (מִשְׁפְּחֹת) of the earth would be blessed through Abram (Gen 12:1–3). As a result, Genesis 10 constitutes an important pillar for properly understanding God's plan for salvation to the nations. In addition to Genesis 10 being a list of מִשְׁפְּחֹת, it also distinguishes among the various descendants by their nations (גּוֹיִם), their language (לְשֹׁנֹת), and their lands (אַרְצֹת). Zunz, in a survey of Jewish geographical literature, asserts, "In the whole range of Jewish literature no branch of knowledge appears to be cultivated more scantily, or to be less known, than that of Geography."[12] Zunz was anachronisti-

---

10. Rad, *Genesis*, 80.
11. Dempster, *Dominion and Dynasty*, 63.
12. Zunz, "Essay on the Geographical Literature," 230.

cally referring to the formal modern-era scientific study of geography. Alexander rebuts, "[Zunz's] essay rather underestimated Rabbinic interest in geographical matters because he has not fully appreciated the fact that geography as an independent field of study hardly existed in the ancient world. Geography was taught in antiquity under forms that are alien to our way of thinking, and once we are alive to this fact we shall find much more of it in the Rabbinic corpus than did Zunz."[13] Geography, while not always the most important factor in national identity, is one of the major distinguishing marks by which people were divided in Genesis 10. Daniel Block asserts,

> Of all the elements which distinguish one nation from another, none seems more obvious than the territorial aspect. One may conceive of a nation that is heterogeneous ethnically, whose government is not monarchical, or which shares a language or other cultural features with another, but it is difficult to imagine either 1) a nation which does not occupy a land that it calls its own, or 2) a nation which shares its territory with another.[14]

The geographical element differs slightly from that seen in Gen 2:4–17 in that the word for land is different (אֶרֶץ rather than אֲדָמָה) and has different connotations.[15] Crüsemann explains, "However, the language in relation to ארץ and אדמה is clearly different. In 12:1, Abraham receives the command 'Get out of your country' (מארצך). ארץ here undeniably denotes a definite and limited area... Conversely, according to 12:3, the blessing applies to all clans of the אדמה. This indisputably means the whole earth."[16] The primary function of the אֶרֶץ in Genesis 10 is that it is allotted to the various nations that are listed and functions in a way by which one nation can be distinguished from another. Sarna explains,

> Racial characteristics, physical types, or the color of skin play no role in the categorizing. Nor is language a guideline since

---

13. P. Alexander, "Toponymy of the Targumim," 11.

14. Block, "Foundations of National Identity," 298.

15. While אֲדָמָה refers to arable land, אֶרֶץ has a more general usage that connotes a sense of universality and sovereignty in that the Lord created the אֶרֶץ along with the heavens. The formula used in Gen 1:1 (אֵת הַשָּׁמַיִם וְאֵת הָאָרֶץ) "expresses the totality of the created order." C. Wright, "אֶרֶץ," *NIDOTTE*, 1:519. אֶרֶץ also may refer to land in contrast to the sea, sovereign territory, or the underworld. Ottosson, "אֶרֶץ," *TDOT*, 1:393; *HALOT*, 1:90–91. The context of Genesis 10 seems to clearly refer to geographical territory allotted to various nations.

16. Crüsemann, "Eigenständigkeit der Urgeschichte," 17.

Canaan, recognized in Isaiah 19:18 to have the same tongue as Israel, is affiliated with Egypt among the Hamites, while the Elamites, who spoke a decidedly non-Semitic language, are classified under Shem... Clearly, geographical proximity, ethnic affiliations, sociopolitical and economic relationships, as well as historical and even literary considerations, were the varied factors that controlled inclusion in the Table that determined its internal divisions and subdivisions.[17]

The precise location of these lands is not relevant for this study. Rost determines that אֶרֶץ should be understood as "in connection with common names and suffixes and also when it is described in more detail by relative clauses, as territory."[18] He further expresses, "For as the individual has possessions, so do the people."[19] What is important in Genesis 10 is that the nations are described as having specific territory of which they could be said to be in possession. It was *their* land as opposed to that of another nation.

Genesis 10 is also written with a geographical orientation. Brueggemann observes, "Genesis 10:1–32 is commonly seen as a verbal 'map' of the world. It pays attention to territorial and political realities."[20] To call the Table of Nations a "map of the world" is not an overstatement. Scott explains that "the main contours of the earth's division among the three sons are relatively clear: the nations of *Japheth* in the northern and western lands, including Asia Minor and Europe (Gen 10:2–5); the nations of *Ham* in Egypt and North Africa (vv. 6–20); and the nations of *Shem* in Mesopotamia and Arabia (vv. 21–31)."[21] The broad geographic nature of the table is also reinforced by references to geographic locations within the Table. Many of the names listed may refer to individuals or ethnic groups, especially where the plural form is used, but some are

---

17. Sarna, *Genesis*, 68–69. Sarna overstates the case in saying that language plays no factor at all since the author explicitly states that language was a factor in the divisions. The examples cited could reasonably be explained with linguistic changes over time or a nation adopting an outside language such as Hellenistic Jews adopting the Greek language. Sarna's emphasis is on the nature of the divisions apart from his dismissal of linguistic distinctions. See also Clements, "גוֹי," *TDOT*, 9:426–27.

18. Rost, "Bezeichnungen für Land und Volk," 136.

19. Rost, "Bezeichnungen für Land und Volk," 139.

20. Brueggemann, *Genesis*, 91. See also Dempster, *Dominion and Dynasty*, 74.

21. Scott, *Paul and the Nations*, 6–8. See also Sarna, *Genesis*, 68. The geographic description offered by Scott is further clarified in the book of Jubilees.

unmistakably geographic references.²² Several geographical sketches are made regarding the inhabited territory of some of Noah's descendants. The sons of Japheth are described as "island nations" (אִיֵּי הַגּוֹיִם) indicating that they generally lived on the islands and the coasts of the Mediterranean Sea.²³ The author explicitly denotes the territory of the Canaanites (Gen 10:19), which is of special interest to the Israelites as they are about to enter that land in fulfillment of God's promise to Abram, Isaac, and Jacob (Gen 12:1; 26:2-5; 28:13). At the conclusion to the final section documenting Shem's descendants, a summary statement describes the territory of Joktan's sons: "The territory [מוֹשָׁב] in which they lived extended from Mesha in the direction of Sephar to the hill country of the east" (Gen 10:30). While scholars have not identified the specific location of Mesha and Sephar, these were known geographic settlements and landmarks to the original audience.²⁴

Ethnicity and language must not be overlooked as essential aspects of national identity, but geography plays an equally important role. The geography of the Bible is more often assumed rather than described, perhaps because both the authors and the audience share an emic geography, but one would be challenged to find a nation in Scripture where a territory of its own is not possessed, anticipated, or longed for. In addition to God confusing languages and dispersing the people over the face of the earth (עַל־פְּנֵי כָל־הָאָרֶץ, Gen 11:9), Moses exposits that God even established the borders of all the nations.

Divine Divisions: Deuteronomy 32:8

Deuteronomy 32:8 indicates that God divided the nations of humanity (אָדָם ... גּוֹיִם) and established their boundaries (גְּבֻלֹת). Prior to addressing the significance of this verse for a biblical understanding of the nations, significant textual issues must be resolved. The main textual

---

22. Among those that appear to be clear geographic references are Tarshish (תַּרְשִׁישׁ), Put (פּוּט), and Shinar (שִׁנְעָר) and Assyria (אַשּׁוּר), including the various cities that Nimrod built (Gen 10:10–12).

23. *HALOT*, 1:38.

24. Wenham, *Genesis 1–15*, 232. Wenham explains, "Sephar might be the coastal town of Ṣaphar in southern Arabia, but the different initial sibilant makes this questionable. Most commentators guess that Mesha represents the western limit of the Yoqtanites and Sephar the eastern, and that the territory lies within southern Arabia, but certainty is impossible."

problem arises in the phrase "according to the number of the sons of God." Differences exist between the Masoretic Text (MT) and the LXX in this verse. The MT indicates that the nations were divided according to the "sons of Israel" (בְּנֵי יִשְׂרָאֵל). The LXX reads that the nations were divided according to the "angels of God" (ἀγγέλων θεοῦ). The debate surrounding the issue seems to have been resolved when Patrick Skehan published his findings from a fragment of Deuteronomy found in cave 4 at Khirbet Qumran. This fragment reads, "the sons of God," indicating that the LXX reading reflects the original.[25] Daniel Stevens explains, "It is thus suggested by many that the fragments of 4QDeut preserve the original reading."[26] If the original reading indicates that God divided the nations according to the number of the sons of God, then an explanation must be given for the variant reading.

The most likely explanation for the variant reading in the MT may be found in Targum Pseudo-Jonathan:

> When the Most High gave the world as an inheritance to the peoples who came from the sons of Noah, when he divided the writings and languages among mankind, in the generation of the division, at that time, he cast lots on seventy angels, the leaders of the nations, with whom it was revealed to see the city; and at that time he established the borders of the nations according to the sum of the number of the seventy souls of Israel who went down to Egypt.[27]

Daniel Block responds, "This text conflates ideas derived from the Table of Nations (Genesis 10), the account of the Tower of Babel (Gen. 11:1–9), and the references to the number of Jacob's household (Gen. 46:26–27; Exod. 1:5). It also appears to incorporate notions from both variants of Deut. 32:8."[28] Jubilees 8–9 helps to further explain the

---

25. 4QDeut; Skehan, "Fragment of the 'Song of Moses,'" 12.

26. Stevens, "Does Deuteronomy 32:8 Refer," 134.

27. E. Clarke, trans., *Targum Pseudo-Jonathan*, 90. A similar interpretation can be found in early Christian literature: "But if anyone should say, 'How then were the people of the Hebrews alone conducted to the supremely Divine illuminations?' we must answer, that we ought not to throw the blame of the other nations wandering after those which are no gods upon the direct guidance of the Angels, but that they themselves, by their own declension, fell away from the direct leading towards the Divine Being, through self-conceit and self-will, and through their irrational veneration for things which appeared to them worthy of God." Pseudo-Dionysius, *On the Heavenly Hierarchy*, 9.3.

28. Block, *Gods of the Nations*, 28–29.

A Biblical Theology of Land in Relation to National Identity

significance of the variant reading found in the MT. In Jub 8:19, Zion is depicted as the center of the earth. Additionally, Noah's curse in Jub 9:14 suggests that Israel considered the boundaries and territories of the nations to be permanent.[29] James Scott concludes, "Thus, the Table of Nations—and Israel's central position in it—is seen to have timeless value and eternal validity, even for the second century B. C., when *Jubilees* was written."[30] He also notes that Deut 32:8 MT refers to the same postdiluvian division of the earth and in the same "Israel-centric way as Jubilees."[31]

The significance of both options focuses on the number seventy. Seventy nations are listed in the Hebrew Table of Nations.[32] Genesis 46:26–27 and Exod 1:5 indicate that Jacob's household that went down to Egypt numbered seventy people. Targum Pseudo-Jonathan and some early Christian literature preserve the tradition that God placed an angel over each of the seventy nations.[33] The intent seems to be in both variants to communicate that God divided the nations and allotted territory to them as depicted in Gen 10:1–32. The poetic form of Deuteronomy 32 may indicate why Moses made this allusion in such an indirect way.[34] Despite the complexities related to the correct original text, Deuteronomy 32 seems to be making a clear reference to the nations listed in Genesis 10.

Building on the geographical allusions to Genesis 10, Moses expresses that he gave the nations their inheritance (נחל), divided the sons of mankind (הִפְרִידוֹ בְּנֵי אָדָם), and set the boundaries of the peoples (גְּבֻלֹת עַמִּים). Both the inheritance (נחל) and the boundaries (גְּבֻלֹת) are strong geographical references.[35] While not exhaustive of its semantic range,

---

29. Charles, trans., *Book of Jubilees*, 77–78. "And thus the sons of Noah divided unto their sons in presence of Noah their father, and he bound them all by an oath, imprecating a curse on everyone that sought to seize the portion which had not fallen (to him) by his lot."

30. Scott, *Paul and the Nations*, 16.

31. Scott, *Paul and the Nations*, 16.

32. The LXX lists seventy-two nations in Gen 10:1–32. How exactly this may impact Deut 32:8 requires further research outside the scope of this book.

33. Clement of Alexandria, *Stromata*, 7.2 (ANF 2:524); Pseudo-Dionysius, *On the Heavenly Hierarchy*, 9.3.

34. Craigie, *Deuteronomy*, 374.

35. In addition to the inheritance and the boundaries, an argument could be made that placing אָדָם in the midst of the references to נחל and גְּבֻלֹת is intended to draw the reader back to the creation of אָדָם from אֲדָמָה in Gen 2:7.

נחל normally refers to allotting land to an heir.³⁶ Wright contends, "The most common literal meaning of both refers to the division of the land within the kinship structure of Israel and thus signifies the permanent family property allotted to the tribes, clans, and households of Israel."³⁷ Wright further observes, "Possibly the oldest occurrence is Deut 32:8–9, in which the origin of the special relationship between Yahweh and Israel is located before even the election of the ancestors, in the cosmic realm of God's sovereignty over all international geography."³⁸ The divine division of the nations by the Most High included where the nations would be geographically located.

Essential to bestowing land to the nations and the division of humanity is establishing geographical boundaries. Boundaries (גְּבֻלֹת) in the Old Testament have an inherent geographic meaning.³⁹ Ottosson explains,

> It is quite natural to find *gebhul* in sections of the OT having to do with defining boundaries: Josh. 66 times, Ezk. 39 times (esp. in chapters 40–48), and Nu. 25 . . . Sometimes the boundaries follow natural topographical phenomena like rivers, lakes, seas, mountains, and valleys; quite frequently cities and villages form boundary points, i.e., the territory between the cities forms the boundary, not the city itself (Ezk. 47:15, 17; 48:1).⁴⁰

Furthermore, "boundary" can also be used as a metonymy for an entire territory.⁴¹ For example, Deut 19:3, establishing the locations for the Cities of Refuge, indicates that the Israelites should "divide into three parts the territory (גְּבוּל) of your land."⁴² Wazana expounds, "In Biblical Hebrew, the term 'border' (גבול) denotes both a demarcated area (cf. Judg

---

36. *HALOT*, 2:686.
37. C. Wright, "נחל," *NIDOTTE*, 3:77. See also Lipiński, "נַחַל," *TDOT*, 9:320–21.
38. C. Wright, "נחל," *NIDOTTE*, 3:79.
39. *HALOT*, 1:173. See also Block, "Foundations of National Identity," 319–27.
40. Ottosson, "גְּבוּל," *TDOT*, 2:365. See also Matties, "גבל," *NIDOTTE*, 1:802–4.
41. Ottosson, "גְּבוּל," *TDOT*, 2:365.
42. Other examples of "boundary" in metonymy with territory include Num 35:26; Josh 16:5; 18:11; 19:10; Judg 2:9; Ezek 47:15. Block explains, "Primarily then, גבול is used to signify 'border, boundary'. But in a derived sense it represents also the territory incorporated within the designated boundaries, whether that area be the private property of an individual, the territory received by a person/clan as his share of the promised land, or areas reserved for religious officials, or associated with the temple, or the ark of the covenant. It is more common, however, to find the word associated with a city (in which case it usually appears to refer to the surrounding territory), a tribe, or a nation." Block, "Foundations of National Identity," 325–26.

A Biblical Theology of Land in Relation to National Identity

19:29: 'He sent them throughout the territory of Israel') and the boundary by which the territory is delimited (cf. Jer 5:22: 'Who set the sand as a boundary to the sea')."[43]

References to the Table of Nations in Genesis 10 and clear geographic identifiers in the inheritance (נחל) and boundaries (גְּבֻלֹת) reinforce the geographic component in the scriptural understanding of the nations.[44] God's plan in creating and establishing the nations includes a geographic territory. While these borders were considered very important in the ancient Near East and unmovable by humans (Deut 19:14), there is no evidence to indicate that these boundaries would not shift or radically change over time.[45] Regardless of the mutability of the boundaries that God established for the nations, Deut 32:8 strongly suggests that geographic boundaries and, by extension, territories are vital to national identity by which one nation is differentiated from another.[46]

Intertestamental Revision: Jubilees 8–9

The opening chapters of the book of Jubilees do not spend considerable amount of time recounting the Genesis creation accounts, preferring to focus more on a defense of the Sabbath.[47] Jubilees does, however, significantly expand the narrative around the Table of Nations in Genesis 10. The influence that Jubilees and other Second Temple Jewish texts may have had on the development of Old Testament geography and influence on New Testament geographical assumptions will be addressed in more detail in chapter 3. For this chapter, it is sufficient to examine how Jubilees maintains and amplifies the geographic component of national identity.

Rather than giving a list of descendant nations, which includes ethnic, linguistic, and geographical designators, Jubilees 8–9 exclusively outlines geographic territory allotted to Noah's sons and their descendants without any reference to ethnicity or the division of languages at Babel. The division of the land corresponds to the three continents, similar to the Table of Nations in Genesis 10. Alexander relates that in Jubilees, "The

---

43. Wazana, *All the Boundaries*, 12.

44. A further point could be made that dividing the sons of mankind (בְּנֵי אָדָם) may be intended to draw attention back to creation, where אָדָם is created from אֲדָמָה.

45. Ottosson, "גְּבוּל," *TDOT*, 2:366; Matties, "גבל," *NIDOTTE*, 1:803.

46. Block, "Foundations of National Identity," 327.

47. Kugel, *Walk through Jubilees*, 29.

earth disc is divided into three climactic regions—a cold northern region, a temperate middle region, and a hot southern region (VIII 30) . . . These zones correspond to a tripartite division of the world among the sons of Noah: Japhet is assigned the northern zone, Shem the middle zone, and Ham the southern zone (VIII 30)."[48] These zones, Alexander further clarifies, correspond to Europe, Asia, and Libya/Africa respectively.[49] The detailed geography of Jubilees 8–9 "offer the largest extra-biblical supplements in the book of *Jubilees*."[50] However, VanderKam observes, "The geography of the book of *Jubilees* not only reflects the author's understanding of where the nations of the earth were located but also where they were supposed to be located."[51] Despite the bias and nationalistic agenda of the author, the abundance of geographic detail reflects how important geography was in the mid-second century BC.[52]

Jubilees 8–9 utilizes a stream of geographic and topological references and numerous lands with varying degrees of certainty regarding their identity.[53] These features include the Egyptian Sea (8:14), Sea of Mâ'ûk (8:22, 26), Sea of 'Atêl (8:22), The Great Sea (8:15; 9:6), which is also divided into four "tongues" (9:11–12), the Sea of Mê'at (8:12, 27; 9:8), the Red Sea (9:4), the "sea which is beyond the mountains of Asshur toward the north" (8:21), the islands of Kaftûr (8:21), "five great islands" allotted for Japheth (8:29), the Tînâ River (8:12, 16; 9:18), the Gihon River (8:15, 22–23), the Euphrates River (9:4–5), the Tigris River (9:5), the Waters of Dêdân (9:2), the "waters of the desert (9:4), the mountains of Râfâ (8:12, 16, 28), the mountains of Qêlt (8:26), the "mountains of fire" (8:22), the mountains of Sanîr and 'Amânâ (8:21; 9:4), the mountains of Asshur (8:21; 9:5–6), the mountains of Ararat (8:21), the mountains of the Red Sea (8:21), and the mountains of Mebrî and 'Êlâ (9:2). In addition to these geographic features, Eden is treated as a physical location in the far east but within the territory of Shem (8:16). Various lands are also referenced: Kârâsô (8:13), 'Afrâ (8:15), India (8:21, 9:2, 3), Bashan, Elam, Asshur, Bâbêl, and Mâ'ĕdâi (8:21), Sûsân (8:21; 9:2), Lebanon (8:21; 9:4),

---

48. P. Alexander, "Notes on the 'Imago Mundi,'" 203.
49. P. Alexander, "Notes on the 'Imago Mundi,'" 204.
50. VanderKam, *Book of Jubilees*, 40.
51. VanderKam, *Book of Jubilees*, 40–41.
52. VanderKam, *Jubilees*, 1:38–39.
53. For treatment regarding the identity of the lands listed in Jubilees 8–9, see Charles, *Book of Jubilees: Notes*, 69–78; P. Alexander, "Notes on the 'Imago Mundi,'" 205–8; Kugel, *Walk through Jubilees*, 77–81.

Gog (8:25), Fârâ, 'Afêrâg (8:27), Asshur, Nineveh, and Shinar (9:3), Sanîr and 'Amânâ (9:4), Mespotomia (9:5), and 'Arârâ (9:5). VanderKam observes, "As with the lists in Genesis 10, in Jubilees there are familiar and unfamiliar or downright unknown names, but in general the author's understanding of world geography emerges clearly enough from the extant textual evidence."[54] Geography, again, while only one component of national identity, is reinforced as an important aspect of a scriptural understanding of what constitutes a nation.

Appointed Times and Boundaries: Acts 17:26

The geographic themes of the Old Testament continue into the New Testament. Paul draws on the geographic aspect of the nations in his address to the members of the Aeropagus council in Acts 17:26. First, Paul refers to Adam as the common ancestor of all the nations. He argues, "He made from one man every nation of mankind" (ἐποίησέν τε ἐξ ἑνὸς πᾶν ἔθνος ἀνθρώπων). This echoes the LXX creation account of Gen 2:7: καὶ ἔπλασεν ὁ θεὸς τὸν ἄνθρωπον χοῦν ἀπὸ τῆς γῆς.[55] Paul is attempting to convince the Athenians that, rather than proclaiming "foreign deities," he is proclaiming the single God who transcends national identities but, at the same time, created the one man from whom all nations arose and spread out over the whole earth.[56]

Paul continues to explain that the nations that arose from one man were to "live on all the face of the earth" (κατοικεῖν ἐπὶ παντὸς προσώπου τῆς γῆς). Scott fervently argues that all of Acts 17:26 is a reference to Genesis 1-10 in abbreviated format. Scott concludes that "the idea of 'every nation' (πᾶν ἔθνος) in Paul's speech clearly alludes to the Table of Nations itself, which concludes with the statement: 'These are the generations of Noah, according to their generations, according to their nations (ἔθνη); from them were the islands of the nations (ἔθνη) scattered over

---

54. VanderKam, *Jubilees*, 1:361.

55. Acts 17:26 does not use ἄνθρωπος as the subject, but rather uses the plural form to emphasize the numerous nations rather than the one man from whom they originated. Paul also uses ποιέω to describe the creation of man rather than πλάσσω; however, LXX uses ποιέω in Gen 2:4 when God created the heavens and the earth (ᾗ ἡμέρᾳ ἐποίησεν Κύριος ὁ θεὸς τὸν οὐρανὸν καὶ τὴν γῆν). See also Marshall, "Acts," 595; Keener, *Acts*, vol. 3, 2645.

56. Keener, *Acts*, 3:2636-48; Bock, *Acts*, 566.

the earth (γῆ) after the flood' (Gen 10:32)."⁵⁷ The LXX allows for some ambiguity related to the term "earth" in Acts 17:26. First, Gen 2:4 and 2:7 use the same word (γῆ) to translate אֶרֶץ in Gen 2:4 and אֲדָמָה in Gen 2:7. Additionally, the LXX uses two different words to translate אֶרֶץ in Gen 10:4, 20, and 31, γῆ in Gen 10:4, and χώρα in Gen 10:20 and 31. Keener observes regarding the "one man" of Acts 17:26, "Although most commentators find here an allusion to Adam, some have argued for an allusion to Noah. This helps explain the mention of 'peoples' and the possible allusions to Gen 10 and 11 in the rest of Acts 17:26 . . . Whichever approach one takes, however, this passage underlines the common origin of humanity, since in Jewish thought all humanity descended from Noah as it did from Adam."⁵⁸ Regardless of the translation or whether the allusions are primarily to Genesis 2 or Genesis 10, Paul is assuming and emphasizing the scriptural understanding of the nations, which includes land and a territory in which to live.

The final portion of this verse, "having determined appointed times and boundaries of their dwelling place" (ὁρίσας προστεταγμένους καιροὺς καὶ τὰς ὁροθεσίας τῆς κατοικίας αὐτῶν), is the focus of much scholarly debate. However, the discussion generally involves Paul's intended meaning of καιροὺς rather than ὁροθεσίας.⁵⁹ "Boundaries" (ὁροθεσίας) seems to be a likely reference to God establishing the boundaries of the peoples in Deut 32:8.⁶⁰ The reference to Deut 32:8 does not necessarily mean that Paul saw the divinely established divisions as permanent. Keener clarifies, "Far from being prescriptive, these boundaries merely depict the geographic

57. Scott, "Luke's Geographical Horizon," 542.

58. Keener, *Acts*, 3:2647. Keener goes on to explain, "The common origin of humanity, like the reversal of Babel in Acts 2:5–11, fits the theme of the Gentile mission in Acts (1:8) and its grounding in salvation history (7:2–53). Rabbis claimed that God created only one person initially so that peoples could not compete as to the superiority of their respective ancestors (*m. Sanh.* 4:5)."

59. Dibelius contends that ὁροθεσία refers to "habitable zones" as opposed to "uninhabitable zones" according to Greek conceptions of world geography, but these are minority positions that go against the normal meaning and usage of this term. Dibelius, *Studies in Acts*. See also LSJ, 1255; Keener, *Acts*, 3:2649–50. Admittedly, the term is not rare in Greek literature (used 249 times) but appears in Scripture only in Acts 17:26. It may be that Paul is intentionally avoiding the alternative term τέρμων to avoid confusion with Τέρμων, the god of boundaries and borders. Of interest, but outside the scope of this study, Paul also avoids using the word πίστις in his Acts 17 address, which may also be due to Πίστις being another Roman god closely associated with Τέρμων. Plutarch, *Num.* 16.1.

60. Bruce, *Book of Acts*, 337–38; Bock, *Acts*, 566; Marshall, "Acts," 497.

separations established—whether in judgment since Babel or otherwise showing humanity's limitations—for various seasons, all to be overturned in divinely appointed times."[61] Boundaries may shift and God providentially directs the movement of peoples and the rise and fall of nations (Job 12:23; Dan 5:25–30; Rom 13:1), but God has also established nations with a sense of belonging to a specific land with specific boundaries.

Nations and the Land in Metonymy

Metonymy is a literary or poetic device "by which one name or noun is used instead of another, to which it stands in a certain relation."[62] Specifically, the authors of Scripture employ a metonymy of subject when they use the land or a nation as a substitute for the people of the nation.[63] In Exodus 7–11, the land of Egypt is described as suffering, but it is the people in the land that are suffering. First and Second Chronicles use a metonymy of subject in several instances to describe David's fame and the fear of God spreading to all the lands (1 Chr 14:17; 2 Chr 17:10; 20:29), God healing the land (2 Chr 7:14), and an enemy king imposing a fine on the land (2 Chr 36:3). Isaiah makes use of a metonymy of subject as the intended audience for one of his oracles (Isa 8:9), the object of God's plan (Isa 14:26), describing the devastating destruction inflicted by the Assyrians (Isa 37:18), and to express the extent of God's salvific plan (Isa 45:22). Ezekiel warns Jerusalem (i.e., the inhabitants of Jerusalem) about engaging in wickedness worse than the lands (i.e., the nations inhabiting those lands) surrounding Jerusalem (Ezek 5:6). Ezekiel also depicts peoples scattered among the lands and gathered from the lands in several locations (Ezek 12:15; 20:23; 22:15; 29:12; 30:26; 36:19, 24). Using land as a metonymy of subject with reference to the nation dwelling within the land further reinforces the tight connection between national identity and an emic perception of geography.[64]

---

61. Keener, *Acts*, 3:2651.

62. Bullinger, *Figures of Speech*, 538.

63. Bullinger defines, "Metonymy of the *Subject* is when the subject is put for something pertaining to it: as the possessor for the possessed; the thing signified for the sign." Bullinger, *Figures of Speech*, 538.

64. Bullinger lists the following passages as metonymy of subject with regard to geography and land: Gen 6:2; 11:1; 28:25; 41:30, 57; 47:15; Deut 9:1; Josh 8:6; Judg 5:7; 1 Sam 14:29; 22:19; 2 Sam 8:2; 25:23; Job 1:15; Ps 9:8; 22:27; 29:8; 66:1, 4; 68:31; 79:7; 105:38; Prov 28:2; Isa 14:31; 23:1; 41:1; 43:3; Jer 3:23; 4:29; 26:2; 48:8; 49:23; Mic 1:4;

The Suffering of the Land of Egypt: Exodus 7–11

Exodus 7–11 is rife with references to land (ארץ). In these five chapters in which the Lord performs signs and brings plagues on Egypt in response to Pharaoh's refusal to let the Israelites depart from Egypt, ארץ is mentioned fifty-three times. Almost half of these references (25) are explicit references to the land of Egypt (אֶרֶץ מִצְרַיִם).[65] A sizeable number of other instances (22) refer just to the land while implying "the land of Egypt" based on the context.[66] Two instances refer to the land of Goshen (8:22; 9:26) (אֶרֶץ גֹּשֶׁן). The remaining four instances (9:14, 15, 16, 29) are variously translated as "land" and "earth" (i.e., the whole earth as in Exod 9:16, כָּל־הָאָרֶץ). The translation of these verses depend largely on whether one sees a universal scope to God's claim on the ארץ in these verses or if the message that the Lord commands Moses to present to Pharaoh is intended to assert the Lord's sovereignty over the land of Egypt in opposition to Pharaoh's claim to dominion over the land. While Wevers argues for a narrower scope based on the fact that elsewhere in this section ארץ refers to the land of Egypt, the general consensus seems to be that ארץ here has a universal connotation.[67] Propp contends that the ambiguity of ארץ in Exod 9:14–16 may be deliberate but ultimately supports understanding "land" as the whole world rather than "the land of Egypt," arguing that the latter reading would be "anticlimactic."[68] Stuart hedges less, asserting that ארץ in Exod 9:14–16 "surely means 'the earth,' that is, the planet, not merely 'the [local] land,' as it can also mean in many contexts. This passage is something of *proto-evangelium*, a call to the whole world (even though it is addressed specifically to Pharaoh) to appreciate what the plagues ultimately showed, that there is one God in control of all things and that he alone can save."[69] Regardless of the contextual mean-

---

6:9; Matt 3:5; 5:13; 11:21, 23; 23:37; Mark 1:5, 33; John 1:10; 3:16–17; 6:33; 7:7; 19:17, 31; 27:21; Acts 8:25; Rom 15:26; I Cor 11:32; 2 Cor 5:19; I John 2:2; 3:1; 5:19. Bullinger, *Figures of Speech*, 567–87.

65. Exod 7:3, 4, 19, 21; 8:5, 6, 7, 16, 17; 9:9, 22, 23, 24, 25: 10:12, 13, 14, 21, 22; 11:3, 5, 6, 9.

66. Exod 7:2; 8:14, 22, 24, 25; 9:5, 29, 33; 10:5, 12, 13, 15, 11:10. LXX supplies the genitive Αἰγύπτου for Exod 11:10, but otherwise translates all of these verses consistent with the Hebrew.

67. Wevers, *Notes on Greek Text of Exodus*, 140. Propp, *Exodus 1–18*, 333; Stuart, *Exodus*, 232; W. Kaiser, "Exodus," 415; T. Alexander, *Exodus*, 190.

68. Propp, *Exodus 1–18*, 333.

69. Stuart, *Exodus*, 232.

A Biblical Theology of Land in Relation to National Identity

ing, if the Lord was asserting authority over the land of Egypt, with the understanding of territorial gods prevalent throughout the ancient Near East, the possible assumption would have been that the Lord was also sovereign over the whole earth.[70]

In addition to the various references to אֶרֶץ, there are four references to גְּבוּל in Exodus 7–11 (8:2; 10:4, 14, 19). גְּבוּל is variously translated as "territory" or "country" in these verses, but never literally as "boundaries."[71] The context of these four verses are the plague of frogs and the plague of locusts. In all of these instances גְּבוּל is used as a parallel reference to אֶרֶץ. In Exod 8:2, the Lord instructs Moses to tell Pharaoh that the Lord will "strike all the territory with frogs" (בַּצְפַרְדְּעִים אָנֹכִי נֹגֵף אֶת־כָּל־גְּבוּלֶךָ), and in Exod 8:5–6 the frogs "come up on the land of Egypt" (וְהַעַל אֶת־הַצְפַרְדְּעִים עַל־אֶרֶץ מִצְרָיִם) and "covered the land" (וַתְּכַס אֶת־אֶרֶץ). In Exod 10:4, Moses and Aaron warn Pharaoh about the impending plague of locusts that the Lord will "bring into your territory" (מֵבִיא מָחָר אַרְבֶּה בִּגְבֻלֶךָ), while one verse later, in 10:5, Moses and Aaron explain that the locusts will "cover the surface of the land so that no one will be able to see the land" (וְכִסָּה אֶת־עֵין הָאָרֶץ וְלֹא יוּכַל לִרְאֹת אֶת־הָאָרֶץ).[72] The parallelism arises again in Exod 10:14, where the locusts "came up over the whole land of Egypt and settled on the whole territory of Egypt" (וַיַּעַל הָאַרְבֶּה עַל כָּל־אֶרֶץ מִצְרַיִם וַיָּנַח בְּכֹל גְּבוּל מִצְרָיִם). The references to גְּבוּל by themselves would increase the geographical aspect of Exodus 7–11. When גְּבוּל is used in literary parallel to אֶרֶץ, the geographical emphasis is further accentuated. Even as the plagues of frogs, locusts, and the other plagues came on and over the land, the land was a metonymy for the actual plague sufferers—the people who dwelled in the land of Egypt.

People and the land in which they dwell frequently share experiences. Heidegger insists, "For as the individual has possessions, so does the people."[73] Scripture illustrates this connection through laws that insist that the land must enjoy Sabbath rests with the people (Exod 23:10–11;

---

70. Block, *Gods of the Nations*, 82–84.

71. LXX renders גְּבוּל as ὅριον in Exod 8:2; 10:4, 14, which has the same generally meaning as גְּבוּל. However, LXX renders גְּבוּל as γῆ in Exod 10:19. No clear consensus is known for the change of terms in Exod 10:19. Wevers, *Notes on Greek Text of Exodus*, 156; Schmidt, "Ὁρίζω," *TDNT*, 5:452.

72. *HALOT*, 818. A literal translation of עַיִן would be "eye," however, *HALOT* suggests a figurative meaning is in view here, explaining that עֵין הָאָרֶץ probably refers to "the surface of the land, probably what is actually visible on it."

73. Heidegger, *Hebel der Hausfreund*, 13.

Lev 25:1–7). Scripture also expresses the connection between people and the land in which they dwell by explaining that the land and the people often share blessings and punishment together. Leviticus 26 explains that if Israel keeps the Sabbath and worships properly, then the Lord will give rain, the land will produce an abundant harvest, and the trees will bear fruit (Lev 26:1–6). If, however, Israel is disobedient to the Lord, then in addition to the people suffering disease and an invasion of enemies, the Israelites will "sow seed in vain" (וּזְרַעְתֶּ֥ם לָרִ֖יק זַרְעֲכֶ֑ם, Lev 26:16) and the "land will not give its produce and the trees of the land will not give fruit" (לֹא־תִתֵּ֤ן אַרְצְכֶם֙ אֶת־יְבוּלָ֔הּ וְעֵ֣ץ הָאָ֔רֶץ לֹ֥א יִתֵּ֖ן פִּרְיֽוֹ, Lev 26:20). Propp observes, "As humanity was created to rule nature (Gen 1:26, 28; 9:2 [P]; cf. 2:19–20 [J]), so may humanity be punished through nature."[74] One may observe this dynamic clearly expressed throughout the plagues on the Egyptian people in Exodus 7–11.

Seven of the ten plagues that God sends on the Egyptians make reference to an impact on the land that serves as a metonymy for the people who dwell in the land.[75] The blood was throughout the land (Exod 7:19), but the Egyptians suffered from the effects (Exod 7:21, 24). The frogs came up on and covered the land of Egypt (Exod 8:5–6), but the people suffered as the frogs came into their houses, into their bedrooms, onto their beds, and into their ovens (Exod 8:3–4). When the frogs died, their bodies were left in the Egyptian houses and courtyards in addition to the open fields (Exod 8:13). Aaron was instructed to strike the "dust of the earth" (עֲפַ֣ר הָאָ֔רֶץ, Exod 8:16–17), but the gnats were on the people and the animals (Exod 8:18). The land of Egypt was "ruined" (שחת) by flies, but swarms of flies came into the houses of Pharaoh, his servants, and all the people (Exod 8:24, 31). Moses threw soot from the brick kiln into the air and it became dust over all the land of Egypt (Exod 9:9), but the people suffered from a painful skin ailment of some kind (Exod 9:11). The hail fell on all the land of Egypt (Exod 9:22, 23–24), but the hail killed the people and animals who were outside in addition to the plants and trees of the field (Exod 9:25). Locusts swarmed over the land and territory (גְּב֖וּל) of Egypt (Exod 10:14), but it was ultimately the people

---

74. Propp, *Exodus 1–18*, 346.

75. The demonstrations of power by God in Exodus 7–11 were likely partially directed towards the Egyptian religious system in order to demonstrate YHWH's sovereignty over the Egyptian gods. However, the way that God manifested these demonstrations of power was upon the land of Egypt with impact upon the people of Egypt. Stuart, *Exodus*, 185.

that suffered from the loss of food. The land of Egypt was covered with darkness (Exod 10:21–22), but it was the people of the land who could not see one another for three days (Exod 10:23). Throughout this section, the distinction between the people and the land in which they live is blurred to the point that the suffering of the land becomes a metonymy for the suffering of the people.

In contrast to the suffering of the Egyptians and the land of Egypt, the people of Israel and the land of Goshen are divinely protected. Exodus 8:22 explains that the land of Goshen is spared from the plague of the flies precisely because it is the land where the people of God "stand" (עָמַד). The land of Goshen is again spared in the plague of hail. While the hail struck down people and animals in the land of Egypt, the land of Goshen, where the "sons of Israel" lived, was spared from the destruction (Exod 9:26). Lastly, the people of Israel were spared from the darkness that weighed on the land of Egypt for three days. Specifically, "all the sons of Israel had light in their area of living (בְּמוֹשְׁבֹתָם)" (Exod 10:23). The Lord treats the land of Goshen differently, but the people who dwell in the land are the object of God's divine grace rather than just the land itself. Yet the land of Goshen is identifiably distinct from the land of Egypt and the people who dwell in the land of Goshen are distinguishable by both the Israelites and Egyptians as distinct at least partially based upon their geographic dwelling. While the name "Goshen" is likely Semitic, an emic name for the region in which the Israelites lived, Sarna explains, "Egyptian texts confirm the presence of Semites and other Asians in the northeastern part of the country, both at the end of the Sixth Dynasty (ca. 2250 B.C.E.) and about 1700 B.C.E., in the wake of the Hyksos invasion."[76] Even at the end of four hundred years of captivity, the Israelites retained a distinct identity from the Egyptians in part because of their geographic location.

The final judgment on Egypt, the death of the first-born (Exod 11:4–5; 12:29–30), also has strong implications for the connection between the land and the people. The Pharaoh was understood as a semi-divine ruler in Egypt.[77] The connection between the ruler of the people and the land of Egypt becomes evident in the coronation ceremony of the crown prince. In a question-and-answer format, the crown prince ceremonially recites the connection between the Egyptian ruler and the Egyptian gods. The Egyptian god, Geb/Seb, plays a pivotal role in the

---

76. Sarna, *Exodus*, 42.
77. Anthes, "Egyptian Theology," 169–212.

divine-human relationship.⁷⁸ Through this ceremony, Anthes concludes that Geb is depicted as both the earth and the prototype of kingship.⁷⁹ Anthes explains,

> Then, in the funerals, the ancestry of both the living and the deceased king was naturally represented by Geb, the father of Osiris. The kingship of both Horus and Osiris, i.e., of Horus-Osiris . . . was reunited in the figure of Geb. Thus Geb became the representative king of the historical past. This interpretation apparently fully accounts for the aspects of Geb as the ruler upon the earth . . . and the ruler of the gods.⁸⁰

The words of the ceremony depicted in the Egyptian Book of the Dead further emphasizes the connection between Geb and the ruler: "Hymns of praise are repeated for [me] by reason of [my] mighty acts, and I am decreed to be the divine Heir of Seb, the lord of the earth, and to be the protector therein. The god Seb refresheth me, and he maketh his risings to be mine."⁸¹ Hart also supports this, explaining, "In the Pyramid Texts we read that Geb actively supports the king in the role of Horus victorious over Seth. The king performs a dance celebrating the belief that Geb will never allow harm to come to the rightful heir of the throne."⁸² Concluding the series of judgments on Egypt with the death of Pharaoh's heir serves as both the final condemnation of the entire Egyptian cultic system and firmly establishing יהוה as God of the ארץ, both the land of Egypt and the whole earth. Geb, serving as the prototype for kingship, ruler of the gods, and ruler upon the earth, combines all of the elements of the previous judgments in one final dramatic moment that affected not only the Egyptian royal family but every household throughout the land of Egypt (Exod 12:30).

Land and the Nations in Metonymy in Chronicles

"Land' (ארץ) is mentioned 114 times in 1 and 2 Chronicles. Frequently (27 times), ארץ is mentioned in a genitive construct referring to a specific land such as the "land of Edom" (1 Chr 1:43), the "land of Judah" (1 Chr

---

78. The god referenced here is variously spelled Geb and Seb in different texts.
79. Anthes, "Egyptian Theology," 175.
80. Anthes, "Egyptian Theology," 209.
81. Budge, *Book of the Dead*, 267.
82. Hart, *Routledge Dictionary*, 59–60.

6:55; 2 Chr 9:11; 11:23; 15:8; 17:2; 19:5), and the "land of the Philistines" (1 Chr 10:9; 2 Chr 9:26). Around nineteen times אֶרֶץ likely has a broader sense of "earth" or "world" (1 Chr 1:10, 19; 16:14, 23, 30, 31, 33; 17:8, 21; 21:16; 29:11, 15; 2 Chr 1:9; 2:12; 6:14, 18, 33; 16:9; 32: 29).[83] A few cases, however, utilize a metonymy of subject where "land" points to the nations in an abstract sense or the people who live in the land. In 1 Chr 14:17, David's name or reputation spreads to other lands. In response to Solomon's prayer at the temple dedication, God promises to heal the land (2 Chr 7:14). The fear of God in the lands surrounding the land of Judah led to peace during the reign of Jehoshaphat (2 Chr 17:10; 20:29). Finally, in the final chapter of 2 Chronicles, King Neco of Egypt imposes a fine on the land after he deposes Jehoahaz (2 Chr 36:3). Each of these passages will be treated separately as the metonymy differs slightly in each passage.

The Name of David Spread Throughout the Lands: 1 Chronicles 14:17

The Chronicler provides a summary statement to conclude all of David's deeds up to that point. The focus of this verse is David's "name" (שֵׁם) going out to all the lands (אֶרֶץ) and "his fear" (פַּחְדּוֹ) being on all the nations (גּוֹיִם). This verse contains a double metonymy. The first is regarding David's "name" and his "fear." The second is found in the parallelism of "lands" and "nations."

First, David's "name went out to all the lands" (וַיֵּצֵא שֵׁם־דָּוִיד בְּכָל־הָאֲרָצוֹת). Allen Ross observes that שֵׁם frequently refers to reputation and carries the nuance of fame.[84] David's fame goes out to all the lands, and the result is that the nations fear him. The "fear" (פַּחַד) of David serves as a metonymy of effect in that the fear is the result of David's name spreading to all the lands. This metonymy is similar to other instances of reputation and fear being related to one another. For instance, Deut 2:25 relates that God intends to put the fear and dread of Israel on the peoples under all the heavens (פַּחְדְּךָ וְיִרְאָתְךָ עַל־פְּנֵי הָעַמִּים תַּחַת כָּל־הַשָּׁמָיִם), or "all the peoples under heaven." The cause for this fear is that the peoples will hear the report (שָׁמַע) about Israel's victories in the wilderness. שָׁמַע, in

---

83. In some cases, the proper scope and translation is not clear and could mean either "land" or "earth" (1 Chr 16:31; 21:12; 2 Chr 6:18; 16:9). However, the change in translation makes little, if any, difference in the meaning of the verse.

84. Ross, "שֵׁם," *NIDOTTE*, 4:147.

its nominal sense, may carry the connotation of reputation or fame in connection with a report of activities.[85]

With the parallelism of פַּחַד and שֵׁם established in 1 Chr 14:17, the parallelism between אֲרָצוֹת and גּוֹיִם becomes evident. As the name/fame of David spread throughout the lands, the Lord brought fear of David upon the nations living within those lands. Japhet observes, "David's victories secure him from additional wars because 'the Lord brought the fear of him upon all nations.' David's greatness has reached its zenith: it is not only he who knows that 'the Lord had established him king' (v. 2), but all the nations around, for his 'fame went out into all the lands.'"[86] Clearly, the "lands" do not literally hear about David's deeds, but the "lands" serve as a metonymy for the nations. The lack of any description of a response from the nations leaves the emphasis on David's fame spreading to all the lands.

Finally, the verb describing the spread of David's name, יצא, reinforces the geographic nature of the expansion of the reputation. While figurative references are present in Scripture (Exod 21:2–5; Lev 25:54; Num 16:46; Deut 24:2; Job 8:10; 15:13; Isa 48:20; Jer 9:3; 11:11), Merrill clarifies the geographic nature of יצא, writing, "The majority of its 1068 occurrences in the OT require a literal, physical meaning of coming or going to some location or other."[87] The Chronicler explains in 1 Chr 14:17 that David's fame spread geographically to the nations. The geographic spread to the nations indicates that David's fame spread out not only from the land of Israel but to other lands that were clearly identifiable with the nations dwelling within defined boundaries.

The Healing of a Land: 2 Chronicles 7:14

Solomon dedicating the Jerusalem temple with prayer and worship provides the setting for God's response in 2 Chronicles 7. God situates his response with the language of covenant and draws upon Solomon's own words used in 2 Chronicles 6.[88] The consequences of Israel's sin have temporal consequences on the land in which they dwell. Drought, famine, pestilence, locusts, and enemies in the land arise in response to

---

85. Aitken, "שָׁמַע," NIDOTTE, 4:175–81; HALOT, 1570–74.
86. Japhet, I & II Chronicles, 290.
87. Merrill, "יָצָא," NIDOTTE, 2:498–99.
88. Japhet, I & II Chronicles, 615; Dillard, 2 Chronicles, 58; Mabie, "1 and 2 Chronicles," 192; Johnstone, 1 and 2 Chronicles, 1:357.

Israel's unfaithfulness to God's covenant (2 Chr 6:26–28; 7:13). Similar to the judgments on the land of Egypt in Exodus 7–11, the judgments anticipated in Solomon's dedicatory prayer are ultimately judgments on people who dwell in the land. Japhet remarks, "God's response [in 2 Chr 7:13–16] is formulated in words taken from the prayer, and relates explicitly three of the calamities mentioned by Solomon, all of which might threaten the people's well-being on the land: drought, locust and pestilence."[89] The land is serving as a metonymy for the nation of Israel. God's covenant promises in 2 Chr 7:14 accentuates the relationship between Israel and the land they inhabit.

After summarizing the curses of covenant violation in 2 Chr 7:13, God begins his covenant promise by addressing "my people" (i.e., Israel), indicating that if they "humble themselves" (יִכָּנְעוּ), "pray" (יִתְפַּלְלוּ), and "seek my face" (יְבַקְשׁוּ פָנָי), then the Lord will "forgive their sin" (אֶסְלַח לְחַטָּאתָם) and "heal their land" (אֶרְפָּא אֶת־אַרְצָם). The actions in the dependent clause all must be taken by Israel. Israel must humble themselves, pray, and seek the Lord. God, in response, will forgive their sin and heal their land. The ultimate object of blessing in this passage is Israel. The land being healed is a result of Israel's response to God. God healing the land is not an end to itself but is intended to bless Israel. Chan, Song, and Brown overlook this when they argue, "While it is possible that 2 Chron 7:14 pictures the drought-stricken and locust-ravaged land as sickly (cf. Deut 29:22) and hence in need of healing, it is hardly proper in Eng. to speak of healing *land*; thus the broader meaning of restore is correct here (accordingly render: 'then will I hear from heaven and forgive their sin and restore their land')."[90] "Heal their land" does make sense in this context if the ultimate object of healing is the nation of Israel. In the same article, Chan, Song, and Brown observe, "Frequently, the prophets used רפא in terms of divine restoration for the nation after a time of judgment and chastisement (e.g., Isa 6:10; Jer 30:17; Hos 5:13; 6:1)."[91] Taking into account that God is the speaker in 2 Chr 7:14, removing the intermediary prophet, and that the context is divine restoration of the nation following covenant curses, "heal their land" should be retained as the proper translation.

God divinely healing the land is parallel to God forgiving Israel's sin. Eichrodt explains that the Old Testament concept of "forgiveness"

---

89. Japhet, *I & II Chronicles*, 615.
90. Chan et al., "רָפָא," *NIDOTTE*, 3:1163.
91. Chan et al., "רָפָא," *NIDOTTE*, 3:1166.

(סלח), both the forgiveness of sin and "the restoration of external good fortune—health, honour, possessions—or defence against external damage from enemies, crop failure, childlessness, early death, and so on."[92] Olivier further contends that the prayer of dedication for the temple (2 Chr 6:3–42) contains five requests for God's forgiveness in response to various situations as a consequence of Israel's sins.[93] He concludes, "Forgiveness entails, accordingly, the removal of sins (cf. Ps 25:11–18), the aversion of punishment, and the restoration of people by means of a redemptive act (Dan 9:19)."[94] The object of God's forgiveness is the nation of Israel, his people who dwell in the land of Israel. God's promise to heal the land from the various afflictions—drought, locusts, and pestilence—portends the holistic nature of God's forgiveness and restoration.[95]

The metonymy between Israel and the land in 2 Chr 7:14 is also very specific in scope. God is referring to a specific land in which Israel dwells. Second Chronicles 7:8 describes the boundary of Israel as "from Lebo Hamath to the Wadi of Egypt" (מִלְּבוֹא חֲמָת עַד־נַחַל מִצְרָיִם). Lebo Hamath marks the northern boundary of Solomon's territory and the Wadi of Egypt serves as the southern boundary.[96] Mabie, arguing against those who are tempted to interpret 2 Chr 7:14 with reference to any other nation or land, emphasizes the limited scope of the land referenced in 2 Chr 7:14, indicating,

> This statement is situated within covenantal particulars related to the Deuteronomic covenant (cf. v. 13), matters of temple theology (and the interwoven Israelite sacrificial system; cf. vv. 15–16), and the Davidic covenant (cf. vv. 17–22). Note that all these features are directly applicable to the nation of Israel located within the specific geographical area of the Promised

---

92. Eichrodt, *Theology of the Old Testament*, 2:455.
93. Olivier, "סָלַח," *NIDOTTE*, 3:261–62.
94. Olivier, "סָלַח," *NIDOTTE*, 3:262.
95. Chan et al., "רָפָא," *NIDOTTE*, 3:1166–67.
96. Mabie, "Geographical Extent of Israel," 321. Some debate exists whether Lebo Hamath is a reference to the "entrance to Hamath" from the perspective of Mesopotamia or from the Israelite perspective. Regardless of the specific location of Lebo Hamath, the two geographic references in 2 Chr 7:8 establish the observed boundaries of the land which serves as the antecedent for the land referenced in 2 Chr 7:14. For further discussion on location of the boundaries in this passage, see Mabie, "2 Chronicles," 314; Mazar, *Early Biblical Period*, 189–202.

A Biblical Theology of Land in Relation to National Identity 39

Land featuring a functioning temple in the city of Jerusalem and having a Davidic king on the throne.[97]

The metonymy between God forgiving the nation of Israel—"my people" (עַמִּי)—and healing the land is clearly delineated in the context of Israel's celebration following the dedication of the temple. The land of 2 Chr 7:14 is not an abstract land, but specifically the land in which Israel inhabits and which is identified by Israel as an essential part of their national identity. The land, therefore, almost certainly functions as a metonymy of subject in parallel to the nation whose sins God promises to heal.

2 Chronicles 17:10 and 20:29

The author of 2 Chronicles provides more information than 1 and 2 Kings regarding the reign of Jehoshaphat. He makes two summary statements regarding Jehoshaphat's victories over the surrounding nations—one at the beginning of the narration (2 Chr 17:10) and one at the end (2 Chr 20:29). The emphasis on these passages is the peace from foreign powers that came as a result of the fear of God spreading to their lands. Within these summary statements, the land again serves as a metonymy of subject.

The geographical emphasis in these two chapters can be observed with the frequency of geographical references. Japhet identifies a heightened emphasis on the land of Judah in 2 Chronicles 17, observing,

> The name "Judah" is, as one would expect extremely common in Chronicles, occurring well over one hundred times. Still, we are struck by the unusual density of its appearance in this chapter, twelve times altogether, in every form: the cities of Judah (vv. 2, 7, 9, 13); the land of Judah (v. 2); all Judah (vv. 5, 19); out of Judah (v. 6); in Judah (vv. 9, 12); of Judah (v. 14); "Judah" alone (v. 10); and the final words of the chapter: "throughout all Judah" (v. 19).[98]

A similar focus on Judah can be found in 2 Chronicles 20, where the name "Judah" is found fourteen times in various forms: all Judah (2 Chr 20:3, 13, 15, 18); Judah alone (2 Chr 20:4, 17, 20, 22, 24); the cities of Judah (2 Chr 20:4); assembly of Judah (2 Chr 20:5); men of Judah (2 Chr

---

97. Mabie, "1 and 2 Chronicles," 192.
98. Japhet, *I & II Chronicles*, 744.

20:27); king over Judah (2 Chr 20:31); and king of Judah (2 Chr 20:35). Japhet further remarks, "Considering that the subject of [chapter 17], king Jehoshaphat, is himself mentioned by name only six times (vv. 1, 3, 5, 10, 11, 12), one wonders whether this stylistic feature is not carefully calculated to highlight the true scene of the events, and the significance of people and land as protagonists on the stage of history."[99] The emphasis on the land of Judah in these chapters is laid in contrast to the "kingdoms of the lands" surrounding Judah.

The author indicates that the fear of the Lord/God (פַּחַד; פַּחַד יהוה אֱלֹהִים) was on all the "kingdoms of the lands" (עַל כָּל־מַמְלְכוֹת הָאֲרָצוֹת). The lands to which the author refers are the lands surrounding Judah. Mabie compares the fear of the Lord spreading to the surrounding nations to the similar way that the fear of David spread with his name in 1 Chr 14:17.[100] At least two insights may be derived from the genitival construct "all the kingdoms of the lands." First, despite "the lands" being identified as the location of the kingdoms, the land still serves as a metonymy of subject. The land is both the location of the kingdoms and also representative of the nations in those lands. While "kingdoms" is probably the best translation in 2 Chr 17:10 and 20:29, this translation can result in the phrase "kingdoms of the lands" appearing redundant since "kingdom" tends to inherently include a territorial aspect in English. The abstract form מַלְכוּת is preferred in Chronicles rather than מַמְלָכָה.[101] The distinction between these terms is subtle, but Nel explains,

> Although the semantic aspects of these words largely overlap, it seems as though a stronger emphasis is put on the activity of ruling in the case of מַלְכוּת. It therefore also refers to the right or office of ruling as king (e.g., 1 Sam 20:31; 1 Kgs 2:12–15, 1 Chron 12:24), royal dignity (Esth 1:4), and even to the period of reign (e.g., Jer 49:34). In 1 Chron 29:30 the two terms are clearly separated in the same context, i.e., מַמְלָכָה (kingdom), and מַלְכוּת (the office of being king).[102]

---

99. Japhet, *I & II Chronicles*, 744. The same contrast is not present in 2 Chronicles 20. King Japhet is mentioned fourteen times in 2 Chronicles 20, even with the number of times that Judah is mentioned. Even so, the even number does not diminish the emphasis on Judah in 2 Chronicles 20.

100. Mabie, "1 and 2 Chronicles," 234.

101. Nel, "מָלַךְ," *NIDOTTE*, 2:957–58.

102. Nel, "מָלַךְ," *NIDOTTE*, 2:957–58.

A Biblical Theology of Land in Relation to National Identity   41

Therefore, while kingdom remains the best translation, the emphasis in 2 Chr 17:10 and 20:29 is on the office of being king. This means that "kingdom" is not a substitute for "nation" in these verses. "Kingdom" refers to the office and institution of the king while the "land" serves as a metonymy for the nation that lives in the land.

The "lands" of 2 Chr 17:10 and 20:29 are also identifiable as distinct lands associated with specific nations. The "lands that surrounded Judah" in 1 Chr 17:10 likely refers to the nations to the west and south of Judah—specifically the Arabs and Philistines who brought gifts to Jehoshaphat (1 Chr 17:11).[103] The lands referenced in 2 Chr 20:29 are broader than in 2 Chr 17:10. Japhet relates,

> While v. 29a is almost a repetition of 17.10, there are several differences. According to 17.10, 'the fear of the Lord fell on all the kingdoms . . . *round about Judah*', and according to the Chronicler's portrait, Jehoshaphat could boast peace only on three sides of his kingdom. In this present chapter, these limitations are no longer necessary, so we read 'the fear of God came on all the kingdoms of the countries.'[104]

The lands, while unspecified in 2 Chr 20:29, are distinctly differentiated from the land of Judah, indicating that there was awareness on both the part of Judah and the other kingdoms that certain geographic territory belonged to each.

Laying a Tribute on the Land: 2 Chronicles 36:3

The author of Chronicles briefly narrates the flurry of royal transitions depending on which foreign power held sway at a given moment leading up to the destruction of Jerusalem and the Babylonian exile. The "people of the land" (עַם־הָאָרֶץ) appoint Jehoahaz as king following the death of Josiah (1 Chr 36:1).[105] However, King Neco of Egypt promptly deposes Jehoahaz after only three months (1 Chr 36:2–3). Neco also imposes a fine or a tribute on the land (וַיַּעֲנֹשׁ אֶת־הָאָרֶץ).

---

103. Japhet, *I & II Chronicles*, 750–51; Dillard, *2 Chronicles*, 134–35; Mabie, "2 Chronicles," 337. For further discussion of the Hebrew term סָבִיב, see chapter 3.

104. Japhet, *I & II Chronicles*, 799; Mabie, "Geographical Extent of Israel," 323.

105. For a discussion regarding the meaning and use of the phrase עַם־הָאָרֶץ, see Oppenheimer, *'Am Ha-Aretz*.

The author does not explicitly identify who is responsible for paying the fine.[106] However, 2 Kgs 23:35 clarifies that Neco imposes the fine on "the people of the land."[107] The clarification is consistent with the normal use of עֹנֶשׁ in Scripture, where it is only used eight times, mostly in Proverbs, and always, except for 2 Chr 36:3, with an individual person as the one to pay the fine (twice in Ex 21:22; Deut 22:19; Prov 17:26; 21:11; 22:3; 27:12). The use of "land" as a metonymy for the "people of the land" is clear in 2 Chr 36:3. The people who dwell in the land of Judah, specifically the people who proclaimed Jehoahaz as king, is the referent in 2 Chr 36:3. Rather than people of any land, King Neco of Egypt lays a fine upon the people of the land of Judah. The singular phrase עַם־הָאָרֶץ contains a geographic reference to the land of Israel. Oppenheimer explains, "When the term 'am ha-aretz occurs in the Bible in the plural, in the form of 'ammei ha-aretz or 'ammei ha-aratzot, it generally denotes foreigners, in contrast to the children of Israel, and it can then mean either the peoples of the world or those living in Eretz Israel."[108] Thus, Neco is specifically placing a fine on Jewish people living in the land of Judah, given that the Northern Kingdom had already fallen to the Assyrians over a century earlier.

The Lands and the Nations in Metonymy in Isaiah

Isaiah engages his audience with a blend of poetry and prose throughout the entire book, so one should expect to find a variety of literary devices.[109] Isaiah 8:9 records an oracle instructing the lands to listen to and obey the commands given. The Lord describes his plan for all the nations in terms of the whole earth (Isa 14:26). Most curiously, Isaiah employs an unusual construct to describe the Assyrian destruction of the lands (Isa 37:18). Finally, in the scope of redemptive history, the Lord calls for all the "all the ends of the earth" to turn to him and be saved (Isa 45:22).

---

106. Dillard, *2 Chronicles*, 299.
107. Japhet, *I & II Chronicles*, 1063.
108. Oppenheimer, *'Am Ha-Aretz*, 11.
109. Motyer, *Prophecy of Isaiah*, 23–25.

The Distant Land Commanded to Listen: Isaiah 8:9

The specific setting of Isa 8:9 is disputed, but likely seems set during the Syro-Ephraimite War.[110] The audience of this passage is similarly disputed primarily depending on the setting. Regardless of who the "peoples" are—whether they are Aramaeans and Israelites of the Northern Kingdom, one of the anti-Assyrian coalitions, or a generic reference to any nations who oppose God—the oracle places the "distant lands" in a poetic parallel metonymy with the peoples.

Scholars debate the proper translation of רֹעוּ. Young argues for a translation of "Be ye evil" based on the thought that רֹעוּ is derived from the base רַע.[111] Motyer rejects this option, preferring to translate רֹעוּ as "Raise the war cry."[112] Kaiser relies on the LXX translation (γινώσκω), contending that the original text of Isa 8:9 was דְעוּ, resulting in a translation of "Mark it."[113] Kaiser, while emphasizing the parallelism between רֹעוּ and הַאֲזִינוּ, argues that a scribal error is not necessary for the parallelism to exist. Relying on a root of רעה, both Williamson and Childs indicate the word should have some sense of gathering or assembling together.[114] This option seems to make sense both linguistically and contextually. "Assemble" or "Band together" maintains the poetic parallelism with the command to "listen" in the second half of the verse but does not rely on a scribal error to maintain the parallelism. The reason that the peoples gather together is to hear the Lord's warning about the devastating consequences that accompany preparing for war against God's people.

The second part of each of the pronouncements uses distant lands (מֶרְחַקֵּי־אָרֶץ) as a metonymy for the "peoples" (עַמִּים) who dwell in those distant lands. God is warning the nations about the consequences of waging war against Judah. Hyun Chul Paul Kim explains, "This hymn mocks all daunting nations in their forming alliances together, announcing that they will be 'shattered.'"[115] Young also observes, "Now [Isaiah] speaks to

---

110. Young, *Book of Isaiah*, 1:300–308; Kaiser, *Isaiah 1–12*, 187–88; Oswalt, *Book of Isaiah: Chapters 40–66*, 195–96; Motyer, *Prophecy of Isaiah*, 71; Watts, *Isaiah 1–33*, 78; G. Smith, *Isaiah 1–39*, 219; Kim, *Reading Isaiah*, 63.

111. Young, *Book of Isaiah*, 1:307. See also Sæbø, "Traditionsgeschichte von Jesaia 8:9–10," 132–44.

112. Motyer, *Prophecy of Isaiah*, 94.

113. O. Kaiser, *Isaiah 1–12*, 187. For a full discussion and refutation of this position, see Williamson, *Commentary on Isaiah 1–27*, 2:260–61.

114. Williamson, *Commentary on Isaiah 1–27*, 2:73.

115. Kim, *Reading Isaiah*, 64.

the remote parts of the earth. All the nations who are regarded as God's enemies are addressed."[116] The metonymy of subject in Isa 8:9 does not seem to be in question. However, many English translations render אֶרֶץ in the plural (e.g., lands or countries). The NASB renders the phrase as "remote places of the earth" (מֶרְחַקֵּי־אָרֶץ), which may make more sense grammatically. Regardless of which translation is more accurate, the general meaning of the statement holds true and the parallel with the "peoples" is the whole phrase מֶרְחַקֵּי־אָרֶץ rather than any one element of it.

The Plan for the Whole Earth: Isaiah 14:26

Isaiah 14:24–27 presents an oath spoken by God initially against Assyria in preparation for their overthrow.[117] The attention shifts from Assyria to all the nations in Isa 14:26. After declaring his authority over Assyria and pronouncing judgment on the nation in Isa 14:25, the Lord reveals that he has a plan for "the whole earth" (כָּל־הָאָרֶץ).[118] The "whole earth" serves as a metonymy of subject for all the nations of the earth.

In Isa 14:26a, the Lord indicates that he has a "plan prepared" (הָעֵצָה הַיְּעוּצָה). Wolters perceives, "An *ʿēṣâ* is a plan of action, both as it is conceived in the mind and as it is communicated to others."[119] Motyer, identifying the transition between the specific incident in Isa 14:24 and the universal scope of the Lord's authority in Isa 14:26, observes, "Isaiah hammers home that the local event—the Assyrian overthrow—is the model of the universal, which is yet to come."[120] The Lord's "plan prepared" parallels the "outstretched hand" (הַיָּד הַנְּטוּיָה). Smith relates, "In these verses [Isa 14:26–27] the prophet relates God's plans to use his powerful outstretched hand (14:26b, 27b, cf. 5:25; 9:12, 17, 20; 10:4), which will carry out his designs for the nations."[121] In other contexts, the Lord stretching out his hands is used in the context of judgment (Prov

---

116. Young, *Book of Isaiah*, 1:308.
117. Kim, *Reading Isaiah*, 88.
118. The phrase כָּל־הָאָרֶץ is better translated as "the whole earth" rather than "the whole land" in this and similar contexts where the emphasis is on the universal sovereignty of God. However, this translation does not diminish or negate the geographic element. "The earth" is not an abstract concept but rather is a real place in which nations dwell. C. Wright, "אֶרֶץ," *NIDOTTE*, 1:518.
119. Wolters, "יָעַץ," *NIDOTTE*, 2:490.
120. Motyer, *Prophecy of Isaiah*, 146.
121. G. Smith, *Isaiah 1–39*, 321.

1:24; Isa 31:3; Jer 15:6; Ezek 6:14; 14:9, 13; 25:7, 13, 16; 35:3; Zeph 1:4; 2:13). Kaiser observes, "The application of this anthropomorphic image to the enemy seems to be influenced by the Deuteronomic set phrase of the mighty hand and outstretched arm of Yahweh."[122] While the metaphorical use of יָד can refer to either judgment or salvation, references to God stretching out his hand are only used in the context of judgment.[123] The oath that God swears concerning his plan to judge Assyria points forward to his plan to judge all the nations of the earth with his outstretched hand.

The parallel pronouncements of judgment emphasize the correlation between "the whole earth" and "all the nations." The structure of the verse emphasizes this parallel utilizing the rare phrase עַל־כָּל־הַגּוֹיִם to parallel עַל־כָּל־הָאָרֶץ.[124] Some scholars argue that Isa 14:26 has a narrower scope in the broader context of Isaiah 14. Childs contends, "The passage further establishes the typological link between Assyria and Babylon. Just as God's plan against Assyria has unfolded and Assyria has been destroyed, so also the promise to include equally arrogant Babylon is part of the selfsame promise."[125] Young suggests, "Sometimes a large empire is hyperbolically represented as being the entire earth, and is so far as that is the case, the determination of God to destroy Assyria may be called a determination against the entire earth."[126] Kim, however, counters, "Even though this subunit concerns Assyria, it thematically connects to its preceding unit on Babylon, while also paving a smooth transition to subsequent oracles against other nations."[127] The promised downfall of Babylon in Isa 14:3–23 transitions to the Lord's oath against Assyria in Isa 14:24–25 to pronouncements against Philistia (Isa 14:28–32), Moab (Isa 15:1—16:12), Damascus (Isa 17:1–3), Israel (Isa 17:4–11), Cush (Isa 18:1–6), Egypt (Isa 19:1–24), Babylon (Isa 21:1–10), Dumah (Isa 21:11–12), Arabia (Isa 21:13–15), Jerusalem (Isa 22:1–14), Shebna (Isa 22:15–25), Tyre (Isa 23:1–18), and a concluding pronouncement

---

122. O. Kaiser, *Isaiah 13–39*, 47.

123. Dreytza, "יָד," *NIDOTTE*, 2:403.

124. Both phrases are relatively rare in Scripture. עַל־כָּל־הָאָרֶץ occurs eight times outside of Isa 14:26 exclusively in the Psalms and the prophetic books (Ps 47:3; 57:6; 83:19; 97:9; Isa 28:22; Jer 1:18; Zech 14:9). עַל־כָּל־הַגּוֹיִם occurs seven times apart from Isa 14:26 (Deut 26:19; 1 Chr 14:17; Isa 25:17; 34:2; Jer 25:13; Obad 1:15; Zech 7:14).

125. Childs, *Isaiah*, 127.

126. Young, *Book of Isaiah*, 1:449.

127. Kim, *Reading Isaiah*, 88.

concerning the judgment and salvation of the nations in Isa 24–25. A second short pronouncement regarding the nations is placed in the midst of these judgments in Isa 17:12–14. The intention of Isa 14:26 is to describe the universality of God's authority rather than over any one portion of the earth, regardless of how extensive a single nation's power may extend. The metonymy of subject with "all the earth" serving as a substitute for "all the nations" further reinforces the scriptural emphasis on a geographic component to national identity even when the scope is so broad as to include all the land and all the nations.

Assyrian Devastation of the Lands: Isaiah 37:18

In isolation from the rest of Scripture, scholars wrestle with the precise meaning and even the textual content of Isa 37:18. Translated literally, the verse would read, "Truly, YHWH, the kings of Assyria have laid waste to all the lands and their lands" (אָמְנָם יהוה הֶחֱרִיבוּ מַלְכֵי אַשּׁוּר אֶת־כָּל־הָאֲרָצוֹת וְאֶת־אַרְצָם). The phrasing forces translators to make contextual decisions with many choosing to render the last portion "all the countries and their lands," or "all the nations and their lands."[128] The Clementine Vulgate swaps the order, placing "lands" first and "their regions" second, so Isa 37:18 is rendered as, "Vere enim, Domine, desertas fecerunt reges Assyriorum terras, et regiones earum." The LXX simply drops וְאֶת־אַרְצָם, but chooses to utilize χώρα rather than γῆ, "ἐπ' ἀληθείας γὰρ ἠρήμωσαν βασιλεῖς Ἀσσυρίων τὴν οἰκουμένην ὅλην καὶ τὴν χώραν αὐτῶν." Similarly, 1QIsaa also shortens the verse to read, אמנם יהוה החריבו מלכי אשור את כול הארצות. The unusual phrasing has led Delitzsch to conclude, "[W]e cannot help regarding the reading אֶת־כָּל־הָאֲרָצוֹת וְאֶת־אַרְצָם as a mistake, when compared with the reading of the book of Kings ... If we read *haggōyīm* (the nations), we get rid both of the reference to their own land which is certainly purposeless here, and also of the otherwise inevitable conclusion that they burned the gods of their own country."[129] Hobbs

---

128. For "all the countries and their lands," see CSB and NASB. For "all the nations and their lands," see CEB, ESV, KJV, NKJV, NRSV. The NIV translates Isa 37:18 as "all these peoples and their lands," which properly sees the connection between peoples and the lands in which they live, but "peoples" seems out of place as a translation in this setting since the parallel verse in 2 Kgs 19:17 reads "all the nations."

129. Delitzsch argues that "their lands" indicates that the Assyrians devastated their own lands in addition to the lands of the nations. Delitzsch, *Isaiah*, 364. See also O. Kaiser, *Isaiah 13–39*, 372.

simply dismisses the כָּל־הָאֲרָצוֹת of Isa 37:18 in place of הַגּוֹיִם from 2 Kgs 19:17 as redundant.[130] Addressing the difficulties associated with this passage, Young explains, "The parallel passage in 2 Kings reads 'all the nations and their land.' Various expedients have been proposed to solve the difficulty, but quite probably Isaiah simply means 'all the nations of the lands and their land.'"[131] Young is close to identifying the metonymy that the author appears to be using in Isa 37:18.

Isaiah 37:18 uses אֶרֶץ in two different ways. The second instance, אַרְצָם, refers to the literal lands of the nations that the Assyrians had devastated in their numerous military victories.[132] The first instance does, as Young indicated, refer to the nations who dwell in the devastated lands. However, the metonymy between the nations and their lands is apparently so clear to Hezekiah as the speaker and Isaiah's readers that they could simply refer to "all the lands," knowing that the audience would understand that the referent would be the nations, especially when immediately followed by a literal reference to the lands. Arguments that rely on the lack of the double wording in the LXX lose considerable weight when taking into account that χώρα frequently refers to either a nation or its territory (Gen 10:20; Isa 19:20; 1 Macc 1:4).[133] It is possible that the LXX translator combined the two references into a single word rather than omitting one of them. Young concludes, "Hezekiah is acknowledging that Sennacherib and his hosts have laid waste the inhabitants of the lands and their lands themselves."[134] Attempts to find an alternative explanation appear unnecessary and overlook the recognized connection that a nation has with its land. Hezekiah is employing כָּל־הָאֲרָצוֹת as a metonymy of subject to refer to the nations who dwell in the various and identifiable lands.

Salvation to the Ends of the Earth: Isaiah 45:22

Isaiah 45:22 employs the phrase "all ends of the earth" (כָּל־אַפְסֵי־אָרֶץ), further demonstrating how אֶרֶץ is used as a metonymy of subject for

---

130. Hobbs, *2 Kings*, 267
131. Young, *Book of Isaiah*, 2: 485.
132. For an account of the military campaigns of Sennacherib and other Assyrian kings see Hawkins, "Neo-Hittite States," 372–441.
133. Silva, "Χώρα," *NIDNTTE*, 4:712.
134. Young, *Book of Isaiah*, 2:485.

nations in Isaiah.[135] In Isa 45:22, the Lord issues the command, "Turn to me and be saved, all the ends of the earth" (פְּנוּ־אֵלַי וְהִוָּשְׁעוּ כָּל־אַפְסֵי־אָרֶץ). Oswalt observes that most commentators agree that this segment is about the salvation of the world, with a few notable exceptions.[136] Whybray suggests that this passage is strictly concerned with encouraging Israelite exiles and regards attempts to see Isa 45:22 as an offer of salvation to all the nations as a "doctrinal innovation."[137] He further asserts that Deutero-Isaiah never "unequivocally" uses the phrase "the ends of the earth" to refer to the nations of the world, preferring to interpret כָּל־אַפְסֵי־אָרֶץ as denoting the created world.[138] However, this interpretation seems to strain the context of Isa 45:18–25, running counter to the assertion that God specifically created the world to be inhabited (Isa 45:18), and, as will be demonstrated, Isa 45:22, employs כָּל־אַפְסֵי־אָרֶץ as a metonymy of subject referring to all the nations of the earth. Watts perceives this scene as a dialogue between YHWH and Cyrus, which leads him to interpret Isa 45:22 as Cyrus offering salvation "to the borderlands of Palestine."[139] However, "borderlands" is not an appropriate translation of אֶפֶס.[140] If the author desired to express "borderlands," גְּבוּל would be a more appropriate term to use. This passage seems to be clarifying that God is the ultimate savior even though Cyrus has been anointed as the instrument of salvation in the immediate context (Isa 45:1–13).

Shalom Paul identifies the similarity between Isa 45:22 and Ps 22:27.[141] Psalm 22:27a reads, "All the ends of the earth will remember and turn to the Lord" (יִזְכְּרוּ וְיָשֻׁבוּ אֶל־יהוה כָּל־אַפְסֵי־אָרֶץ). The similarities in motif and vocabulary appear to support Paul's assertion that Psalm 22 possibly influenced the phrasing of Isa 45:22–25.[142] If Paul is correct, then

---

135. "The ends of the earth" is a common phrase and motif in Isaiah. Only Isa 45:22 and Isa 52:10 read כָּל־אַפְסֵי־אָרֶץ. Other places in Isaiah use קָצֶה or כָּנָף rather than אֶפֶס (Isa 5:26; 23:17; 24:16; 41:9; 42:10; 43:6; 48:20; 49:6; 62:11). All three words have similar meanings referring to the "end" or "extremity." *HALOT*, 79, 486, 1120; Hill, "אֶפֶס," *NIDOTTE*, 1:481–82; Matties and Longman, "קָצֶה," *NIDOTTE*, 3:959–60; Klein and Matties, "כָּנָף," *NIDOTTE*, 2:670–71.

136. Oswalt, *Book of Isaiah: Chapters 40–66*, 220.

137. Whybray, *Isaiah 40–66*, 111–12.

138. Whybray, *Isaiah 40–66*, 112.

139. Watts, *Isaiah 34–66*, 705, 707.

140. *HALOT*, 79.

141. Paul, *Isaiah 40–66*, 271.

142. Paul, *Isaiah 40–66*, 271.

Ps 22:27b provides the referent for כָּל־אַפְסֵי־אָרֶץ. The psalmist declares, "And all the families of the nations will bow down before you" (וְיִשְׁתַּחֲווּ לְפָנֶיךָ כָּל־מִשְׁפְּחוֹת גּוֹיִם). Ross, commenting on Ps 22:27, explains, "'All the ends of the earth' will turn to the LORD, that is, the people who live in the ends of the earth (a metonymy of subject)."[143] Charles and Emilie Briggs also identify the similarity between Ps 22:28 and Isa 45:22, further explaining that "all the families of the nations" likely refers back to the patriarchal blessings of Gen 12:3 and Gen 28:14.[144] The vocabulary of Ps 22:27 points back further to the fourfold formulas of Gen 10:5, 20, and 31, where אֲרָצֹת, מִשְׁפְּחֹת, and גּוֹיֵ are used together to describe all the various peoples to the farthest reaches of the earth. While כָּל־אַפְסֵי־אָרֶץ is a broad reference and poetically refers to all the nations of the earth rather than any specific, identifiable nations, the fact that the nations can be referenced in such a way infers the close connection between the nations and the land in which they dwell. Furthermore, the apparent connection becomes more clear in the context of Isa 45:18, which proclaims that God formed and made the אֶרֶץ specifically to be inhabited by the nations. Clements explicitly relates the meaning of this passage, writing, "In the greatest and most openly evangelical invitation which the Old Testament anywhere contains, God makes his own appeal to all the nations and peoples to turn to him: 'Turn to me and be saved, all the ends of the earth! For I am God, and there is no other' (Isa. 45:22)."[145]

The Lands and the Nations in Metonymy in Ezekiel

The book of Ezekiel uses less poetic structure than other prophets. In defense of Ezekiel as the primary author, Block opines, "In my view, there is no reason to doubt that many of Ezekiel's oracles were recorded immediately. Indeed, the autobiographical narrative (as opposed to poetic) style suggests the prophet probably recorded them himself."[146] Despite the lack of emphasis on poetry, Ezekiel does make extensive use of metonymies of subject regarding land and the nations, but in a more limited way than Isaiah or Chronicles. Ezekiel situates Jerusalem in the middle of the lands in Ezek 5:5–6. Apart from this, Ezekiel has a significant number of instances

---

143. Ross, *Commentary on the Psalms*, 1:546.
144. Briggs and Briggs, *Book of Psalms*, 1:199–200.
145. Clements, "Isaiah 45:20–25," 393.
146. Block, *Book of Ezekiel: Chapters 1–27*, 21–22.

describing how Israel and various other nations would be scattered among the lands as punishment but regathered from among the lands in response to their faithfulness (Ezek 12:15; 20:23; 22:15; 29:12; 30:26; 36:19, 24).

Jerusalem in the Middle of Rebellious Lands: Ezekiel 5:5–6

Two metonymies of subject occur in Ezek 5:5–6, where Ezekiel delivers a message of condemnation on Jerusalem. First, God reveals that he placed Jerusalem "in the center of the nations and lands all around her" (זֹאת יְרוּשָׁלַם בְּתוֹךְ הַגּוֹיִם שַׂמְתִּיהָ וּסְבִיבוֹתֶיהָ אֲרָצוֹת). This verse has resulted in considerable discussion regarding the view that Jerusalem formed the "center of the earth" in Jewish cosmography.[147] This debate will be addressed in chapter 3. The focus for this section is the way that גּוֹיִם and אֲרָצוֹת are used in a parallel construct so that אֲרָצוֹת constitutes a metonymy of subject referring to the גּוֹיִם. Apart from whatever theological or cosmographic implications may or may not be intended, the immediate context of the passage is primarily geographical, with missiological implications.[148] Jerusalem did exist in a geographically central location. Wright comments, "This description might be considered appropriate in purely geographical terms. Jerusalem, and the land in which it was situated, did indeed stand at the hub of the ancient world of empires, if one considers Mesopotamia to the east, Egypt to the west, the Anatolian empires to

---

147. Many see the reference to Jerusalem as the "center" or "navel" of the world in Ezek 38:12 (עַל־טַבּוּר הָאָרֶץ) as a parallel statement to Ezek 5:5. Scott, *Paul and the Nations*, 9–10, 131, 138; Cooke, *Book of Ezekiel*, 58; L. Allen, *Ezekiel 1–19*, 72; L. Allen, *Ezekiel 20–48*, 206; Eichrodt, *Ezekiel*, 88, 524; Olley, *Ezekiel*, 499; Sweeney, *Reading Ezekiel*, 40. Block rejects the view that Ezek 5:5 is suggesting that Jerusalem is the "navel" of the whole world based on linguistic differences with Ezek 38:12 and contextual considerations. Block, *Book of Ezekiel: Chapters 28–48*, 448. See also Tuell, "טַבּוּר," *NIDOTTE*, 2:333–34; Tuell, "תָּוֶךְ," *NIDOTTE*, 4:279–80; Woodward, "Medieval Mappaemundi," 340. For more of the "navel of the earth" motif in ancient literature, see Zimmerli, *Ezekiel 1*, 174–75; Zimmerli, *Ezekiel*, 2:310–11.

148. Wright observes, "For Jerusalem or Israel to be *in the centre of the nations*, then, meant much more than a territorial grid-reference. It was a shorthand way of expressing all the universality of God's purposes among the nations that was bound up in the particularity of Israel's election. That is, if Israel were the hub at the centre of the wheel, it was for the sake of the spokes and the rim that they were there at all." C. Wright, *Message of Ezekiel*, 88. Cooper also relates, "Israel was set in the 'midst' of the nations as a kingdom of priests, and thus they were supposed to be instruments of God's missionary purpose." Cooper, *Ezekiel*, 102.

the north, and the Ethiopian and Arabian cultures to the south."[149] The Lord then makes the same statement, but reverses the order in the second half of the verse: "and the lands all around her" (וּסְבִיבוֹתֶיהָ אֲרָצוֹת). Olley contends, "In LXX it is Jerusalem together with the surrounding regions that have been placed in the midst of the nations."[150] However, the "lands" most likely is a metonymy of subject referring to the nations that surround Jerusalem and among which Jerusalem has been placed in the center. Block explains that Ezek 5:5 is situating Jerusalem's position in the context of her neighbors.[151] Wright further observes, "The combinations of 'nations and countries', or 'peoples and lands' is a favourite expression of Ezekiel."[152] Furthermore, סָבִיב in Hebrew and κύκλῳ in LXX tend to have the meaning of surrounding a central location.[153]

Second, in Ezek 5:6, Jerusalem is condemned for rebelling against God's "ordinances" (מִשְׁפָּטַי) and "statutes" (חֻקּוֹתַי) more than the גּוֹיִם and אֲרָצוֹת that surround (סְבִיבוֹתֶיהָ) her. "The lands" serve as a parallel to "the nations" as a metonymy of subject. The parallel becomes evident when we see the close connection between "ordinances" and "statutes." Hummel points out, "The two words (מִשְׁפָּט and חֻקָּה) are a nearly constant pair throughout the Bible, together virtually forming a hendiadys."[154] Applying one side of the hendiadys to "the nations" and the other side to "the lands all around her" forms a poetic parallel that should lead the reader to naturally draw a connection between "the lands" and "the nations." Furthermore, the poetic allusion to the nations as "the lands" is strengthened by the fact that land cannot rebel against statutes. The Lord is saying that the nations who dwell in those lands are rebelling against his statutes. A metonymy of subject only works in poetic construct when both sides are so closely connected that the author can refer to one and mean the other. While the Lord does not explicitly identify the nations surrounding Jerusalem, it is clear that the nations are identifiable at least in part by the lands in which they dwell.

149. C. Wright, *Message of Ezekiel*, 86–87.

150. Olley, *Ezekiel*, 265.

151. Block, *Book of Ezekiel: Chapters 28–48*, 447–48.

152. C. Wright, *Message of Ezekiel*, 86 n. 62.

153. The geographical meaning of סָבִיב and κύκλῳ will be addressed at length in chapter 3.

154. Hummel, *Ezekiel 1–20*, 170. While the pair do occur thirty-six times throughout the Old Testament, Ezekiel contains fifteen of מִשְׁפָּט and חֻקָּה as a pair (Ezek 5:6, 7; 11:20; 18:9, 17, 19, 21; 20:11, 13, 16, 19, 21, 24; 37:24; 44:24). Even if the words do not necessarily form a hendiadys through Scripture, they certainly do in the book of Ezekiel.

Scattered and Gathered: Ezekiel 12:15; 20:23; 22:15; 29:12; 30:26; 36:19, 24

Ezekiel uses "nations" and "lands" together frequently, but most commonly these words are expressed in the context of either scattering rebellious people among the nations and lands or promising to graciously gather them from among the nations and lands.[155]

Ezekiel alludes to the fulfillment of the covenant curse of Lev 26:33–45 describing the dispersion of Jerusalem's residents among the nations in exile.[156] The prophet repeatedly warns that the Lord will "disperse" (פּוּץ) the residents of Jerusalem among the nations and "scatter" (זָרָה) them among the lands (Ezek 12:15; 20:23; 22:15; 36:19). Ezekiel additionally addresses punishing Egypt in similar terms (Ezek 22:12; 30:26). פּוּץ and זָרָה are used together seven times in Ezekiel, and each time are used in the formulaic expression "I will disperse them among the nations and scatter them among the lands" (הֲפִיץ אֹתָם בַּגּוֹיִם וְלְזָרוֹת אוֹתָם בָּאֲרָצוֹת).[157] Both of these terms, פּוּץ and זָרָה, are roughly synonymous in that both terms are used extensively to describe scattering people in judgment.[158] The synonymous nature of these terms is reinforced by LXX rendering פּוּץ as διασκορπίζω and זָרָה as διασπείρω, which are also roughly synonymous.[159] The parallelism in the verbs continues to parallelism in the nouns: גּוֹיִם and אֲרָצוֹת. The אֲרָצוֹת (sometimes translated "countries") serves as a metonymy of subject for the גּוֹיִם in these formulaic pronouncements throughout Ezekiel.

In contrast to the dispersion of Israel among the nations, Ezekiel communicates God's promise of gathering Israel from among the nations following the exile in Ezek 36:24. Wright observes, "The restoration of Israel to their own land is described in terms that echo the original exodus in which God had taken Israel 'out' of Egypt and brought them into the promised land."[160] Ezekiel 36:24 also represents the fulfillment of the covenant promise of restoration following exile given in Deut 30:3–5. Given

---

155. C. Wright, *Message of Ezekiel*, 86n. 62.

156. Block, *Book of Ezekiel: Chapters 28–48*, 347.

157. Ezek 22:15 is addressed directly to Jerusalem so the second-person feminine singular pronoun is used rather than the third-person plural pronoun.

158. Carrol R. and Futano, "זָרָה," *NIDOTTE*, 1:1145; Carrol R., "פּוּץ," *NIDOTTE*, 3:585–89.

159. Silva, "Διασπορά," *NIDNTTE*, 4:705; Silva, "Σκορπίζω," *NIDNTTE*, 4:318.

160. C. Wright, *Message of Ezekiel*, 293.

the apparently intentional reversal of fortunes for Israel, it is completely appropriate for Ezekiel to utilize a similar formula for the reversal of the scattering. Ezekiel 36:24 expresses God's promise to "take you from the nations and gather you from all the lands" (וְלָקַחְתִּי אֶתְכֶם מִן־הַגּוֹיִם וְקִבַּצְתִּי אֶתְכֶם מִכָּל־הָאֲרָצוֹת). In the promise of this new exodus, Israel would be taken out from the אֲרָצוֹת in which the גּוֹיִם dwell and taken to a land of their own (וְהֵבֵאתִי אֶתְכֶם אֶל־אַדְמַתְכֶם).[161]

Conclusion

This lengthy section through significant portions of the Old Testament has been an attempt to show how closely a nation and its land are interconnected in Scripture. While all of the references in this section are found in the Old Testament, the Old Testament was the Bible of the early church, and it served as the theological foundation for the church, including its theology of mission.[162] The New Testament content is more limited in this particular aspect, but the overwhelming Old Testament evidence on this particular matter almost certainly impacted the first-century approach to missions.

National Identity and the Land

The connection between national identity and the land in which the nation lives is a complex relationship but undoubtedly essential. Daniel Block illustrates national identity as a triangle with "deity," "people," and "land" at each of the points. Block explains, "In this scheme of things each element is vital, not only because it is related to both of the other elements, but also because it has a significant bearing on the bond that unites the opposite members."[163] Scripture generally depicts land as an important element of national identity, both in the impartation and the loss of land in exile. Additionally, the New Testament describes the

---

161. Block suggests, "The major importance of the אדמה is seen in the role it plays in providing the foundation for man's welfare." Block, "Foundations of National Identity," 315. The choice of אדמה rather than ארץ is a fascinating contrast that bears further examination but is outside the scope of this book.

162. C. Wright, *Knowing Jesus*, 142–83.

163. Block, *Gods of the Nations*, 20.

church, a "holy nation" (1 Pet 2:9), as spreading geographically to "the end of the earth" (Acts 1:8).

Loss of Land and Loss of National Identity: Deuteronomy 19:1 and Jeremiah 12:17

The loss of land is frequently associated with the loss of national identity in Scripture. Block explains that the connection between national identity and territory "lies at the heart of the common ancient Near Eastern practice of guaranteeing the submission of vassal states by their wholesale deportation of populations from their native lands."[164] A similar concept is demonstrated in God's promises to "annihilate" (כרת) the nations (הַגּוֹיִם) in the land (אֶרֶץ) he was going to give to the Israelites in Deut 19:1. כרת can have a literal meaning of to cut something such as a tree (Judg 9:48) or idolatrous pillars (Exod 34:13; 1 Kgs 15:13). The word can also be used in the descriptive sense of making a covenant (Deut 29:12, 14).[165] However, כרת is frequently used in the negative sense of killing a person or exterminating a nation by cutting them off from the community or the land in which they dwell. This sense is typically expressed with the hifil stem and God is normally the subject in such situations (Lev 17:10; 29:3, 5–6; 26:30; Deut 12:29; 19:1; 1 Sam 2:33; 1 Kings 9:7; Ps 101:8; 109:13, 15; Jer 51:62; Ezek 14:8, 17, 19, 21; 29:7, 13 Amos 2:3; Mal 2:12).[166] In Deut 19:1, the expression is used in reference to literal killing in warfare. However, the implication behind it is also that Israel would inhabit the land in which the Canaanite nations lived. The combination of both elements heightens the connection between a specific territory and national identity in that losing a war leads not only to the loss of territory but often to the complete loss of national identity.

Jeremiah records a similar admonition to the nations surrounding Israel in Jer 12:17, where he records God's warning that if they will not obey the Lord, then he "will uproot that nation, uproot and destroy it" (נָתַשְׁתִּי אֶת־הַגּוֹי הַהוּא נָתוֹשׁ וְאַבֵּד). "Uproot" (נתשׁ) originally referred to the physical act of uprooting plants but shifted to refer to people being removed from lands.[167] God's threat to uproot disobedient nations amounts

---

164. Block, "Foundations of National Identity," 392.

165. This sense may arise from the custom of "cutting" a sacrificial animal in the ceremony, formalizing the covenant, such as in Gen 15:9–20. *HALOT*, 500.

166. Carpenter, "כרת," *NIDOTTE*, 2:729.

167. *HALOT*, 737.

to a threat of removal from their land, which leads to their destruction (אבד) as a nation. Brueggemann draws the correlation between uprooting and judgment, relating, "One may identify what seems to be a key theme that recurs at important places in the total literature: 'to pluck up and tear down, to plant and build.' The theme articulates God's decisive judgment and God's resilient hope."[168] The emphasis in Jer 12:17 is on removal from the land as the means of annihilation as expressed by the repetition of נתש first in the finite form followed by the infinitive absolute. The loss of land does not simply mean that the nation is relocated. National identity is so tightly connected with a specific land that a nation would be destroyed. God could providentially preserve a nation through exile according to the divine will, but the fact that it took a divine act further emphasizes the devastating effects of exile from the land.[169]

Endowing Land and Establishing National Identity: Genesis 12:1–3

Wright describes Gen 12:1–3 as "pivotal in the book of Genesis: it moves the story forward from the preceding eleven chapters which record God's dealings with all nations . . . , into the patriarchal narratives that lead to the emergence of Israel as a distinct nation."[170] These verses emphasize the role that the future Israel would play in the redemption of "all the families of the earth." However, before God can make Abram "into a great nation" (לְגוֹי גָּדוֹל), Abram must leave his own land and go to the "land that I will show you" (הָאָרֶץ אֲשֶׁר אַרְאֶךָּ). Speiser identifies establishing Abram in a designated land as essential for him receiving status as a "nation" rather than as a "people." He explains, "The term in question [in Gen 12:2] is *gōy*, not *ʿam*; and rightly so. For Abram was an *ʿam* to begin with, in the primary sense of the word, so long as he had a nephew named Lot . . . But to carry out God's purpose, as that purpose is expressed by the Bible as a whole, the *ʿam* was not enough; what was needed was the added status and stability of nationhood in a land specifically designated for that purpose."[171] While Speiser seems to overstate the distinction between עַם and גּוֹי, his point that land was an essential aspect of nationhood is well made.

---

168. Brueggemann, "Book of Jeremiah," 119.
169. Van Dam, "אָבַד," *NIDOTTE*, 1:224.
170. C. Wright, *Mission of God*, 194.
171. Speiser, "'People' and 'Nation' of Israel," 163.

That the Lord does not specify the land does not diminish that the land had already been identified and demarcated. Wazana observes that the lack of description of the land in Gen 12:1–3 is not what one would expect in a promise to make someone a great nation. He contends,

> This sort of association would logically appear to require an explicit designation of the nature of 'this land'—the scope of its territory and the lines of its borders. Precisely this kind of definition is absent from the promissory texts, however. Surprisingly, despite the fact that the command 'Go forth' contains no unambiguous geographical identification or detailed instruction(s), Abraham correctly deciphers God's intention and directs his steps toward the destined land. This move creates the impression that ha-'areṣ was a defined geographical unit well known to all concerned—the writer, his readers, and the patriarch—thus precluding any need to specify its location, span or borders.[172]

Lending further credibility is the repetition of certain key locations. Sailhamer remarks, "The account of Abraham's entry into the land of Canaan is selective. Only three sites in the land are mentioned: Shechem (12:6), the area between Bethel and Ai (v. 8), and the Negev (v. 9)."[173] He further perceives that "it can hardly be accidental that these are the same three locations visited by Jacob when he returns to Canaan from Haran (Gen 34–35) as well as the same sites occupied in the account of the conquest in the land under Joshua."[174] While certainly far from the comprehensive demarcations provided in Josh 13–21, these locations could possibly represent the northern, central, and southern regions of the land.

God's selection of Israel and promising a specific land does not quite align with other conceptions of the relationship between a nation, the land, and their god(s). Block relates that the other nations of the ancient Near East related to their deities strictly on the basis of living in the deity's land.[175] He differentiates the Hebrew understanding, explaining, "This is in sharp contrast to the Hebrew notion that, having selected Israel to be

---

172. Wazana, *All the Boundaries of the Land*, 88–89. Burge is mistaken in his assertion that no promise of land is made until Abraham sees the land for the first time in Gen 13:14–17. The implication behind Abram leaving the land of his own land and God leading him to a new land in order to make him a great nation is that the nation would possess the land. Burge, *Jesus and the Land*, 2.

173. Sailhamer, *Pentateuch as Narrative*, 140.

174. Sailhamer, *Pentateuch as Narrative*, 140.

175. Block, "Foundations of National Identity," 457.

A Biblical Theology of Land in Relation to National Identity

his own people, Yahweh also reserved a specific piece of land for them, and that, centuries before they appeared as a nation on their own soil."[176] Land is not the only factor required for national identity, but it certainly is an essential element. In order to be made into a great nation, the future Israel would need a large population, a distinct spiritual identity, and a large territory.[177]

Redefinition of National Identity and the Geographical Spread of the Gospel: 1 Peter 2:9; Luke 24:47; and Acts 1:8

First Peter 2:9 describes the church as a "holy nation" (ἔθνος ἅγιον), a reference originally applied to Israel in Exod 19:6. Forbes's narrow definition of ἔθνος as referring to "those who share a common culture" seems inappropriate in this passage since the focus is on Christians being united in Christ rather than sharing common culture.[178] Grudem contends, rather, that "just as believers are a new spiritual race and a new spiritual priesthood, so they are a new spiritual *nation* which is based now neither on ethnic identity nor geographical boundaries but rather on allegiance to their heavenly King, Jesus Christ, who is truly King of kings and Lord of lords (Rev 19:16)."[179] Christians as a "holy nation" are not restricted to any specific ethnicity, language, family, or geography. Rather than diminishing these various aspects of national identity, Christians identifying as a "holy nation" universalizes these components, including the geographic, as illustrated in Luke's versions of the Great Commission in Luke 24:47 and Acts 1:8.[180]

Luke offers two slightly varied accounts of his version of the Great Commission. Luke 24:47 indicates that the disciples would bear witness about repentance and the forgiveness of sins "to all nations, beginning at

---

176. Block, "Foundations of National Identity," 457.

177. Wenham, *Genesis 1–15*, 275.

178. Forbes, *1 Peter*, 69; Schmidt, "Ἔθνος in the NT," *TDNT*, 2:369. This strict definition of ἔθνος also has the very real potential of distorting the mission of the church from making disciples to the kind of "civilizing" mission that was prominent during the colonial period. Schreiter, *New Catholicity*, 1–2; Wrogemann, *Intercultural Hermeneutics*, 73–74.

179. Grudem, *1 Peter*, 117.

180. Universalizing these components does not mean that all become one in a way that ignores distinctions. Rather, it emphasizes the classic understanding of catholicity—unity in diversity.

Jerusalem" (εἰς πάντα τὰ ἔθνη. ἀρξάμενοι ἀπὸ Ἱερουσαλήμ). Acts 1:8 also records that the disciples would be witnesses but more specifically "in Jerusalem, and in all Judea and Samaria, and to the end of the earth" (ἔν τε Ἱερουσαλὴμ καὶ [ἐν] πάσῃ τῇ Ἰουδαίᾳ καὶ Σαμαρείᾳ καὶ ἕως ἐσχάτου τῆς γῆς). Both accounts complement one another and clarify the task that the risen Lord gives to the church. Merkle summarizes, "To be obedient to Jesus's charge, the gospel is to go to all nations or to the end of the earth. That is, the message of the good news of Jesus Christ is to cross all *geographic* and thus also all *ethnic* barriers. There is *no place* and *no people* that should be excluded."[181] Luke almost certainly means the same thing when he says that the gospel must go to πάντα τὰ ἔθνη and to ἐσχάτου τῆς γῆς. It would make little sense for Luke to change definitions between his two volumes.

The geographic element is not exclusive to Luke's version of the Great Commission, but it is certainly emphasized more clearly than Matt 28:18–20 and John 20:21.[182] Several scholars have observed that Acts 1:8 establishes a "table of contents" of sorts for the rest of Acts.[183] Bock also observes a similar geographic format in Luke's Gospel, noting, "Geographic progression reveals the movement's growth under God's plan. The outline of the Gospel [of Luke] from Galilee to Jerusalem shows this growth, as does the necessity of Paul's going to Rome in Acts (Acts 19:21; 23:11)."[184] In both passages, Luke indicates that proclamation of the gospel would start from Jerusalem. This is an appropriate location for the mission to begin since Jerusalem was the ultimate destination for Jesus in Luke's Gospel. Edwards notes, "For the first time Jerusalem appears as the starting point of the church's mission rather than as the terminus of Jesus' mission (Acts 1:8; Rom 15:19)."[185] Schnabel explains, "Jerusalem is the capital of Israel, the center of the people of God, the goal and finish of Jesus' ministry, the place where God poured out the

---

181. Akin et al., *40 Questions About the Great Commission*, 202–3.

182. The geographic element is not completely absent from Matt 28:18–20 and John 20:21. As evidenced by Luke's version, ἔθνος implies a geographic component, and John's use of πέμπω relates a geographic sense in that the inference is that the disciples are sent from one location to somewhere else. Rengstorf, "Ἀποστέλλω (Πέμπω)," *TDNT*, 1:398–406; Silva, "Ἔθνος," *NIDNTTE*, 2:89–93; Silva, "Πέμπω," *NIDNTTE*, 3:703–4.

183. Köstenberger and Alexander, *Salvation*, 121; Schnabel, *Acts*, 78–79; Keener, *Acts*, 1:697; Bruce, *Book of Acts*, 36–37; G. Osborne, *Acts*, 23.

184. Bock, *Luke*, 1:29.

185. Edwards, *Gospel According to Luke*, 735.

promised Holy Spirit, the location of the first community of follower of Jesus after Easter."[186] Köstenberger and Alexander further observe, "The holy city, with its unique place in salvation history, is not only the place where Jesus suffers and dies (Luke 9:51; 13:33; 18:31) and rises from the dead (24:1–11, 36–49). It is also the place where the church's mission to the nations is launched."[187] Jerusalem is the indisputable starting point for the mission of the church. However, the destination is less clear.

Luke says that the disciples would be witnesses in Jerusalem, and in all Judea and Samaria, and to the end of the earth.[188] Judea and Samaria can be clearly identified, but significant debate surrounds the phrase "to the end of the earth" (ἐσχάτου τῆς γῆς). A minority position is that Ethiopia in the south is the intended destination, but this is unlikely since the gospel is taken to Ethiopia in Acts 8:26–39, less than halfway through the book.[189] Schwartz argues that ἐσχάτου τῆς γῆς ought to be translated as "to the end of the land" with reference to the land of Israel.[190] However, his method of reaching such a conclusion is based on translating the Greek text into Hebrew while rejecting or ignoring significant evidence from Greek literature and the New Testament account, even in Luke-Acts. Γη may certainly mean either "earth" or "land," just as ארץ in Hebrew. However, context determines the meaning, and since the land of Israel is sufficiently covered with the formula "all Judea and Samaria," the intended meaning is almost certainly the "end of the earth."

The most common argument is that ἐσχάτου τῆς γῆς in Acts 1:8 refers to Rome since that is where the book of Acts ends.[191] Barrett argues, "The truth probably is that the phrase does refer to Rome, but to Rome not as an end in itself but as representative of the whole world."[192] The

---

186. Schnabel, *Early Christian Mission*, 1:390.

187. Köstenberger and Alexander, *Salvation*, 120.

188. Regarding the omission of Galilee, Schnabel explains that by the time that Luke wrote Acts Galilee had been integrated into the Roman province of Judea. Schnabel, *Acts*, 78.

189. Cadbury, *Book of Acts in History*, 15; Thornton, "To the End of the Earth," 374–75; Hengel, *Acts and the History*, 80.

190. Schwartz, "End of the Γη (Acts 1:8)," 669–76.

191. Burchard, "Fussnoten zum Neutestamentlichen Griechisch," 161–63; Filson, "Journey Motif in Luke-Acts," 75–76. For an in-depth discussion of this topic, see Unnik, "Ausdruck Ἕως Ἐσχάτου Τῆς Γῆς," 386–401.

192. C. Barrett, *Acts of the Apostles*, 80. Bock references Barrett, arguing, "Acts does show an interest in Rome (19:21; 23:11; chap. 28). From a literary standpoint within Acts, the reference to Rome after a long providential sea journey in Acts 27 would

argument that ἐσχάτου τῆς γῆς refers to Rome rests almost entirely on an interpretation of Pss. Sol. 8:16 (LXX), where the incident mentioned is believed to be that of Pompey the Great's attack on Jerusalem.[193] Assuming that the attack is the Roman invasion of Jerusalem in AD 63, ἐσχάτου τῆς γῆς is still not a clear reference to the city of Rome since Pompey spent almost all of his political and military career immediately prior to the Third Mithridatic War in Hispania.[194] Furthermore, Rome was commonly understood as the *Umbilicus Romae*, the center of Roman world.[195] It makes little sense to refer to the recognized center of the first-century world as ἐσχάτου τῆς γῆς.

The overwhelming evidence from Greek and Roman literature shows that ἐσχάτου τῆς γῆς was a common way to refer to the very edge of the known world, with some first-century writers suggesting that the "end of the earth" may refer to Spain. Strabo refers to Spain, specifically Cadiz (Γάδειρα), as the "end of the earth."[196] Lucan also narrates, "But Caesar could not brook this protracted warfare before the walls [in Gaul]: he turned to the army in Spain and the limits of the world, leaving orders that the operations should go on."[197] Pliny the Elder similarly begins his geographical account starting from Cadiz.[198] Ἐσχάτου τῆς γῆς could also have a more general reference to the geographical limits of the known world. Strabo describes the geographical map of Eratosthenes as depicting the "Pillars of Hercules" as the western boundary and the "farthest mountains which bound India on the north" as the eastern boundary.[199] Philostratus records a similar understanding of the geographical limits of the world as he describes the various geographical limits in all directions.[200]

The best explanation for ἐσχάτου τῆς γῆς is that it is a general phrase referring to the entire known world. Schnabel asserts, "[Ἐσχάτου τῆς γῆς]

---

mean that the message has now reached the hub of the Gentile world, from which it can proceed everywhere. Thus the difference between interpreting 'end of the earth' as specifying Rome or as looking at the broader edges of the world is not great." Bock, *Acts*, 65.

193. C. Barrett, *Acts of the Apostles*, 80.
194. Seager, "Rise of Pompey," 208–28.
195. McRay, *Archaeology and the New Testament*, 344.
196. Strabo, *Geog.* 3.1.4; 3.1.8.
197. Lucan, *Pharsalia*, 3.454.
198. Pliny the Elder, *Nat.* 2.167.
199. Strabo, *Geog.* 2.1.1; See also Romm, *Edges of the Earth*, 17.
200. Philostratus, *Vit. Appol.*, 6.1.

does not refer to Rome, Spain, or Ethiopia, nor to the Jewish diaspora, nor simply to the Gentiles, but literally to the farthest reaches of the inhabited world known at the time."[201] Scott argues that Luke is relying on the Table of Nations from Genesis 10, but reaches a similar conclusion, saying,

> 1 Chronicles 1 lists the nations of the world 'in a circle' which proceeds counterclockwise—from the North, to the West, to the South, and to the East—with Jerusalem in the center. Likewise in Ezek 5:5, Jerusalem is in the center of a 'circle' of nations. This would correlate with the normal meaning of the 'ends of the earth' as the furthest points on the edge of the inhabited world, including the Scythia in the North, India in the East, Ethiopia in the South, and Spain in the West.[202]

The expectation from Luke 24:47 and Acts 1:8 is that the gospel would go to every place in the world, crossing geographic boundaries until there was literally no boundary left to cross.

Conclusion

The geographical aspect is one of the most obvious components of national identity.[203] The connection between people and the land in which they live began at creation and has persisted. Scripture records that land was integral in the identity of the nations from their formation. The land is also so closely connected with national identity that the land can be used as a metonymy of subject for the nation that dwells in it. Furthermore, divine bestowal of land, among other factors, could result in the creation of a new nation. In contrast, divine punishment could result in removal from the land, which could also lead to a loss of national identity. Additionally, the New Testament describes the church as a "holy nation" that is described as expanding geographically to the "end of the earth." Far from being the only aspect of national identity, geography plays a significant role in how a nation sees itself. Chapter 3 will examine one way that the land-nation relationship can be applied by mission strategists to effectively develop and communicate mission strategy.

---

201. Schnabel, *Acts*, 79.
202. Scott, "Luke's Geographical Horizon," 526–27.
203. Block, "Foundations of National Identity," 298.

3

A Biblical Case Study for Implementing Contextual Geography in Missions Strategy

Paul's Use of ΚΥΚΛΩ in Romans 15:19

A PEOPLE GROUP'S WORLDVIEW and culture informs their perception of geography. J. B. Harley counsels, "Any appreciation of the historical importance of maps depends upon a clear conception of their nature, of the factors that have shaped their making and transmission, and of their role within human societies."[1] Paul makes frequent geographic references in his letters.[2] Romans 15:19 is one such example of a geographic reference. This particular instance stands apart because Paul is explicitly describing his missionary activity, which makes it particularly relevant for the current study. Paul writes in the second half of the verse, "[S]o that from Jerusalem and all the way around to Illyricum I have fulfilled the ministry of the gospel of Christ." Since geography and the culture in which it develops are connected, a critical question arises when the apostle Paul makes geographical references: which geography is Paul using? Paul is a culturally complex person: the child of a Jewish family living in a Roman provincial city situated in the Hellenistic eastern portion of the Roman

---

1. Harley, "Map and the Development," 1.
2. 1 Cor 16:1; 2 Cor 1:1; 9:2; 11:9; Gal 4:25; Eph 1:1; Phil 1:1; 4:14; Col 1:1; 4:15; 1 Thess 1:7–8; 2:1; 3:1; 1 Tim 1:3; 2 Tim 1:15, 17–18; 3:11; 4:10, 12, 20; Titus 1:5; 3:12.

Empire. Answering the question of which geography Paul is referencing in Rom 15:19 requires analysis of each aspect of Paul's context.

The previous chapter developed a biblical theology of land in relationship to national identity. This chapter will serve as a case study for applying a biblical theology of land and national identity in a missions context, and will argue that because Paul was contextualizing his message in Rom 15:19 for a Roman audience, κύκλῳ serves as a key geographical term denoting the circuitous route that he took between Jerusalem and Illyricum over the course of his missionary labors in the eastern portion of the Roman Empire.

This chapter will begin by first examining the etymology and usage of κύκλῳ along with its corresponding terms in contemporaneous Hebrew and Latin literature. After establishing the possible linguistic options available, this chapter will then examine the potential geographies upon which Paul could have relied. The final section of this chapter will investigate the audience to whom Paul was writing in Rome with the intent of showing that Paul's Roman audience played a major factor in Paul's decision to rely on Roman geography in this instance.

The Content of Romans 15:19: Etymology and Usage

The etymology of the key term for this study will focus on the three languages and cultures that influenced Paul's thinking and writing.[3] Greek was the language in which Paul composed his letters and transmitted much of his theological thought and practice to the early church. Hebrew was the traditional language of Judaism even though many first-century Jews no longer spoke Hebrew, especially in the diaspora.[4] Paul did speak Hebrew (Acts 22:2–3), since it would have been necessary for his education in Jerusalem under Gamaliel (Acts 22:3). Latin is not a language used in Scripture, but it was used extensively throughout the Roman Empire during the first century, and some in Paul's audience in Rome almost

---

3. Wallace and Williams, *Three Worlds of Paul of Tarsus*, 3–7; Porter, "Paul as Jew, Greek, and Roman," 1–6.

4. Even where Hebrew was still in use, it was used alongside other languages. Rajak illustrates, "The Greek Bible translation was above all a book for the diaspora. The translation served diasporic communities extraordinarily well to connect their constantly renewed tradition, as they understood it, and the world of the ruling power with its dominant Greek culture." Rajak, *Translation and Survival*, 92. See also Keener, *Acts*, 3:3194; Porter, "Did Paul Speak Latin?," 290.

certainly were proficient in both Greek and Latin.[5] Some argue that any time that Paul may have spent in Illyricum was partially in preparation for his trip to Latin-speaking Spain.[6] The etymology and usage of the key term will provide insight into Paul's intention and meaning in Rom 15:19.

Greek Content: κύκλῳ

The Greek etymology will focus exclusively on the dative singular form of the noun κύκλος for two primary reasons. First, it is the form that Paul utilizes in Rom 15:19 (ὥστε με ἀπὸ Ἰερουσαλὴμ καὶ κύκλῳ μέχρι τοῦ Ἰλλυρικοῦ πεπληρωκέναι τὸ εὐαγγέλιον τοῦ Χριστοῦ). Second, the dative singular form is the most common single form of the word κύκλος found in Greek literature, being used 8,458 times.[7] Part of the reason for the high incidence of the dative singular form is likely due to it being used as both a preposition and an adverb of place.[8] Due to the prevalence of this form across Greek literature, this study will focus on works of cultural significance where the word occurs frequently or influences Greek thinking. This section will also examine occurrences and usage in the New Testament.

Homer

A discussion on the usage of κύκλῳ in Homer may appear strange since the form only appears twice—once in each of his epics, the *Iliad* and *Odyssey*. However, any examination of a word potentially related to Greek geography must begin with Homer since that is where many ancient Greeks and contemporary scholars trace the origins of Greek geography.[9]

---

5. Rochette, "Language Policies," 554–55. Evans, "Paul and the Pagans," 126–29; Christidis, *History of Ancient Greek*, 649. Christidis observes, "In the administrative sphere, a relatively small number of Latin words were borrowed (e.g., δηνάριον 'denarius,' Καῖσαρ, 'Caesar,' κεντυρίοων, 'Centurio,' λεγιών 'legion,' πραιτώριον 'praetorium')."

6. Chapple, "Paul and Illyricum," 20–35; Porter, "Did Paul Speak Latin?," 289–308; Bruce, *Paul*, 316.

7. This search was conducted using *Thesaurus Linguae Gracae* (http://stephanus.tlg.uci.edu). Other forms occurring in high quantity are the nominative singular, found 4,858 times; the genitive singular, found 6,419 times; and the accusative singular, found 4,705 times. All plural forms occur less than 1,500 times and usually in similar ways to their singular counterparts.

8. "κύκλῳ," in Swanson, *Dictionary of Biblical Languages*; "Κύκλος," in LSJ; Pompeo, "Dative," 415.

9. Purcell, "Geography," 632–33; Harley et al., "Foundations of Theoretical

Strabo, in the opening paragraphs of his *Geography*, explains that "[B]oth I and those before—among whom is Hipparchos—assume correctly that Homer was the originator of the art of geography . . . Thus he was interested not only in human activities . . . but also in each of the places of the entire inhabited world, both land and sea. Otherwise he would not have gone to its farthest limits in his writings."[10] Homer also represents the earliest documented instance of κύκλῳ.[11]

The occurrence κύκλῳ in the *Iliad* is found in the context of elders sitting "on their seats of stone in a solemn circle" (οἳ δὲ γέροντες εἴατ' ἐπὶ ξεστοῖσι λίθοις ἱερῷ ἐνὶ κύκλῳ) as they pronounce judgment in a dispute between two men.[12] The dative of place is further emphasized by Homer using the dative preposition ἐνὶ (ἐν).[13] Homer's use here is similar to later instances that use κύκλῳ to describe something existing in an indeterminate area around a geographical center.

The single instance of κύκλῳ in the *Odyssey* is found in the story of Hephaestus forging bonds and placing the bonds all around the bedposts (ἀμφὶ δ' ἄρ' ἑρμῖσιν χέε δέσματα κύκλῳ ἁπάντῃ) in order to capture Ares while engaged in an amorous encounter with Aphrodite.[14] Homer's usage here is again a dative of place and is supplemented by the intensive adverb ἁπάντῃ (ἅπας), reinforcing that Hephaestus places bonds everywhere surrounding the bedposts. Even though the geographic space around the central location (bedposts) is more narrowly defined, Homer again uses the word to denote something existing around a geographical center.

Aristotle

Aristotle wrote his treatise *On the Heavens* in the fourth century BC, offering the earliest extant work that uses κύκλῳ in significant numbers.[15] In all

---

Cartography," 131; Dilke, *Greek and Roman Maps*, 20, 55–56.

10. Strabo, *Geogr.* 1.1.2.

11. Herodotus estimates that Homer lived approximately four hundred years prior him, which would place the dating of Homer somewhere in the eighth century BC. Herodotus, *Hist.* 2.53.

12. Homer, *Il.* 18.505.

13. Ἐν used with the dative of location is usually used to indicate someone or something resting at the attained goal. Beekes and van Beek, *Etymological Dictionary of Greek*, 419.

14. Homer, *Od.* 8.279.

15. Other earlier writers use κύκλῳ, but none match the frequency of the word in

of Aristotle's various works, he uses κύκλῳ 274 times. The highest density of use—74 times—comes in *On the Heavens*. Aristotle utilizes the word as a technical term to describe one of the two different forms of motion and, more specifically, to the circular movement of the heavenly bodies.

He asserts early in the work, "Now all motion in space [locomotion] is either straight or circular or a compound of the two" (πᾶσα δὲ κίνησις ὅση κατὰ τόπον, ἣν καλοῦμεν φοράν, ἢ εὐθεῖα ἢ κύκλῳ ἢ ἐκ τούτων μικτή·).[16] Aristotle further defines κύκλῳ, explaining, "By 'circular motion' I mean motion around the center" (κύκλῳ μὲν οὖν ἐστὶν ἡ περὶ τὸ μέσον).[17] Aristotle's technical use is not immediately helpful in completely understanding Paul's use in Rom 15:19, but at least one insight may be garnered. Aristotle observes that an object moving in a circle moves around a central geographic location.

Κύκλῳ occurs far less frequently in some other works by Aristotle but is not completely absent. In *History of Animals*, Aristotle's longest single work, he describes a defensive tactic of bonitos, who swim around a predator "in a circle" in order to drive it off (συστρέφονται δὲ καὶ αἱ ἄμιαι ὅταν τι θηρίον ἴδωσι, καὶ κύκλῳ αὐτῶν περινέουσιν αἱ μέγισται).[18] In a similar activity, Aristotle also observes that a stallion, when approached by another stallion, will gather his mares into a central position and run in a circle around them before going to fight the intruder (ὅταν δὲ προσίῃ τις ἄρρην, συστρέψας εἰς ταὐτὸ καὶ περιδραμὼν κύκλῳ, προσελθὼν μάχεται·).[19] These two brief examples are consistent with Aristotle's technical use of κύκλῳ. Whether it is a heavenly body encircling other heavenly bodies, fish swimming in a circle in self-defense, or a stallion fending off a competitor by running in a circle around a drove of mares, κύκλῳ refers to something existing or, more technically, moving in a circle around another object or a geographic center.

Aristotle and especially in *On the Heavens*. Euclid, writing approximately a century after Aristotle, uses κύκλῳ only twenty-nine times in his geometrical treatise, *Elements*. Every instance except for two has the preposition ἐν attached to it, and each is used in identical ways, referring to mathematical components of a geometric circle. However, the extent to which Euclid's geometry influenced early cartography may further prove that κύκλῳ was used mainly as a geographical term. Harley et al., "Growth of an Empirical Cartography," 148.

16. Aristotle, *Cael.* 268b.
17. Aristotle, *Cael.* 268b.
18. Aristotle, *Hist. an.* 621a.
19. Aristotle, *Hist. an.* 572b.

Strabo

Strabo is the preeminent source when it comes to first-century geography, partially because his is the only work of its kind from this period to survive in full.[20] Strabo built his *Geography* on the model of Eratosthenes' seminal *Geography*, which is preserved primarily in Strabo's work.[21] Strabo's *Geography*, consisting of seventeen books, contains the most instances of κύκλῳ in a single work until Proclus' *Commentary on Plato's Timaeus*, written in the fifth century AD.[22] Strabo's *Geography* was completed between late AD 23 and AD 24.[23] The relatively close proximity to Paul writing the book of Romans in the mid-to-late-50s in conjunction with the frequent use of κύκλῳ makes Strabo's work extremely important for this case study.[24]

Of the eighty-four occurrences of κύκλῳ in Strabo, sixty-one of these has the meaning of "surrounding" or "around."[25] Strabo, citing Posidonius, explains that "the inhabited earth is entirely surrounded by the ocean" (ἡ οἰκουμένη κύκλῳ περιρρεῖται τῷ ὠκεανῷ).[26] Describing the area around Aricia along the Appian Road, he describes a temple and water being surrounded in a circle by a ridge of mountains (κύκλῳ δ᾽ ὀρεινὴ συνεχὴς ὀφρὺς περίκειται).[27] These fairly literal and concrete descriptions locate landmarks that surround other features. The inhabited earth is the central geographic feature, and the ocean surrounds it in a circle. The temple and body of water near Aricia, the central geographic features, are surrounded in a circle by a ridge of mountains.

Strabo uses κύκλῳ to refer to less-defined boundaries as well. Strabo depicts Mount Vesuvius as being surrounded in fruitfulness (τάχα δὲ καὶ

---

20. Purcell, "Strabo," 1447; Elvers, "Strabo," *BNP*, 13.866–69; Roller, *Eratosthenes' Geography*, x.

21. Roller, "Introduction," 16; Roller, *Eratosthenes' Geography*.

22. Exceptions to this would be the Septuagint, which will be treated below, and Plutarch's collection of Roman biographies, if those were taken as a single work.

23. Roller, "Introduction," 16.

24. Longenecker, *Epistle of the Romans*, 6; Kruse, *Paul's Letter to the Romans*, 13; Jewett, *Romans*, 18.

25. Other instances have the meaning of "in a circle/circuit" (twelve times), "circle of the earth" (three times), "boundary/circumference" (two times), and six other times when the word carries a technical meaning like "tropical circle" or "circle of the ocean."

26. Strabo, *Geogr.* 2.3.5.

27. Strabo, *Geogr.* 5.3.12.

τῆς εὐκαρπίας τῆς κύκλῳ τοῦτ' αἴτιον).[28] He also describes several places as being surrounded or encircled by plains or fields (τῶν κύκλῳ πεδίων/ τῆς κύκλῳ χώρας).[29] Even when the term is used without clear boundaries it still conveys the same general meaning: something existing in a circle, or more generally surrounding, whether exactly circular or not, another object or geographic center.

New Testament

The New Testament writers use κύκλῳ only seven times in addition to Paul's single use in Rom 15:19. Mark's Gospel contains three instances (Mark 3:34; 6:6, 36), one occurrence is in Luke (Luke 9:12), and the final three are found in Revelation (Rev 4:6; 5:11; 7:11). Since the single occasion in Luke is a parallel account from Mark, only the six uses from Mark and Revelation will be examined.[30]

The instance of κύκλῳ in Mark 3:34 is in the context of Jesus addressing those who were sitting around him (καὶ περιβλεψάμενος τοὺς περὶ αὐτὸν κύκλῳ καθημένους λέγει). Voelz observes that Jesus highlights the physical location by addressing those in a circle (κύκλῳ) around him in contrast to his family members outside (ἔξω, Mark 3:31, 32).[31] France comments, "There is no reason to think that Mark intended κύκλῳ to be taken in other than a purely literal sense; the dative is used as an adverb, meaning 'all round him.'"[32] Mark places Jesus at the physical center of his followers physically surrounding him. Even if some emphasize a metaphorical significance in Mark's narrative, the immediate context is referring to the physical location of Jesus and his followers.[33]

The second, in Mark 6:6, mentions Jesus going to the villages surrounding Nazareth (Καὶ περιῆγεν τὰς κώμας κύκλῳ διδάσκων). Most English translations lose the nuance of κύκλῳ in this verse. Several

---

28. Strabo, *Geogr.* 5.4.8.

29. Strabo, *Geogr.* 5.3.7, 6.2.7, 17.1.5.

30. Luke 9:12 is in the same context as Mark 6:36. Some argue that Luke may be relying on Mark as a source in this instance. Even if Luke is writing independently, the same analysis for Mark 6:36 would also hold true for Luke 9:12. Marshall, *Gospel of Luke*, 359–60; Bock, *Luke 1:1—9:50*, 829–30; Bovon, *Luke 1*, 352–56.

31. Voelz, *Mark 1:1—8:26*, 269. See also Guelich, *Mark 1–8:26*, 182; Marcus, *Mark 1–8*, 286.

32. France, *Gospel of Mark*, 179–80.

33. Edwards, *Gospel According to Mark*, 124–25; Strauss, *Mark*, 171–74.

translations render this phrase as Jesus "going around [or round about] the villages teaching" (NASB, CSB, KJV, WEB). Others vary slightly, but still lose the full effect of κύκλῳ in this context.³⁴ Both the NKJV and CEV are the only two versions that render this phrase in a way that captures some of the meaning of κύκλῳ in this context. The NKJV reads, "Then He went about the villages in a circuit, teaching." This is a possible translation but does not seem to use the term accurately in context.³⁵ The CEV rendering is better, but lacks the circular element, reading, "Jesus taught in all the neighboring villages." A better translation would be: "And he was going around to the surrounding villages teaching." France explains that "κύκλῳ indicates that he remained in the hill country around Nazareth rather than returning yet to the lake."³⁶ The translation submitted here communicates that Jesus was going to other places after being rejected in Nazareth but maintaining a geographic centerpoint of Nazareth in Galilee for the subsequent events.

The third occurrence, in Mark 6:36, has a clear geographic reference as Jesus prepares to feed five thousand men and the apostles urge Jesus to send the crowd away into the surrounding countryside and villages (ἀπόλυσον αὐτούς, ἵνα ἀπελθόντες εἰς τοὺς κύκλῳ ἀγροὺς καὶ κώμας ἀγοράσωσιν ἑαυτοῖς τί φάγωσιν.). Voelz indicates that κύκλῳ is being used as an adverb modifying both "fields" (ἀγρούς) and "villages" (κώμας).³⁷ The isolated location where the crowd found Jesus meeting with his disciples formed the central geographic location for the surrounding fields and villages, where food could be found.³⁸ All three instances of κύκλῳ in Mark maintain and even emphasize a geographic meaning.

The three uses of κύκλῳ in Revelation occur in similar contexts and can be treated together. All three passages describe beings in heaven surrounding the throne of God:

- Καὶ ἐν μέσῳ τοῦ θρόνου καὶ κύκλῳ τοῦ θρόνου τέσσαρα ζῷα γέμοντα ὀφθαλμῶν ἔμπροσθεν καὶ ὄπισθεν (Rev 4:6)
- καὶ ἤκουσα φωνὴν ἀγγέλων πολλῶν κύκλῳ τοῦ θρόνου καὶ τῶν ζῴων καὶ τῶν πρεσβυτέρων (Rev 5:11)

---

34. The ESV and RSV read, "And he went about among the villages teaching." The LEB reads, "And he was going around among the villages teaching."
35. Collins, *Mark*, 293, 296.
36. France, *Mark*, 244. See also Guelich, *Mark 1–8:26*, 315.
37. Voelz, *Mark 1:1—8:26*, 420.
38. Bock, *Mark*, 212.

- Καὶ εἶδον, καὶ ἤκουσα φωνὴν ἀγγέλων πολλῶν κύκλῳ τοῦ θρόνου καὶ τῶν ζῴων καὶ τῶν πρεσβυτέρων (Rev 7:11)[39]

Brewer draws on the imagery of a Greek amphitheater to describe this circular scene, but Mounce argues that Brewer is relying too much on Greek imagery when Jewish imagery of Isaiah 6 and Ezekiel 1 seem to be John's likely referents.[40] Brighton observes that the double spatial designations ἐν μέσῳ and κύκλῳ indicate that the four living creatures (ζῷα) "form an immediate and inner circle around the throne of God."[41] The three instances of κύκλῳ place the throne of God not only at the theological and doxological center of heaven but also at the geographical center of those surrounding the throne to worship.

All six unique uses of κύκλῳ in the New Testament apart from Paul's use in Rom 15:19 further reinforce the geographical reference that this word consistently conveys throughout Greek literature. Even though the New Testament writers rarely use κύκλῳ, it was used extensively in broader Greek literature and, as will be shown below, in the Septuagint.

The Jewish Content: סבב

Despite his Roman citizenship and his Greek primary education, Paul was almost certainly comfortable and fluent in the Hebrew language.[42] Luke narrates that Paul spoke to the Jews in the Hebrew language in Acts 22:2.[43] Paul also describes himself as a "Hebrew of Hebrews" (Ἑβραῖος ἐξ Ἑβραίων) in Phil 3:5. Bruce explains that this distinction was more precise and specialized than "Israelite" or "Jew."[44] Paul may be using "Hebrew" in distinction from the "Hellenists." Bruce defends this view, saying, "The distinction was probably linguistic and cultural: the Hebrews ...

---

39. These passages echo Isa 6:2 where κύκλῳ is used to describe the seraphs around the throne, but is an unusual rendering from the Hebrew to the Greek. See the section on Hebrew below. Aune, *Revelation 1–5*, 297.

40. Brewer, "Revelation 4:6 and Translations," 227–31; Mounce, *Book of Revelation*, 123. See also Aune, *Revelation 6–16*, 47; Beale, *Book of Revelation*, 328–29; Vogelgesang, "Interpretation of Ezekiel in Revelation," 178–79.

41. Brighton, *Revelation*, 123.

42. Hild, "Tarsus," *BNP*, 14.155–56; Strabo, *Geogr.*, 14.5.13–15; Cf. Bruce, *Paul*, 32–36, 43; Murphy-O'Connor, *Paul*, 46–51.

43. Some scholars question whether Paul spoke Hebrew or Aramaic when he addressed the crowd in Acts 22. This debate is summarized in Keener, *Acts*, 3:3191–95.

44. Bruce, *Paul*, 42.

A Biblical Case Study for Implementing Contextual Geography   71

attended synagogues where the service was conducted in Hebrew and used Aramaic as their normal mode of speech, while the Hellenists spoke Greek and attended synagogues where the scriptures were read and the prayers recited in that language."[45] Regardless of whether Bruce is correct in his assessment of Paul's self-designation, Paul advancing beyond many his own age (Gal 1:14) while studying under Gamaliel, the leading scholar of Jewish law in the mid-first century, would have necessitated extensive knowledge in Hebrew.[46]

Paul's Jewish context is not limited to the Hebrew language. The Septuagint (LXX) extensively uses κύκλῳ. This section will briefly examine the Hebrew word that κύκλῳ generally translates in all but a few instances, followed by a summary of the three main categories in which κύκλῳ is used in the LXX.

Hebrew Bible

The Hebrew word סבב in its substantive or adverbial forms (סָבִיב) carries roughly the same semantic range as κύκλῳ.[47] As a substantive or adverb, סָבִיב occurs 333 times.[48] As a verb, the word can mean "to turn, go around, or surround."[49] As a verb, the word is used in a variety of contexts.[50] However, most of these different uses can be attributed to various subjects forming the central focus surrounded by different objects or concepts.[51] Most commonly, the central subject is something substantive.[52] Hebrew poetry, however, sometimes places abstract concepts at the center, such as "iniquity" (Ps 49:6), "steadfast love" (Ps 32:10), "trouble" (Ps 55:11), or geographic boundaries (Josh 15:3, 10; 16:6; 18:14). When סָבִיב occurs as an adverb, it has a much narrower semantic range. The contexts for its use

---

45. Bruce, *Paul*, 42.

46. Keener, *Acts*, 2:1222–26; Youngblood, "Gamaliel," 393–94; Bruce, *Epistle to the Galatians*, 90.

47. Garcia-López, "סבב," *TDOT*, 10:130.

48. Garcia-López, "סבב," *TDOT*, 10:128. The root verb occurs only 161 times in all its forms in the Old Testament. It primarily appears in its qal form (90 times), mostly in the Deuteronomistic History (37 times) and the Writings (36 times).

49. *HALOT*, 738–40; *BDB*, 685–87; L. Allen, "סבב," *NIDOTTE*, 3:219.

50. Dietrich et al., eds., *Cuneiform Alphabetic Texts*, 1.4 VI, 34, 1.16 III, 3,1.19 II, 12.

51. Garcia-López, "סבב," *TDOT*, 10:129.

52. Garcia-López, "סבב," *TDOT*, 10:129.

as an adverb can be grouped into four main categories: military, cultic, religious-theological, and general geographical description.[53] However, the semantic range of the instances in which κύκλῳ is used to translate סָבִיב is even narrower still.

Septuagint

Several different words translate סָבִיב in the LXX. Most of the words are related to the κυκλ- root.[54] Of the 333 instances of סָבִיב, κύκλῳ is used to render it 200 times. Two main categories emerge as the primary use of κύκλῳ in the LXX—geographical and cultic.[55] The cultic category may further be divided based on the main object in question, namely, the various elements of the tabernacle/temple and the altar.

Of the two main categories, the geographical category constitutes the most common use. The Old Testament writers use κύκλῳ 123 times in an exclusively geographic context. Apart from the Pentateuch and the closing chapters of Ezekiel, the geographic use of κύκλῳ is the normal use of the term. The two most frequent geographic uses involve various objects or locations surrounding a city or camp (e.g., "walls," "fields," "villages," "pastures," etc.) and various designations for the nations surrounding Israel (e.g., "lands," "peoples," "nations," "enemies," "kings").[56]

---

53. Garcia-López, "סבב," *TDOT*, 10:131–38; L. Allen, "סבב," *NIDOTTE*, 3:219–20.

54. The unrelated words used to translate סָבִיב are μεταβαλών (Job 10:8), σμίλακά (Jer 26:14), περιοίκου (Jer 30:5), περιφερές, Ezek 41:10), ἐπέστρεψεν (Ezek 42:17), and ἀνεστράφησαν (1 Sam 14:21). None of these occur more than a single time as a translation of סָבִיב.

55. Other uses include abstract concepts in the Writings, such as LXX Ps 17:12; 49:3; 97:2; Job 18:11 and the three instances in Daniel that do not easily fit into any category, since in one case κύκλῳ is clearly not translated from the Hebrew text, and the other two instances seem to use κύκλῳ idiomatically to express a "remainder" by translating the Hebrew שאר (Dan 7:7, 12).

56. For objects surrounding a city: LXX Gen 41:48; Exod 16:13; Lev 25:31; Num 1:50, 53; 2:2; 11:31–32; 16:24, 27, 34; 32:33; 35:2, 4; Josh 15:12; 19:8; 21:11, 42; Judg 7:18, 21, 29;1 Kgdms 26:5; 2 Kgdms 5:9; 4 Kgdms 25:1, 4; 1 Chr 4:33; 6:55; 11:8; 2 Chr 14:14; 34:6; Ps 43:14; 77:28; 78:3; 124:2; Jdt 1:2; 15:3; Jer 1:15; 6:3; 27:14, 32; 39:44; 40:13; 52:4, 7, 14; Ezek 4:2; 5:2; 8:10; 27:11; 31:4; 1 Macc 1:31, 54; 7:17; 10:84; 2 Macc 4:32. For nations surrounding Israel: LXX Lev 25:44; Deut 12:10; 17:14; 25:19; Josh 24:33b; 1 Kgdms 14:47; 2 Kgdms 7:1; 3 Kgdms 2:35k; 4 Kgdms 25:4; 2 Esd 15:17; 16:16; Zech 12:2; Jer 25:9; 52:7; Bar 2:4; Ezek 5:5–7, 14–15, 16:57; 23:24; 36:3, 36; 1 Macc 1:11; 3:23; 5:10, 38, 57; 12:13, 53; 14:36.

The cultic context forms the only other frequent use of κύκλῳ in the LXX. Found mostly in the Pentateuch and the closing chapters of Ezekiel, κύκλῳ describes the construction of the tabernacle, the temple, and their articles. The word is used in the Pentateuch to describe overlaying gold on the various items (LXX Exod 25:10, 23–24; 30:3), placing items around the tabernacle court (LXX Exod 27:17; 28:28; 37:18; 39:9; 40:6, 27; Num 3:37; 4:32), and crafting the priestly garments (LXX Exod 28:29–30; 36:31, 33–34). Exodus and Leviticus also describe sprinkling blood from sacrifices around (κύκλῳ) the altar (LXX Exod 29:16, 21; Lev 1:5, 11; 3:2, 8, 13; 6:32, 8:15, 19, 24; 9:12, 18; 16:18; 17:6). In addition to the instances in the Pentateuch, the closing chapters of Ezekiel pick up the cultic use of κύκλῳ as he describes his vision of the temple (LXX Ezek 40:5, 14, 16–17, 29, 33, 36, 43; 41:6–8, 10, 16–17; 42:20; 43:20; 46:23). Some of the ways that Ezekiel uses κύκλῳ could overlap with the geographical use, but since he used it in the context of the temple vision and in ways parallel to the Tabernacle construction in the Pentateuch, it seemed best to include all of these occurrences in the cultic category.

Both the geographic and the cultic uses form an overwhelming majority of the instances of κύκλῳ in the LXX. While serving as a word translating סָבִיב, the LXX use of κύκλῳ is consistent with what has been seen in other Greek literature. Whether the center consists of a camp, city, village, king, the nation of Israel, the tabernacle, the temple, the altar, or the articles used for Israelite worship, κύκλῳ normally describes something that physically surrounds the central object. Walls, fields, and villages surround cities, the nations surround Israel, and gold surrounds the wood used to craft the objects for cultic use.

The Roman Content: *Circuitus*

Considerable debate continues regarding whether Paul spoke Latin.[57] While Paul may have spoken Latin as a Roman citizen, the translation of Rom 15:19 into Latin in the late fourth century provides a starting point for evaluating Roman literature in the first century. Romans 15:19b in the Vulgate reads: "ita ut ab Jerusalem *per circuitum* usque ad Illyricum repleverim Evangelium Christi." This translation uses the rare combination

---

57. For a thorough summary of the debate, see Porter, "Did Paul Speak Latin?," 289–308.

of the preposition *per* with the accusative case of *circuitus*.[58] Other cases, primarily the ablative, are more common in influential works from the first century BC through the first century AD. The three works from this time period in which the lemma *circuitus* most frequently occurs are Julius Caesar's *The Gallic Wars* and *The Civil War* and Pliny the Elder's *Natural History*. One may not be surprised to find *circuitus* twenty times in Pliny's thirty-seven-book treatise attempting to catalog the total knowledge of the natural world of the mid-first century, but Julius Caesar's shorter commentaries on the Gallic and Civil Wars initially seem to be a less-likely source. The common factor between the two is that Caesar, in describing his military campaigns, includes extensive geographic details. Pliny dedicates books 3–6 to describing the geography of the world.

Julius Caesar, The Gallic Wars and The Civil War

Julius Caesar's two works *The Gallic Wars* and *The Civil War* served as propaganda raising his popularity among the senate and people of Rome while also leading to and legitimizing his claims as dictator.[59] In providing a narrative of his military campaigns from the mid-first century BC, Caesar provides detailed accounts of the tactics used, which necessarily include numerous geographic references.

Caesar uses the lemma *circuitus* a total of twenty-two times in both books. The ablative singular case is the most common, occurring seventeen times, the nominative singular three times, and the accusative singular only twice. Half of the references involve taking a certain route around a geographical object or the enemy.[60] The other half describes certain fortifications built in a circumference of various sizes, evaluates a mountain on each side for the best path of ascent, depicts an enemy

---

58. Most of the occurrences of *per circuitum* are found in the third century or later. The only first-century references are found in Columella, *Rust.* 5.6.15; 8.15.3–4; Frontinus, *Stratagems* 1.1.6; Seneca the Younger, *De remediis fortuitorum* 1.3. The three references from Columella refer to a circumference of a tree, pond, or garden. This is certainly a much narrower area than Paul refers to from Jerusalem to Illyricum. Even so, Columella's use resembles the use of κύκλῳ in Homer. Frontinus uses *per circuitum* to describe a barbarian army taking a circuitous route (itinere per circuitum).

59. Goldsworthy avers, "To say that the Commentarii were not simply factual narratives of campaigns, but also works of propaganda and self-justification, is stating the obvious." Goldsworthy, "'Instinctive Genius,'" 193. See also Gardner, "Gallic Menace,'" 181–89.

60. Caesar, *Bell. gal.* 1.41; 7.45–46; *Bell. civ.* 1.59, 61, 63–64. 68; 2.24; 3.30, 41.

stronghold as being reinforced by steep rocks all around, and conveys the supposed circumference of Britain.[61]

The different uses of *circuitus* in Caesar have many parallels with how the Greeks utilized κύκλῳ, but first-century Latin writers seem to prefer the ablative case to the dative. Caesar tends to use *circuitus* to describe an object moving around a central object—whether that is an enemy, a city, or a marsh land—or an environment surrounding a central object such as a fortification of some type. The only unusual instance in Caesar is in reporting the size of Britain (Ita omnis insula est in circuitu viciens centum milium passuum).[62] It would go beyond the immediate evidence to argue that Britain forms the central object of the circumference. Even so, this case represents an exception in Caesar rather than a general trend.

Pliny the Elder, Naturalis Historia

Gaius Plinius Secundus (Pliny the Elder) completed the thirty-seven books of *Natural History* in AD 77, two years before his death at Pompeii in the aftermath of the Mount Vesuvius eruption.[63] Having been born in either AD 23 or 24, he would have been a rough contemporary of the apostle Paul.[64] Similar to Strabo, Pliny attempted to catalog details regarding knowledge of the known world, but he has a broader scope than Strabo. Pliny describes the subject of his work as "the world of nature, or in other words life" (rerum natura, hoc est vita).[65] However, Pliny dedicates books 3–6 to describing the geography of the known world. Throughout all thirty-seven books, Pliny only uses *circuitus* twenty times, but eight instances appear in his books on geography. As with Caesar, the ablative case is far more common, occurring fifteen times. Two specific references in *Natural History* are particularly insightful for the current study.

First, Pliny uses similar language as Paul uses in Rom 15:19. In describing the navigable extent of the western portion of the Roman Empire, Pliny writes, "Today, the whole west is navigated from Cadiz

---

61. Caesar, *Bell. gal.* 2.30; 5.42; 7.69, 83; *Bel. civ.* 3.44–45, 63; *Bel. gal.* 1.21; *Bel. gal.* 2.29; *Bel. gal.* 5.13.

62. Caesar, *Bell. gal.* 5.13.

63. Zirkle, "Death of Gaius Plinius Secundus," 553–59.

64. Murphy-O'Connor, *Paul*, 4

65. Pliny the Elder, *Nat.* P.13.

and the Columns of Hercules round Spain and Gaul" (A Gadibus columnisque Herculis Hispaniae et Galliarum circuitu totus hodie navigator occidens).[66] While Paul describes an arc of territory on the northeastern end of the Mediterranean Sea, Pliny describes a similar arc on the northwestern end.[67] Additionally, Pliny's phrase establishes the starting point for his geographical work as it moves from Cadiz and around the Mediterranean, similar to Paul "fulfilling the gospel of Christ" (πεπληρωκέναι τὸ εὐαγγέλιον τοῦ Χριστοῦ) from Jerusalem round to Illyricum. Pliny quite clearly sees the Mediterranean, and more specifically Rome, as the center of the inhabited world.[68]

Second, Pliny offers further insight regarding his geographical understanding of the world with Rome at its center in book 9. In this volume on zoology, Pliny relates that the best pearls were located in Sri Lanka [Taprobane] and Stoidis, and he refers his readers back to *NH* 6.81 and 110 by stating, "as we said in our circuit of the world," (ut diximus in circuitu mundi).[69] Taking the normal meaning of *circuitus* as referring to a circumference or a circular route around an object, the likely object being referenced is either the Mediterranean Sea or, more likely, Rome.

---

66. Pliny the Elder, *Nat.* 2.167.

67. Paul's arc from Jerusalem to Illyricum is slightly longer based on a rough measurement, but both measure from a point on opposite ends of the Mediterranean Sea and plot a general course that would take a traveler up to the borders of Roman *regiones* in Italy.

68. Instead of continuing in the circle started in books 3–4, Pliny backs up to Cadiz and traces an arc around the African portion of the Mediterranean in book 5 before moving on to the lands further east and north in book 6. Murphy describes the importance of Rome in *Naturalis historia*: "Rome is the place to which everything flows, where everything is present for the having, where the value of the good things of all countries is unequivocally established. In this the *Natural History* is like an ancient map of the world: taking Rome as its centre, it surrounds the kingdom of certain knowledge with a border of exotic and wonderful tales." Murphy, *Pliny the Elder's Natural History*, 20. Gaius Julius Solinus, a third-century geographer, relied so much on Pliny that he earned the moniker "Pliny's Ape." Brodersen observes that approximately three-quarters of Solinus' work is drawn directly from Pliny. Solinus begins his account with the city of Rome as the "head of the world" (a capite orbis, id est ab urbe Roma principium capessemus), and moves outward. While Solinus is less subtle than Pliny in declaring Rome as the center of the world, that Solinus relies so much on Pliny is evidence that Pliny had a similar view. Mommsen, *C. Iulii Solini*, 2; Brodersen, "Mapping Pliny's World," 63–88.

69. Pliny the Elder, *Nat.* 9.106.

The Context of Romans 15:19: Geography

Just as with the various linguistic influences on Paul, various geographies that existed in the three cultures also exerted influence on how Paul saw the world and communicated to others about the world. Christian Jacob perceives, "One can argue that all maps have the same purposes: the display of geographical or topographical data, giving orientation and distances and providing a view of a territory... It could also be contended that the map as artefact... presents us with some clues about the way its users would have looked at it."[70] Herodotus is often credited with being the "father of history," but his work contains so much geographical content that he could also possibly be called the "father of geography."[71] Claudius Ptolemy, while writing in Roman Egypt in the second century, continued the Greek geographic tradition. Other significant Greek and Roman geographical works survive only in fragments and primarily through Strabo in the first century AD and Claudius Ptolemy in the early second century AD, but the influence of Hellenistic thought on Paul cannot be overlooked. From a Jewish perspective, Genesis 10 and the book of Jubilees provide insight into first-century Jewish geography. Paul asserts his Roman citizenship several times during his missionary journeys (Acts 16:37-38; 22:25-29; 23:26), and so the geography constructed by Marcus Agrippa under the orders of Caesar Augustus and the contemporary *Geography* of Strabo must also be taken into account.

The Greek Geographical Context

The Greeks were much different in their thinking than the Jews or the Romans regarding geography. Stahl explains, "The theoretical-minded Greeks regarded cartography as a mathematical science and understood that maps could attain accuracy only if terrestrial positions were determined from observations of the heavens."[72] Even though the Greeks often engaged in theoretical or philosophical geography, Herodotus provides an example of early practical geography in the context of his *Histories* while Claudius Ptolemy demonstrates how to use the theoretical foundations of geography to build both practical and accurate maps.

---

70. Jacob, "Toward a Cultural History of Cartography," 192.
71. Podossinov, "Introduction," 1-5.
72. Stahl, "By Their Maps," 146.

Herodotus

The concept of a map as a representation of the real world arose much earlier than Herodotus. Homer describes the earth as a circular disk surrounded by the ocean, but it is not until the rise of the Hellenistic historical writings that one can find a form of systematic geography.[73] Hecataeus wrote a two-volume set in the sixth century BC describing the ethnography of Europe and Asia.[74] A century earlier, Anaximander of Miletus allegedly wrote a geography to accompany his globe.[75] Hecataeus and Anaximander offer some evidence that maps and geography in some form existed as early as the seventh century BC, but the fragmentary nature of Hecataeus and the loss of both Anaximander's map and his geographical summary allow for little analysis.[76] Additionally, Hecataeus and Anaximander were doing philosophical geography. Golden observes, "There is little evidence before Herodotus and Thucydides of the kind of practical application of geographic theory that might aid an army or tradesman in getting from 'point a' to 'point b.'"[77]

Herodotus, writing in the fifth century, narrates a story about how Aristagoras, a Milesian tyrant, attempts to use a bronze map to fool the Lacedaemonian king, Cleomenes, into undertaking a foolhardy military campaign against the Persians.[78] Even though Herodotus criticizes Aristagoras for his attempt at deceit and bribery, the historian immediately corroborates, and even improves upon, the tyrant's bronze map relating precise measurements, rate of travel along the routes, and calculating the total time of the travel down to the day.[79]

---

73. Homer, *Il.* 18.395–409; *Od.* 20.65; Purcell, "Geography," 632–33; Talbert, "Geography," *BNP*, 5.772–76; Dilke, *Greek and Roman Maps*, 22–27; Harley, Woodward, and Aujac, "Foundations of Theoretical Cartography," 135–40.

74. Jacoby, *Fragmente der Griechiscen Historiker*, 1: Fr. 1–373.

75. Diogenes Laertius, *Vit.* 2.1.1–2.

76. Schnabel, *Early Christian Mission*, 1:449–50.

77. Golden, "Geography of Thucydides," 200.

78. Herodotus, *Hist.* 5.49–51 (Rawlinson).

79. Herodotus, *Hist.* 5.52–54 (Rawlinson). Whether Herodotus had firsthand knowledge of all the places he went is still a matter of debate. See *Hist.* 4.42; Armayor, "Did Herodotus Ever Go to Egypt?," 59–73; Armayor, "Did Herodotus Ever Go to the Black Sea?," 45–62. While a thorough analysis of Herodotus is outside the scope of this book, it is hard to overlook that Aristagoras is from Miletus, which was also the home of Anaximander and Hecataeus. For further analysis of Herodotus, see Branscome, "Herodotus and the Map of Aristagoras," 1–44; Bakker et al., eds., *Brill's Companion to Herodotus*.

In addition to this famous episode, Herodotus provides a broader picture of the known world amid describing the Scythian conquest by the Persian king, Darius. Herodotus follows the three-continent approach that continued into the Middle Ages with Europe to the west, Asia to the east, and Libya (Africa) to the south.[80] More importantly for this chapter, Herodotus writes his geography with reference to Persia at the center.[81] Even the story of Aristagoras relates a road map describing the precise route from Sparta to Persia reflecting the political reality of Persian dominance over the Greeks, and especially Halicarnassus, Herodotus' home.[82] Whether Herodotus begrudgingly placed Persia at the center of his geography or he was merely attempting to present accurate information to his audience so that they could understand the geographical setting of the historical events he described is a question for classic historians to answer. However, since Herodotus almost certainly recognized that he was writing a work under the authority of the Persians, and that the Persians would likely read it, placing Persia at the center and situating all other locations in reference to the center seems to make the most sense.[83]

Claudius Ptolemy

If Herodotus marks the dawn of Hellenistic geography, then Claudius Ptolemy in the early second century AD marks high noon.[84] At the same

---

80. Herodotus, *Hist.* 4.37–58 (Rawlinson). Herodotus is skeptical about the origin of these divisions and whether these divisions are even accurate (*Hist.* 4.45). However, he still relies on these divisions as he develops the geographical context of Darius' conquest.

81. Prontera, "Centre et Périphérie," 16.

82. Nicolet explains, "The first maps in Western history appeared during the Persian Wars as visualizations of the distances that were destined to mark, or to mask, the balance of power. Even with reproduction made easy by engraving and printing, the map will preserve the rare and prestigious trait of a work of art used not only by the authorities but by sciences or pedagogy. It can easily be utilized as a monumental display in which the decorative effect is combined with ideological meaning, stressing the will to know, to conquer, to exploit or to convert." Nicolet, *Space, Geography, and Politics*, 5–6.

83. There is some evidence that even his attempts to write favorably about the Persians where possible (e.g., *Hist.* 3.159–60) did not result in a uniformly positive reception by the Persians. Gould, "Herodotus," 696–98.

84. Scott suggests, "Greek conceptions of the world developed primarily in the period from approximately the sixth century BC, when Greek science emerged, to the second century AD, culminating in work of Ptolemy." Scott, "Luke's Geographical

time, Claudius Ptolemy also represented the end of ancient cartography.[85] Ptolemy's detailed instructions in his Γεωγραφίας Ὑφήγησις ("Guide to Drawing a World Map") "achieved a reputation for infallibility and completeness."[86] Ptolemy carries some of the blame for this perception because, even though he urged his readers that a good cartographer will continue to gather data and refine measurements, he often presents his work with an air of finality when it comes to his calculations.[87]

Ptolemy differentiates between γεωγραφία, defined as "an imitation through drawing of the entire known part of the world together with things that are . . . connected with it," and χωρογραφικός, defined as an impression of a single part of the whole picture.[88] He explains that the difference is "as one makes an image of just an ear or an eye . . . to making a portrait of the whole head."[89] Ptolemy's goal is to develop a theoretical method for building both an accurate and practical map of the known world.

Ptolemy's method, although theoretical and post-dating Paul's letter to the Romans by approximately a century, reveals some insights relevant to the present study. First, Ptolemy relies on earlier sources, some of which originated in the middle of the first century. Marinos of Tyre is the source of most of Ptolemy's geographical data, but likely post-dates Paul's letter to the Romans by half a century.[90] However, both the *Parthian Stations* by Isidoros of Charax and the anonymously authored *Periplus of*

Horizon," 484.

85. Olshausen, *Einführung in die Historische Geographie*, 76.

86. Berggren and Jones, *Ptolemy's Geography*, 3–4; Stahl, "By Their Maps" 148.

87. Berggren and Jones, *Ptolemy's Geography*, 63. One of Ptolemy's greatest errors was in adopting Posidonius' calculation of eighteen thousand miles for the circumference of the earth rather than using Eratosthenes' practically accurate calculation of twenty-five thousand miles. Stahl, "By Their Maps," 152.

88. Berggren and Jones, *Ptolemy's Geography*, 63. Berggren and Jones translate γεωγραφία and χωρογραφικός as "world cartography" and "regional cartography." This translation certainly captures Ptolemy's emphasis on developing a world map but obfuscates the broader semantic range of χωρογραφικός, which includes the descriptive geography found in Herodotus, Strabo, and Pliny the Elder but was not focused on necessarily developing a visual map.

89. Berggren and Jones, *Ptolemy's Geography*, 57.

90. Berggren and Jones, *Ptolemy's Geography*, 23, 62–64; The Arabic historian al-Masʿūdī believed that Marinos lived during the reign of Nero, but Wieber convincingly argues that all Arabic knowledge of Marinos is through Ptolemy. Masʿūdī, *Al-Masʿūdī's Kitāb Al-Tanbīh Wa l-Išrāf*; Wieber, "Marinos von Tyros," 161–90.

the Erythraean Sea both date to the early-to-middle first century AD.[91] Therefore, even though Ptolemy's original data could be dismissed as too late, Ptolemy cannot be completely regarded as irrelevant.

Second, Ptolemy demonstrates that his geography, like other geographies of the age, whether theoretical or practical, relies on arbitrary points of reference. Ptolemy's theoretical points of reference for his cartography are the equator and the Islands of the Blessed at the furthest western edge of his map.[92] However, Ptolemy does not use the Islands of the Blessed as he was providing a "summary caption" (ὑπογραφὴ κεφαλαιώδης) to help a person understand how to interpret what they were seeing. In describing the eastern and western limits of the map, Ptolemy uses Alexandria as the central reference point. He summarizes, "Again, the eastern limit of the known world is bounded by the meridian drawn through the metropolis of the Sinai, which is 119 1/2° on the equator . . . east of the meridian drawn through Alexandria. The western limit [is bounded by] the meridian drawn through the Islands of the Blest, which is 60 1/2° . . . from the meridian through Alexandria."[93] Ptolemy most likely did not actually see Alexandria as the center of the world since the meridian line at the visual and geographical center of his map (90°) runs through Persia and the Caspian Sea. Ptolemy is aware of where his map will be seen and to whom he is writing in his summary caption. Ptolemy knows that his audience consists of Alexandrians, and he provides them with the most familiar geographic reference point. Although Ptolemy's method can be flexibly applied, he accommodates his explanation to his audience.

The Jewish Geographic Context

It does not appear that Judaism had geographers like the Greeks and Romans did, but the Old Testament contains significant geographical information.[94] Second Temple Judaism finds its primary geographical foundation in the early chapters of Genesis. James Scott explains, "The so-called Table of Nations in Genesis 10, along with a few other biblical

---

91. Schoff, trans., *Parthian Stations by Isidore of Charax*, 17; Casson, *Periplus Maris Erythraei*, 6–7. Ptolemy may also have relied upon sources that significantly predate Paul. See Geus, "Claudius Ptolemy" 218–31.

92. Berggren and Jones, *Ptolemy's Geography*, 14.

93. Berggren and Jones, *Ptolemy's Geography*, 110.

94. Schnabel, *Early Christian Mission*, 1:468.

givens, provides the basis for subsequent Jewish tradition that seeks to represent the world and its inhabitants."[95] This section will focus specifically on the Table of Nations of Genesis 10 and how later Jewish literature interpreted this chapter. Additionally, this section will examine how the Table of Nations is presented anew in the book of Jubilees.

Genesis 10

Genesis 10:1–32, often called the Table of Nations, constitutes a summary of the Jewish understanding of the world. Genesis 10 covers a threefold division of the nations from the three sons of Noah, with "the nations of *Japheth* in the northern and western lands, including Asia Minor and Europe (Gen 10:2–5); the nations of *Ham* in Egypt and North Africa (vv. 6–20); and the nations of *Shem* in Mesopotamia and Arabia (vv. 21–31)."[96] The Old Testament primarily is the story of God's relation with Israel. However, Donaldson indicates,

> From beginning to end the biblical narrative deals focally with a particular people, but always within a larger setting that embraces all nations. In Genesis, the story of Abraham and his descendants is prefaced by a narrative (Gen 1–11) that begins with the creation of the world and culminates in the list of Noah's descendants, from whom "the nations spread abroad on the earth after the flood" (Gen 10:32).[97]

One must take seriously Scott's claim that the Table of Nations strongly influenced Paul's geographical view of the world.[98]

The Table of Nations uses a variety of designators for the "families" (מִשְׁפְּחֹת) listed throughout the chapter. Some of the designations refer to family divisions (e.g., Canaan, Nimrod, and Peleg), others refer to geographical locations (e.g., the coastlands, Babel, Shinar, Nineveh, and Gaza), and still others reflect ethnic and linguistic divisions. Osborne suggests that these different designations are "an indication of

---

95. Scott, "Geographical Perspectives in Late Antiquity," 412.

96. Scott, *Paul and the Nations*, 6–8. See also Delitzsch, *New Commentary on Genesis*, 1:307–46; Schnabel, *Early Christian Mission*, 1:478; P. Alexander, "Geography and the Bible," *ABD*, 2:980.

97. Donaldson, "Nations," 231.

98. Scott, *Paul and the Nations*, 5–56; See also Magda, *Paul's Territoriality and Mission Strategy*, 9.

family relations, language groupings, geography, political relationships and ethnicity."[99] Geography, while not the only grouping, is certainly a factor in the Jewish division of the nations. Regarding the families of Japheth, Sailhamer writes, "They are the nations that make up the geographical horizon of the author, the outer fringe of the known world."[100] Block also asserts, "Of all the elements which distinguish one nation from another, none seems more obvious than the territorial aspect."[101] The geographical focus continued into Second Temple Judaism.

Geographical locations played an important part of the Old Testament narratives, and their identification was important to properly understanding Scripture. Alexander, describing the importance of geography among Jewish teachers in the first century BC, writes, "Just as in 'topical history' the Greek student learned the positions of places mentioned in Homer, so too Jews learned the identification of places mentioned in the Bible."[102] Additionally, Alexander shows that the writers of the Targumim made attempts to update some of the geographic locations with their contemporary names.[103] Philo, in his narration of his diplomatic trip to Rome, attempts to recast the Table of Nations in a Greek and Roman world. He presents Agrippa I as saying,

> Concerning the holy city I must now say what is necessary. It, as I have already stated, is my native country, and the metropolis, not only of the one country of Judaea, but also of many, by reason of the colonies which it has sent out from time to time into the bordering districts of Egypt [Αἴγυπτος], Phoenicia [Φοινίκη], Syria [Σύρος] in general, and especially that part of it which is called Coelo-Syria [Κοίλη], and also with those more distant regions of Pamphylia [Παμφυλία], Cilicia [Κιλικία], the greater part of Asia Minor [Ἀσία] as far as Bithynia [Βιθυνία], and the furthermost corners of Pontus [Πόντος]. And in the same manner into Europe [Εὐρώπη], into Thessaly [Θεσσαλία], and Boeotia [Βοιωτός], and Macedonia [Μακεδονία], and Aetolia [Αἰτωλία], and Attica [Ἀττική], and Argos [Ἄργος], and

---

99. W. Osborne, "Nations, Table of," 593; See also Block, "Foundations of National Identity," 631.
100. Sailhamer, *Pentateuch as Narrative*, 131.
101. Block, "Foundations of National Identity," 298.
102. P. Alexander, "Toponymy of the Targumim," 13.
103. P. Alexander, "Toponymy of the Targumim," 106–62.

Corinth [Κόρινθος] and all the most fertile and wealthiest districts of Peloponnesus [Πελοπόννησος].[104]

Philo places geographical categories among his "harmonious order" (τάξεις ἐναρμονίους) that proceeds from the individual (ἀνήρ), to families (οἶκοι), to cities (πόλεις), to countries (χώρεις) and nations (ἔθνη), and to the great regions of the earth (κλίματα γῆς μεγάλα).[105]

The tradition of emphasis on geographical knowledge continued into the first century AD with Josephus. Josephus, similar to Philo and the book of Jubilees, updates the names of the nations for Roman audience.[106] However, Josephus placed the blame on the Greeks for changing the names of nations rather than the Romans. Josephus follows Genesis 10 in listing the nations in the order of the descendants of Japheth, the descendants of Ham, and the descendants of Shem.[107] Josephus, writing several decades after Paul's death, demonstrates that the Table of Nations continued to be influential in Jewish thought into the late first century AD, and, along with it, the geographical view of the world that originated from the Table of Nations.

The Book of Jubilees

The book of Jubilees offers an important insight into the geographical view of the world in Second Temple Judaism. Kugel asserts, "The book of *Jubilees* is arguably the most important and influential of all the books written by Jews in the Second Temple period."[108] Especially as it relates to the exposition of Genesis 10 in Jubilees 8–9, Jubilees blends the geography of the Near East with the geography of the Greeks. Alexander observes,

---

104. Philo, *Legat.* 281; Scott contends, "In describing the places to which these Jewish colonies had been sent, Agrippa proceeds systematically according to three categories, supplying in the process a *pars pro toto* table of nations: The Mainlands . . . , The most high esteemed of the Islands . . . , [and] the Countries beyond the Euphrates." Scott, *Paul and the Nations*, 88–89.

105. Philo, *Praem.* 7

106. Scott, *Paul and the Nations*, 40. Feldman insists that Josephus is presenting biblical geography "in terms intelligible to his Greek audience." While Josephus wrote in Greek, his audience was Roman, specifically the Flavian emperors Vespasian and Titus. Feldman, "Hellenizations' in Josephus' Portrayal," 336–53; Whiston, trans., *Works of Josephus*, ix; Inowlocki, "Josephus Rewriting of the Babel Narrative," 169–91.

107. Josephus, *Ant.* 1.121–47.

108. Kugel, *Walk through Jubilees*, 1.

"Jubilees VIII–IX offers a remarkably complete and coherent picture of the inhabited world. The account is so full of precise, visual detail that it is hard to avoid the suspicion that the author was describing not merely an image which he saw with his mind's eye, but one which lay physically before him in the shape of a world map."[109] Rather than merely providing a list of descendants, Jubilees goes into considerable detail regarding the specific locations of each descendant. Important for the current study, Jubilees 8:12 explains, "And there came forth on the writing as Shem's lot the middle of the earth [ὀμφᾰλός] which he should take as an inheritance for himself and for his sons for the generations of eternity."[110] Alexander suggests that Jubilees draws from Hellenistic geography, but that instead of placing Delphi at the ὀμφᾰλός, Jerusalem fills that position.[111]

In addition to placing Jerusalem at the center, Jubilees describes the descendants of Shem, Ham, and Japheth in circular paths. Scott explains, "The descriptions of Shem and Japheth make a counterclockwise circuit beginning at the sources of the Tina, while the description of Ham makes a clockwise circuit beginning at a place beyond the Gihon, to the right of the Garden of Eden."[112] Placing the territory of Shem, and specifically Jerusalem, at the center while describing all the other descendants of Noah (i.e., the nations) in circles themselves but also in a circle around Jerusalem is the way that Second Temple Judaism understood the world. It is plausible, perhaps even likely, that Paul would have been influenced by this work, and he possibly held to this view personally.

The Roman Geographic Context

The Romans were thoroughly practical in their cartographic depictions of the world. Stahl maintains, "To the practical Romans correct location by longitude and latitude was of no importance; in fact they did not much care about gross distortions of land masses or even about directions."[113] That is not to say, however, that the Romans had no purpose for maps or

---

109. P. Alexander, "Notes on the 'Imago Mundi,'" 197.

110. Charles, trans., *Book of Jubilees*.

111. P. Alexander, "Notes on the 'Imago Mundi,'" 199; Scott, *Paul and the Nations*, 15; Kugel, *Walk through Jubilees*, 77–78; Cf. Strabo, *Geogr.* 9.3.6; Agathemerus 1.2.

112. Scott, *Paul and the Nations*, 15. See also P. Alexander, "Notes on the 'Imago Mundi,'" 208–9; Kugel, *Walk through Jubilees*, 77–81.

113. Stahl, "By Their Maps," 146.

for geography. The Romans were, indeed, practical, and therefore sought to develop geography that not only accurately described the world in which they lived but also met the standards of literature of the day.[114]

During the Augustan period, a "mapping impulse" arose that continued through the remainder of the Julio-Claudian dynasty (27 BC–AD 68).[115] The emphasis on geography arose from the *Princeps Civitatis* during the so-called *Pax Augusta* in the aftermath of a long period of expansion.[116] One should not be surprised to find that the first map of the known world was initiated by Augustus' son-in-law and friend, Marcus Vipsanius Agrippa. Approximately three decades later, Strabo completed his monumental *Geography*, leaving a comprehensive description of the known world for posterity.

Agrippa's Pinax and Commentarii

The documentation and descriptions of the *pinax* that Marcus Vipsanius Agrippa initiated is both feeble and frustrating. The documentation is sufficient to conclude that a map and commentary of some kind existed in the Porticus Vipsania, but the precise nature and appearance of the map is nearly impossible to know.[117] Shipley, in his seminal work on

114. Syme, "Military Geography at Rome," 227–51.

115. The impulse to catalogue and depict the world may have also persisted through later dynasties since archaeologists have identified at least seven geographical monuments that date from the Augustan period into the fourth century. The mapping impulse is also not limited just public monuments depicting geography or formal written works dedicated to the study of geography. The obsession with geography carried over into the poetry and literature of the day. Boatwright, "Visualizing Empire in Imperial Rome," 235; Lindheim, "Pomona's Pomarium," 163–94; Pogorzelski, "Orbis Romanus," 143–70; Ziogas, "Topography of Epic Narrative" 325–48; Nicolet, *Space, Geography, and Politics*, 8–9.

116. Crook relates that "Augustus, it is often alleged, placed limits on the extension of territory and advised that the empire be held within fixed bounds. But evidence for that conclusion is slim and dubious." Crook, "Augustus," 188.

117. Brodersen argues that no such map existed, and that the *pinax* and the *commentarii* were synonymous. Brodersen suggests that the Agrippa's geographical monument consisted of something similar to Augustus' *Res Gestae*. However, the existence of a map is documented by numerous eye-witnesses, and several scholars dismiss Brodersen's argument as unconvincing. Even if a map in the modern sense did not exist, something both visually remarkable and geographic in nature was on public display in the Porticus Vipsania. Brodersen, *Terra Cognita*, 280–84; Dueck, *Strabo of Amasia*, 128. Cf. K. Clarke, *Between Geography and History*; Strabo, *Geogr.* 2.5.17; Pliny, *Nat.* 3.17.

Agrippa's building accomplishments, explains, "We have no information as to whether the map was cut in the marble of a wall, or in the pavement of the portico," but this does not prevent him from concluding that, "It was [Agrippa's] original project to display to the Romans, and visitors to Rome, on a huge scale and in a special building, the known world of which the Roman Empire formed so large a part."[118] Although, little can be concluded about the specific contents and size of the map, some conclusions can be reached based on the evidence available.

First, the map was geographic in nature with the intention of depicting the entire known world (*orbis terrarum*) rather than just the *orbis Romanum*.[119] Nicolet explains that "it was the most complete (a map 'of the world'), the most spectacular, and certainly the most exact for its day: Agrippa had traced it from numerous measurements taken on location, some of the results of which have come down to us."[120] Agrippa's map appeared at a time when Augustus was securing his dynasty and instilling a character of permanence.[121] Agrippa's *pinax*, constructed in a period for consolidating peace and celebration, visually located Rome within the larger world for every person to see, whether they were living in or merely visiting Rome.[122]

Second, the commentary accompanying the map allowed for others to reconstruct the map. Pliny cites Agrippa's measurements and figures more than thirty times in books 3–7 of his *Natural History*.[123] One can assume that Agrippa's figures were still available to Pliny in the second half of the first century. If Agrippa's full commentary was still available to the public, one may reasonably also speculate that other copies could have been made and maps reproduced even if these maps are not extent today, especially if the Porticus Vipsania was located in a well-traveled

---

118. Shipley, *Agrippa's Building Activities in Rome*, 77.
119. Pliny, *Nat.* 3.17.
120. Nicolet, *Space, Geography, and Politics*, 7.
121. Crook indicates, "It hardly needs saying that building programmes advertising the ruler were not confined to the capital. Nor, in the Roman world in general, were they confined to structures erected at government expense, for there was a great mass of building on local and private initiative as the municipal wealthy responded to the stability of the 'Augustan Peace.'" The Porticus Vipsania housing Agrippa's map was among these building programs. Crook, "Augustus," 139.
122. Arnaud, "Texte et Carte de Marcus Agrippa," 121.
123. Nicolet, *Space, Geography, and Politics*, 98.

residential neighborhood.[124] Nicolet similarly asserts, "Such were Agrippa's *Commentarii*: a written text (certainly brief but discursive) from which the map was drawn."[125] If copies of Agrippa's *pinax* or commentary were known or available to Paul, it is possible, although speculative, that he could have drawn upon knowledge of Roman-produced maps when communicating to a Roman audience.

Agrippa's map originated in a specific cultural context. Jacob explains, "Maps in a given society should be considered as rooted in a visual culture... On a general level, visual artefacts reflect a culturally bound perception."[126] This means that regardless of how diligent Agrippa was in his work and how practical the Romans were in general, Agrippa's map was still a cultural artifact that reflected the Roman worldview. The Roman worldview was undoubtedly fascinated with mapping and transforming the landscape. Talbert observes, "Roman land divisions were marked by boundary stones of one kind or another—very tangible, immovable objects—and similarly conspicuous milestones confirmed the courses of many of their roads. Under Roman rule, too, many communities and regions acquired new, Latin names... displacing the earlier nomenclature of indigenous languages."[127] However, the mapping impulse in Augustan Rome is reflective of deeper cultural values. Lindheim perceives, "The impulse to gain control of space, the desire to impose boundaries and to create a coherent unified whole out of the empire's territory and its people spills over into almost every aspect of Roman public life. Political, social and cultural discourses in Augustan Rome, rotating around questions of what it means to be Roman, especially Roman and male, display a striking tendency towards order, stability and fixity."[128] Given that a geographical awareness was such a clear mark of Roman culture, it is difficult to imagine that Paul, a Roman citizen who traversed the eastern Roman Empire and grew up in the Roman education center of Tarsus, would be unfamiliar with Roman geography.

---

124. Boatwright, "Visualizing Empire," 240.

125. Nicolet, *Space, Geography, and Politics*, 101. Some scholars have long-speculated that Agrippa's map is the ultimate source of the thirteenth-century *Tabula Peutingeriana*. See Talbert, *Rome's World*, 136–42; Salway, "Nature and Genesis," 119–35; Hunt, "2000 Years of Map Making," 4; Stahl, "By Their Maps," 152.

126. Jacob, "Toward a Cultural History of Cartography," 193.

127. Talbert, "Roman Worldview," 252.

128. Lindheim, "Pomona's Pomarium," 169–70.

Strabo

Strabo, known only by his Roman cognomen, was an Anatolian Greek from the city of Amasia, near the Black Sea coast, who wrote a survey of the entire inhabited world (οἰκουμένη).[129] He most likely completed his *Geography* close to his death in the AD 20s.[130] Strabo's aim is not merely to compose a narrative of geography of the entire world. Rather, he explicitly only focuses on the inhabited portions (καλοῦμεν γὰρ οἰκουμένην ἣν οἰκοῦμεν καὶ γνωρίζομεν).[131] Strabo recognizes that he is writing a "colossal work" (κολοσσικὸν ἔργον), and he encourages readers to not merely evaluate the individual parts but rather to see how the individual parts contribute to the whole project as one would with an artistic piece.[132] However, few, if any, people read Strabo's colossal work for at least a century. Roller explains, "The *Geography* vanished from sight at his death, presumably lying unattended in his study. It was not published (in the ancient sense of creating multiple copies that were placed in private collections or libraries)."[133] Despite the lack of early publication and distribution, Strabo offers insight into first-century geography.

First, Strabo contextualized Greek geography to a Roman audience. Strabo, a Greek writing in the Greek language and relying primarily on Greek sources, was explicitly writing with an awareness of the Roman hegemony on the formerly Greek world.[134] Strabo traveled to Rome several

---

129. Strabo, *Geogr.* 1.1.2; Dueck, *Strabo of Amasia*, 1; Roller, "Introduction," 1–5.

130. For a summary of the debate surrounding the date of Strabo's composition, see Dueck, "Date and Method of Composition." Dueck concludes that Strabo likely took notes throughout his life's travels and relied on earlier sources, but that Strabo probably wrote his *Geography* within the years AD 18–24.

131. Strabo, *Geogr.* 1.4.6.

132. Strabo, *Geogr.* 1.1.23. Connors observes a curious link between the verb ἐπισκοπεῖν used to describe his undertaking of the "colossal work" and the "all-seeing gaze over the earth" depicted in the colossal status of Helios at Rhodes. Connors, "Eratosthenes, Strabo," 147–48. See also, Dueck, *Strabo of Amasia*, 156.

133. Roller, "Introduction," 27. Koelsch also explains that, "Unlike Ptolemy or Aristotle, Strabo's work went untranslated into Arabic and was probably unknown to medieval Arab scholars, which explains why no copies are known to have survived in Spain or Sicily. It went unmentioned by Pliny the Elder (AD 23–79), the Roman natural historian, and by Plutarch (ca. AD 45–120). But portions of Strabo's manuscript dating to the second century AD have been found among Egyptian papyri, and it was also known in Byzantium. Koelsch, "Squinting Back at Strabo," 504.

134. Dueck, *Strabo of Amasia*, 31–84; Roller, "Introduction," 3; Nicolet, *Space, Geography, and Politics*, 8; Paassen, *Classical Tradition of Geography*, 9.

times, staying for approximately thirteen years on one stay (20–7 BC), and perhaps writing his *Geography* while in Rome.¹³⁵ Dueck explains,

> Strabo's contacts with Romans and his sojourn in Rome enabled him to absorb the atmosphere at the centre of the empire. He shows how the vast Roman conquests and with them the expansion of the empire to the ends of the inhabited earth contributed to the widening of geographical knowledge while they established the position of Rome as a world power. Imperial might induced changes in the political map of the world and in the cultural character of remote Barbaric tribes who adopted the Roman way of life.¹³⁶

Strabo demonstrated this by organizing his *Geography* to resemble a Roman *periplus*.¹³⁷ He begins his narration from the ἱερόν ἀκρωτήριον at the far western end of the Mediterranean and travels clockwise around the Mediterranean, arriving back in Northwest Africa.¹³⁸ Strabo is unquestionably Greek, but he is able to clearly communicate the history of Greek geography and contextualize a Greek geographical genre to a thoroughly Roman audience.¹³⁹

Second, the clear center of Strabo's geography is Rome. Strabo bookends his entire work with an eye toward Rome. Strabo begins with the observation that "The manifest usefulness [of geography] for political activities and for those of commanders, as well as the understanding of the heavens and things on the earth and sea . . . , assumes the same type of man as the one who gives consideration to the art of life and happiness."¹⁴⁰ He soon qualifies this observation by acknowledging that "geography for the most part exists for political needs" (τὰς χρείας τὰς πολιτικάς).¹⁴¹ Strabo, after completing his circuit of the inhabited world, leads his readers back to the center.¹⁴² Clarke argues that Strabo employed

---

135. Strabo, *Geogr.* 6.2.6; 7.1.4; 10.5.3; 12.6.2; 17.1.44; Roller, "Introduction," 10–11; Dueck, *Strabo of Amasia*, 85–86.
136. Dueck, *Strabo of Amasia*, 107.
137. K. Clarke, *Between Geography and History*, 198.
138. Strabo, *Geogr.* 3.1.4; 17.3.1–23.
139. K. Clarke, *Between Geography and History*, 335.
140. Strabo, *Geogr.* 1.1.1.
141. Strabo, *Geogr.* 1.1.16.
142. Strabo, *Geogr.* 17.3.24.

a "centre-periphery model" that was interested in commodity flows to the center (i.e., Rome).¹⁴³

Strabo is an example of a Pontic Greek who was born in the province of Asia, writing in Greek about the geography of the οἰκουμένη to a Roman audience. He locates Rome at the cultural and geographical center. Despite his work laying undiscovered for at least a century, Strabo is a prime example of how an individual from the eastern portion of the Roman Empire might accommodate himself to the Roman geographic view.

Contextualized Geography in Romans 15:19: Paul's Background and Foreground

The word κύκλῳ in Rom 15:19 suggests travel in an arc around a central location. Various geographical centers existed in the ancient world depending on one's cultural or religious presuppositions. Fredriksen insightfully observes, "Paul's textual homeland was the Jewish scriptures in Greek. Paul's social homeland (and eventual apostolic ambit) was the multiethnic, thus multireligious, Greco-Roman city."¹⁴⁴ How one answers the question of the center of Paul's geography in Rom 15:19 often depends upon how one primarily identifies Paul. If Paul is primarily Jewish, then it is assumed that Jerusalem must sit at the center of Paul's geographical scope in Rom 15:19. Paul's audience, however, is rarely considered. As one who sought to "become all things to all people, that by all means I might save some" (1 Cor 9:22), it is not unthinkable that Paul would consider the geography of his audience especially when writing to receive support for his journey to the Roman province of Spain (Rom 15:24, 28).¹⁴⁵

Paul's Jewish Background

Porter pithily observes, "No one would dispute that Paul was a Jew."¹⁴⁶ Paul's Jewish background is beyond legitimate questioning given the biblical evidence that would have to be either refuted or ignored to hold a contrary position. In addition to Paul spending years in Jerusalem

---

143. K. Clarke, *Between Geography and History*, 212, 221, 333.

144. Fredriksen, *Paul*, 61. See also N. T. Wright, *Paul*, 3–6; Wallace and Williams, *Three Worlds of Paul of Tarsus*, 3–7.

145. Bird, *Romans*, 504; Moo, *Epistle to the Romans*, 17.

146. Porter, "Paul as Jew, Greek, and Roman," 1.

studying with Gamaliel, he visited Jerusalem numerous times over the course of his ministry (Acts 9:26; 15:4; 18:22; 21:15–18). It should come as no surprise that Paul explains that his ministry arose "from Jerusalem" (ἀπό Ἰερουσαλήμ). Schnabel explains why Jerusalem was central to, but not necessarily at the center of, Paul's missionary work. Theologically, Jerusalem was the center of God's people and the eschatological destination of the pilgrimage of the nations. Historically, Jerusalem was the location where Jesus died and was raised from the dead. Practically, the Christian community in Jerusalem was the largest church and remained the home of the other apostles.[147] Some, however, conclude that Jerusalem was not only important to Paul, but was the center of his missionary geography.

A. S. Geyser

Albert Geyser argues that Paul places the origin of his ministry in Jerusalem in order to provide Paul with the "authenticity of his apostleship."[148] He also contends that Paul does not intend to provide a geographical or historical account of his ministry, and κύκλῳ in Rom 15:19 simply refers to spreading the gospel in the area immediately around Jerusalem and radiating out from Jerusalem up to Illyricum, which, in Geyer's argument, corresponds to the ends of the earth in Acts 1:8.[149] Both Knox and Morris astutely find Geyser's argument deficient primarily on the grounds of the geographical context. Morris rebuts, "[I]n the context Paul is referring to real places like Rome, Spain, and Jerusalem."[150] Geyser's attempt to explain Paul's geographic statement in symbolic terms does not consider Paul's context or the purpose of Paul's letter to the Roman Christians.

F. F. Bruce

F. F. Bruce, taking a slightly different approach than Geyser, argues that Jerusalem occupied a critical position in Paul's eschatological thinking.

---

147. Schnabel, *Early Christian Mission*, 2:1422–23. Commenting specifically on Rom 15:19, Schnabel does identify Jerusalem at the middle of the arc. Schnabel, *Brief des Paulus an die Römer*, 826.

148. Geyser, "Essai d'Explication de Rom 15:19," 158.

149. Geyser, "Essai d'Explication de Rom 15:19," 158.

150. Morris, *Epistle to the Romans*, 514; Knox, "Romans 15:14–33 and Paul's Conception," 8–9.

He concludes, "Not only was the Gentile mission to be, in the purpose of God, the precursor of Israel's salvation; Jerusalem was to be the place from which this crowning phase of the salvation of mankind would be displayed."[151] Bruce argues that Paul writes that he fulfilled the gospel ἀπό Ἰερουσαλήμ because, "For Paul, in fact, as for Luke, Jerusalem is the place where the gospel begins."[152] Paul, he continues, sees Jerusalem as "the earthly metropolis of the new Israel."[153] Bruce contends that Paul viewed Jerusalem through the lens of Isa 60:5 and 66:20, where the contributions made by the churches throughout the eastern Roman Empire constituted a fulfillment of the Old Testament prophecy of the wealth of the nations coming to Jerusalem.[154]

Bruce may be at least partially correct in his assessment of Jerusalem in Paul's thinking. However, he draws conclusions that cannot be wholly supported based on the evidence. First, he argues that the role of Jerusalem in Rom 15:19 can be established by examining Paul's emphasis on Jerusalem in the Epistle to the Galatians.[155] The problem that arises is not necessarily one of Paul's personal emphasis but of the letter's audience and occasion. Regardless of whether or not one holds to a Northern or Southern Galatian audience, it can likely be safely assumed based on Paul's early missionary pattern that the churches being addressed had a significant number of Jews in the congregation (Acts 13:14; 14:1; 17:2, 10; 18:4).[156] Even if Paul is addressing a mostly non-Jewish audience in Galatians, he is indirectly addressing Jewish opponents whose core theology focused on circumcision and the law.[157] The audience and occasion of Paul's Epistle to the Romans stands in noticeable contrast. Following Claudius' expulsion of the Jews from Rome around AD 49, the church would have undergone a cultural shift. Moo explains that "[T]he Gentile

---

151. Bruce, "Paul and Jerusalem," 25.
152. Bruce, "Paul and Jerusalem," 4.
153. Bruce, "Paul and Jerusalem," 4.
154. Bruce, *Paul*, 322.
155. Bruce, "Paul and Jerusalem," 5.
156. Schnabel, *Early Christian Mission*, 2:1300–1. Schnabel stresses, "Paul always understood himself as a Jew, even and especially as a missionary among the Gentiles... Seen from a mission-tactical point of view, Gentiles who believed in Israel's God were the best candidates for successful evangelism. This alone suggested that a Jewish-Christian missionary to the Gentiles should begin missionary work in the local synagogue, where he would encounter not only Jews but also Gentiles."
157. Schreiner, *Galatians*, 49.

element in the churches, undoubtedly present before the expulsion, would have come into greater prominence as a result of the absence for a time of all (or virtually all) the Jewish Christians."[158] In addition to the notably dissimilar audience, Paul's occasion for writing to the Romans was noticeably friendlier. Instead of being astonished to hear of false teachers and issuing a harsh rebuke (Gal 1:6), Paul is thankful for the renowned faith of the Roman Christians, expressing an eagerness to visit them so that they can assist him on his way to Spain (Rom 1:8, 11; 15:22–24).

Second, Bruce claims,

> It appears, then, that while Paul was born into a Jewish family which enjoyed citizen rights in a Greek-speaking city, Aramaic and not Greek was the language spoken in the home and perhaps also in the synagogue which they attended. Unlike many Jews resident in Anatolia, this family was strictly observant of the Jewish way of life and maintained its links with the home country. Paul would have been given little opportunity of imbibing the culture of Tarsus during his boyhood: indeed, his parents made sure of an orthodox upbringing for him by arranging for him to spend his formative years in Jerusalem.[159]

There is little, if any, evidence supporting the details that Bruce offers, while there is significant evidence that contradicts several of his claims. First, Tarsus, as Paul described, was a "not insignificant city" (οὐκ ἄσημος πόλις, Acts 21:39). Strabo provides some context for Paul's claim:

> The people there are so eager about philosophy and everything else in terms of general education that they have surpassed Athens and Alexandria or any other place that can be named where there have been schools or discourses of philosophers. But it is different, for those who study there are all natives, as foreigners do not readily stay. Moreover, the former do not remain there, but finish abroad, and having finished they are pleased to live abroad, although a few return.[160]

If Paul spent a portion of his childhood in Tarsus in the family of Jewish Roman citizens, then it seems likely that Paul would have received some education in the Greco-Roman schools.[161] Even in the plausible case that

---

158. Moo, *Epistle to the Romans*, 5; See also Schreiner, *Romans*, 10–16.
159. Bruce, *Paul*, 43.
160. Strabo, *Geogr.* 14.5.13
161. Willem van Unnik rejects this view arguing that Paul's family relocated to Jerusalem early in his childhood, and that Paul, subsequently, received all of his

Paul's family did exclusively speak Aramaic in the home and synagogue, there is not enough evidence to conclude that Paul received an exclusively Jewish education. Murphy-O'Connor asserts, "The hypothesis of a highly conservative and deeply religious family ever concerned to keep pagan influences at bay is not impossible in itself, but it cannot be harmonized with the type of education that Paul received."[162]

Paul's education in Tarsus almost certainly involved the kinds of subjects that Strabo described in addition to his Jewish education. Murphy-O'Connor observes, "Jewish students in Tarsus had to learn how to function in the Hellenistic world to which they belonged. The Greek they learnt at home had to be refined into the ability to read and write. Their basic curriculum would have been that of pagan children their age. These latter would certainly not have used the LXX as a reader, but Jewish children in addition read Euripides or Homer."[163] Craig Evans identifies over two hundred parallels between Paul's writings and Greco-Roman literature. Few of the parallels are direct quotations, and, he explains, "[I]n most cases we have at most parallels that probably reflect no more than the way educated people spoke Greek."[164] Evans also relates that not all of these allusions are literary, but that some concern geographical or scientific matters.[165]

James M. Scott

James Scott builds an original and strong argument regarding Paul's understanding of world geography based on the Table of Nations. Drawing on evidence from Rom 15:19, Scott rejects that κύκλῳ refers to either a semicircular path between Jerusalem and Illyricum or the area surrounding Jerusalem.[166] He argues that "if Paul had wanted to describe the path from Jerusalem to Illyricum and all that lay in between, then ἀπὸ ... μέχρι would have sufficed, for the infinitive πεπληρωκέναι itself

---

education in Jerusalem. Others such as Martin Hengel and Murphy-O'Connor find van Unnik's proposal unlikely due to Paul's excellent use of Greek and his use of the Greek translation of the Hebrew Bible. Unnik, "Tarsus or Jerusalem," 259–320; Hengel, "Vorchristliche Paulus," 238; Murphy-O'Connor, *Paul*, 46.

162. Murphy-O'Connor, *Paul*, 37.
163. Murphy-O'Connor, *Paul*, 48.
164. Evans, "Paul and the Pagans," 118.
165. Evans, "Paul and the Pagans," 118.
166. Scott, *Paul and the Nations*, 138.

indicates that the intervening territory was covered. It is likely, therefore, that Paul added καὶ κύκλῳ in order to emphasize the centrality of Jerusalem to his mission rather than to describe the path that he took to Illyricum."[167] There is much to appreciate about Scott's general argument. His argument for the South Galatian theory, drawing heavily on evidence in Second Temple Jewish geography, may provide a definitive answer to the long-debated question regarding the destination of Paul's letter to the Galatian churches. However, Scott misreads the evidence that he finds in Rom 15:19.

First, Scott dismisses the argument for κύκλῳ referring to a semicircular path from Jerusalem to Illyricum based on a questionable linguistic argument. He claims that the normal meaning of κύκλῳ refers literally to "in a circle."[168] He concedes that William Bowers does cite three instances where κύκλῳ refers to "a curving route alone, with no thought of a complete circuit," but he dismisses this evidence without further comment.[169] Scott is partially correct in that κύκλῳ certainly has a normal meaning of "in a circle" or "around" as shown from Homer, Aristotle, Strabo, the LXX, and other New Testament instances. However, the normal use does not exhaust the semantic range, since Strabo does use the word to refer to a circuitous route that does not necessarily include a circle.[170]

Second, like Bruce, Scott draws evidence from Galatians to interpret Rom 15:19. He asserts, "The fact that Paul views Jerusalem as the center of the world can be shown already in Gal 4:21–31, where he provides geographical information intended to support his typological argument... Even the idea of the Jerusalem above as 'our Mother' in Gal 4:26 may be based on this Jerusalem-centric perspective."[171] The response above to Bruce's similar reliance may also be applied here to Scott's argument. Unless it can be shown that Paul wrote to similar audiences for a similar purpose in his letters to the Romans and Galatians, the conclusions drawn do not seem to logically hold.

---

167. Scott, *Paul and the Nations*, 138.

168. Scott, *Paul and the Nations*, 138.

169. Scott, *Paul and the Nations*, 138; Bowers, "Studies in Paul's Understanding," 23–25. The three references that Bowers cites are Xenophon, *Anab.* 7.1.14; Appian, *Mithrid.* 101; Philo, *Legat.* 250. The last of these uses the accusative singular case (κύκλον) rather than the dative singular.

170. Strabo, *Geogr.* 13.1.7; 17.1.19.

171. Scott, *Paul and the Nations*, 139–40.

Third, Scott acknowledges the position offered by John Knox, who argued that Paul was thinking in terms of a full circle around the Mediterranean Sea, and that ἀπὸ Ἰερουσαλὴμ καὶ κύκλῳ μέχρι τοῦ Ἰλλυρικοῦ reflected the portion of that circle he had already completed.[172] Knox, similar to Scott, reads Paul's use of κύκλῳ here in the normal Greek use, but he takes into account the immediate Roman geography rather than an implied Jewish geography. Knox explains that the phrase "from Jerusalem . . . around to Illyricum" refers to "Syria, Cilicia, Asia Minor generally, Macedonia, and Achaia."[173] Knox clearly has Roman geography in mind. Scott argues that Knox fails "to consider the OT and Jewish background," and, "misses the relationship between the circle of nations and their center in Jerusalem."[174] However, a similar argument could be made that Scott overlooks the audience of Romans and the immediate context of Rom 15:19, which suggests a reference to Roman geography. Scott makes a valuable contribution in demonstrating that the Table of Nations constitutes an important passage that deserves significant attention in biblical theology. Scott may even be correct to argue that Paul's personal geography is based on Genesis 10. However, Paul having a foot in both the Jewish and Roman world allowed him to communicate in both of those worlds. Paul's multicultural worldview allowed him to naturally transition from the Old Testament references about the place of the ἔθνη in the kingdom of God (Rom 15:9–12) to references of Roman geography in Rom 15:19.

Paul's Roman Foreground

Fredriksen urges those who would understand Paul to situate him within both his Jewish and Roman contexts.[175] Porter observes, "While Paul was not preoccupied with Rome as the sovereign power of the day, he did acknowledge and live within the empire, which was pervasive in its culture and social backdrop to the developing Christian movement."[176] Paul's Jewish heritage and his Roman citizenship permitted him to live and communicate in two cultures. By establishing the intended audience,

172. Knox, "Romans 15:14–33," 11.
173. Knox, "Romans 15:44–33," 6.
174. Scott, *Paul and the Nations*, 139.
175. Fredriksen, *Paul*, 7.
176. Porter, *Apostle Paul*, 23; See also Harrill, *Paul the Apostle*, 76–94.

Roman Audience

Scripture is silent on the origin of the church in Rome. The view endorsed by Eusebius that Peter personally established the church in Rome is generally rejected today.[177] However, the church in Rome almost certainly developed out of the synagogue in Rome. Luke mentions οἱ ἐπιδημοῦντες Ῥωμαῖοι present at Peter's preaching at Pentecost (Acts 2:10). Schnabel hesitantly suggests that these Jewish Christians from Rome could be the origin of the church in Rome.[178] James Dunn also proposes that "Christianity in Rome probably emerged first within the Jewish community there. This is what we might have expected anyway in the case of a movement which began as a sect within the spectrum of first-century Judaism and whose first missionaries were all Jews."[179] However, the church in Rome did not remain primarily Jewish for very long.

A radical shift in the Roman church would have occurred following the Claudian expulsion of the Jews.[180] Schnabel explains, "It appears, therefore, that Jews of Rome who believed that Jesus of Nazareth was the Messiah, the *Christos*, and who wanted to convince their fellow Jews of the messianic dignity and ministry of Jesus provoked unrest in the Jewish community. These disturbances may be linked with outreach to Gentiles in Roman synagogues, particularly perhaps the God-fearers."[181] The departure of the Jewish presence in Rome would have left the church noticeably changed over the five years until Claudius died in AD 54.

---

177. Eusebius, *Eusebi Chronicorum Liber Prior*; Schnabel, *Early Christian Mission*, 1:722.

178. Schnabel, *Early Christian Mission*, 1:805. This theory also has the benefit of explaining the development of the later tradition that Peter personally established the church in Rome. Still, this is speculation since no definitive evidence exists.

179. Dunn, *Romans 1–8*, xlvi. Dunn also observes the "strong links" between Jerusalem and Rome under Caligula and Claudius. Whether these links were mutually friendly or strengthened by fear of the unpredictable Caligula is a matter of debate. The wife of Herod Agrippa I allegedly gifted a map to Caligula which lends further evidence to the Roman obsession with maps in the first century. *Anth. Gr.* 9.778.

180. Suetonius, *Claud.* 25.3–4; Cf. Acts 18:2; Orosius, *Historiarum adversum paganos* 7.6.

181. Schnabel, *Early Christian Mission*, 1:809. See also, Cranfield, *Romans*, 1:16.

A Biblical Case Study for Implementing Contextual Geography

Even if some Jews had made their way back to Rome between Claudius' death and Paul's letter, the church would have necessarily taken on a remarkedly Roman identity even while the foundation of Jewish scripture remained. Dunn contends, "Following the expulsion of (many of?) the Jews in 49 most of the house churches would have become largely Gentile in composition; and in their continuing growth they would have drawn in other Gentiles who had not previously been attracted to or been familiar with Judaism."[182] This should not be a revolutionary insight. As the church has spread to different cultures and languages around the world, the Jewish background communicated through the Old Testament was carried with them. The church in Rome that Paul was writing to, while counting some Jews among its composition, was primarily Gentile, more specifically Roman.[183]

Linguistic Parallel

Without evidence to the contrary, it seems reasonable to conclude that Paul received some education in his childhood home, and that part of that education was Hellenistic. Murphy-O'Connor describes that "The focus of Hellenistic education was not the development of a critical spirit, but the transmission of a whole culture in the works of such writers as Homer, Euripides, Menander, and Demosthenes."[184] Paul demonstrated an ability to navigate the higher social circles throughout his ministry, quoting from Hellenistic literature and utilizing hundreds of stylistic parallels to Greco-Roman sources.

Craig Evans identifies sixty parallels with "pagan literature" in the book of Romans.[185] Most of these parallels are formal in nature in that Paul uses phraseology or draws on themes similar to those found in pagan literature. Romans contains the highest number of these parallels,

---

182. Dunn, *Romans 1–8*, liii.

183. Cranfield asserts, "That the church in Rome included some Jews may be taken as certain... But the evidence adduced as proving that the church was predominantly Jewish falls a long way short of being conclusive. Thus neither the constant engagement with the OT to be seen throughout the epistle nor the use of the words γινώσκουσιν γὰρ νόμον λαλῶ in 7.1 proves that Paul was writing to a predominantly Jewish-Christian church; for the OT was the Bible of the Gentile, as well as of the Jewish, Christian..." Cranfield, *Romans*, 1:19.

184. Murphy-O'Connor, *Paul*, 48. See also Schnabel, *Early Christian Mission*, 2:926.

185. Evans, "Paul and the Pagans," 118–20.

followed closely by 1 Corinthians with fifty-five. Both Romans and 1 Corinthians have a similarity in that they are both letters written to churches in cities with a distinctly Roman identity.[186] Evans does not list any parallels for Rom 15:19, and it would be impossible for Paul to rely on Pliny the Elder, but the parallel between Paul's ἀπὸ Ἰερουσαλὴμ καὶ κύκλῳ μέχρι τοῦ Ἰλλυρικοῦ and Pliny's "A Gadibus columnisque Herculis Hispaniae et Galliarum circuitu" is too similar to overlook. It would go beyond the available evidence to argue that Paul is using a Latinism, but the similarity in phrases may reflect a Roman view of geography, which Paul apparently references in Rom 15:19.

Geographical References

Paul chose to use geographic designations rather than ethnic designations in Rom 15:19. Paul certainly used ethnic designations in Romans (1:16), but in this instance he chose to use exclusively geographic references. If Paul had wanted to refer specifically to ethnic groups, he could have done so by writing ἀπὸ Ἰουδαίων καὶ κύκλῳ μέχρι τοῦ Ἰλλυριῶν. Paul did not, and most likely could not have said such a phrase in a way that had any sort of specificity. By the time Paul was writing in the middle of the first century, Illyricum had become an ethnically diverse province.[187] Šašel Kos expresses, "For administrative purposes, numerous tribes and peoples who had no ethnic ties to the Illyrians, were counted as belonging to Illyricum and called Illyrian, because they lived in Illyricum. Greek and Latin authors of the time after the establishment of the Illyricum protectorate in the 2nd century BC, who mentioned Illyris/Illyria or Illyricum and Illyrians, did so *only with regard to the administrative organizations of the Balkan or in a geographical sense*."[188] An ethnic designation in Rom 15:19 would have made little or no sense to a Roman reader.

More specifically, Paul used Roman geographic designations rather than Hellenistic. Paul was not referring to the Hellenistic region of Ἰλλυρία

---

186. While Corinth is geographically located in the traditional territory of Greece, Corinth was a distinctly Roman city after being reestablished by Julius Caesar in 44 BC. Strabo, *Geogr.* 8.6.23. See also Murphy-O'Connor, *St. Paul's Corinth*, 3–4; Sanders et al., *Ancient Corinth*, 18–19.

187. Strabo, *Geogr.* 7.5.2–3;

188. Šašel Kos, "Illyricum," *BNP*, 6.732–35, emphasis added. See also James, "Illyricum," 35–39.

A Biblical Case Study for Implementing Contextual Geography 101

but rather the Roman province of Ἰλλυρικόν.[189] Paul, once again, chooses to use a Roman reference rather than a Greek descriptor. Additionally, Hahn claims that "[Paul] probably specifies [Illyricum] as representing for him primarily the ancient boundary separating the eastern and western halves of the empire."[190] When commentators mention Hahn's claim at all, they summarily dismiss it.[191] However, Hahn's statement requires further consideration. Even if there is no evidence for Hahn's interpretation in Rom 15:19 or in Paul's other letters, there is evidence found in Roman geographic history.

Appian narrates, "Octavian and Antony now, on their own authority, made a new division of the whole Roman empire, the boundary between them to be the town of Scodra in Illyria, which was thought to be about midway on the Ionian gulf. Antony was to have all provinces and islands east of this, as far as the river Euphrates, and Octavian everything to the west, as far as the Atlantic."[192] Even though Octavian conquered Antony, and put down rebellions in Illyricum, the traditional boundary between East and West persisted.[193] When Diocletian divided the empire around 293, Illyricum was once again the boundary between the eastern and western portions of the Roman Empire.[194]

Taking Roman geographic history into account, Chrysostom's interpretation of Rom 15:19 seems to fit comfortably. He preached,

> Wherefore he adds, "So that from Jerusalem, and round about unto Illyricum, I have fully preached the Gospel of Christ." Count up then cities, and places, and nations, and peoples, not those under the Romans only, but those also under barbarians. For I would not have you go the whole way through Phoenicia, and Syria, and the Cilicians, and Cappadocians, but reckon up also the parts behind, the country of the Saracens, and Persians, and Armenians, and that of the other savage nations. For this is

---

189. Chapple, "Paul and Illyricum," 21. Schnabel, *Early Christian Mission*, 2:1295–98.

190. Hahn, *Mission in the New Testament*, 96.

191. Fitzmyer, *Romans*, 714. Fitzmyer insists, "There is no need to think with Hahn . . . , that Paul was considering Illyricum as 'the ancient boundary separating the eastern and western halves of the empire.' There is no evidence for that interpretation here or elsewhere in Paul's letters."

192. Appian, *Bell. civ.* 5.65.

193. *Res gest. divi Aug.* 30. See also Wilkes, "Danubian and Balkan Provinces," 545–85.

194. Dunstan, *Ancient Rome*, 428–29.

why he said, "round about," that you might not only go through the direct high road, but that you should run over the whole, even the southern part of Asia in your mind.[195]

Erasmus likewise offers an alternate Latin translation of Rom 15:19: "in circumiacentibus regionibus" ["in the surrounding regions"].[196] Erasmus' updated Latin translation corresponds even more to Paul's intentions than Chrysostom, who draws upon some ethnic designations.

Conclusion

It seems evident that in Rom 15:19 Paul is drawing on Roman geography rather than ethnic designations, Hellenistic geography, or even his own Jewish geographical background. When Paul says that he has fulfilled the gospel ἀπὸ Ἰερουσαλὴμ καὶ κύκλῳ μέχρι τοῦ Ἰλλυρικοῦ, he is not indicating a strictly circular path, but rather that he has covered the territory consisting of the entire eastern portion of the Roman Empire. Paul did not travel straight from Jerusalem to (or up to) Illyricum, but he traveled "round about" throughout the eastern Roman Empire. Paul perhaps personally held his own Jewish geography, but when he was communicating to a mostly non-Jewish Roman audience, Paul adopted Roman geography, which placed either Rome or the Mediterranean Sea at the center of the known world, in order to accurately communicate the scope of his missionary journeys and plan further journeys to the ends of the earth.

Paul's use of contextual geography demonstrates a willingness to communicate with his audience using their emic understanding of geography. The discovery process for Paul was more intuitive since he had spent the formative years of his life in the Jewish diaspora of a Greek-speaking province in the eastern half of the Roman Empire. His model for using contextual geography while developing and communicating missions strategy to the Roman church is one that can and should be followed. However, as will be demonstrated in the following chapter, geography has become an increasingly less important category for many developing missions strategy.

---

195. *NPNF1* 11:544. Cf. Hengel and Schwemer, *Paul between Damascus and Antioch*, 260–67.

196. Sider, ed., *Collected Works of Erasmus*, 408.

4

What Is a People Group?

MISSIOLOGISTS HAVE MADE MANY attempts to define, describe, analyze, and categorize the nations of Scripture. Since the middle of the twentieth century, Western Christians, particularly evangelicals, have engaged in a concerted effort to provide precise definitions and distinctions to varying degrees of success. Much of the impetus to formulate such definitions has been with the intention of properly defining the nations so that Christians can take the gospel to those who have never heard it, make disciples of Jesus where disciples do not exist, and plant churches among peoples where the church has not yet been planted. This chapter will survey the major definitions and descriptions that have been proposed, demonstrating that there is little, if any, significant consideration of emic geography in the current proposals. The criticism offered in this chapter should not be interpreted as indicating that the contributions of these missiologists lack value. In almost every instance each one advanced the conversation, and made indispensable contributions to the development of missions strategy. Many overcorrected from the predominantly geopolitical missions strategy that universally prevailed before the Lausanne Congress for World Evangelization in 1974, but the correction they offered was an essential step in a better understanding of the nations in the world today.[1] The intention here is not to abandon their contribution but rather

---

1. Winter, "Highest Priority," 213.

to reintroduce geography, and especially emic geography, as an essential component of national identity.

The chapter will begin with an analysis of homogeneous units and various understandings of people groups. Next, this chapter will examine two alternatives to "people group" terminology: unimax peoples and ethnic solidarities. Some have attempted to incorporate geography into missions strategy. Youth with a Mission's Project 4K is one evangelical organization that has made an attempt to include geographic considerations into their global missions strategy. Roman Catholic missions strategy, while founded on a radically different soteriology and theology of missions from evangelical theology, emphasized geography as a major aspect of its approach long before the twentieth century, but it has undergone some revision since the Second Vatican Council. This chapter will conclude with a brief survey of recent articles that make attempts to address new developments in people group thinking.

Homogeneous Units and People Groups

Various definitions for people groups have been proposed since the middle of the twentieth century. Donald McGavran launched the conversation with his proposal of homogeneous units in *The Bridges of God*. This definition was picked up by the Lausanne Congress for World Evangelization, but in less than a decade the Lausanne Working Group shifted to the term "people groups." Over time, several definitions have been proposed for people groups. Some make attempts to base their definition in Scripture while others rely more exclusively on sociological categories.

Homogeneous Units

Donald McGavran did not use the term "homogeneous unit" in his seminal work, *The Bridges of God*, but the origin of people group thinking can be traced to this book. McGavran explains, "A true people is a social organism which, by virtue of the fact that its members intermarry very largely within its own confines, becomes a separate race in their minds."[2] McGavran adapted this definition in his first edition of *Understanding Church Growth*. He explains, "The homogeneous unit is simply a section of society in which all the members have some characteristic

---

2. McGavran, *Bridges of God*, 9.

in common."³ McGavran provides several examples such as culture, language, and tribe or caste.⁴ Although McGavran does suggest that geography may be a factor, he limits this to a geopolitical context. He indicates that a homogeneous unit "might be a political unit or subunit, the characteristic in common being that all the members live within certain geographical confines."⁵ By itself, this statement would not necessarily impose etic geographical standards on the definition, but he goes on to give an example for the total number of Christians in the Indian province of Kerala, and he indicates, "Sometimes the unit will be a country or city."⁶ By the third edition, however, McGavran had removed the reference to geography as a major division, completely listing only the examples of culture, language, and tribe or caste.⁷ He relegated geography to a secondary division among the subunits of tribes.⁸

The shift in McGavran's thinking toward strictly sociological, and primarily ethnic, groupings may be demonstrated in his case study on the Indian church, where he unequivocally equates ἔθνη in Matt 28:19 with Hindu castes and subordinates geography to secondary importance. McGavran asserts that "the powerful meaning of contextualization is that which has to do with the new Christian's relationship to his people, his tribe, his caste, his *ethnos*."⁹ He further expresses, "The task is to disciple the castes and the tribes. In Hindi, Matthew 28:19 reads, '*Sab jatiyon ko chela karo*.' *Jati* is the Hindi word for caste."¹⁰ In describing the distribution of the church in India, he surveys the geopolitical states of India and the status of Christianity within those states. He observes, "In only twenty-one of the more than three thousand ethnic groups of India (castes and tribes) do Christians form any considerable proportion of the total population. In perhaps fifty more, small arrested people movements to Christ have taken place, leaving tiny sealed-off congregations here and there. *In more than 2900 castes and tribes there are practically no Christians at*

---

3. McGavran, *Understanding Church Growth*, 85.
4. McGavran, *Understanding Church Growth*, 85.
5. McGavran, *Understanding Church Growth*, 85.
6. McGavran, *Understanding Church Growth*, 85.
7. McGavran, *Understanding Church Growth* (3rd ed.), 69.
8. McGavran, *Understanding Church Growth* (3rd ed.), 70.
9. McGavran, *Ethnic Realities and the Church*, 13.
10. McGavran, *Ethnic Realities and the Church*, 22.

all."[11] While the situation has changed some since McGavran was writing in 1979, the status of Christianity in India should compel us to engage in missions. However, McGavran makes at least one significant error in his assessment.[12] He rejects geography as a major category on the grounds that the geopolitical divisions of India do not provide an accurate picture of the status of Christianity in India. On the surface, McGavran is correct that the *geopolitical* divisions do not provide an accurate picture, but in many and perhaps most cases the geopolitical divisions of states in India reflect etic geography rather than emic geography.[13] The states encompass far too large an area and far too many distinct groups, which is precisely the point that McGavran is making, but the manner in which he presents the argument assumes the antecedent. There are more ways of looking at geography than just the large geopolitical subdivisions of a country. Each of the 2,900 castes and tribes that McGavran identifies perhaps has their own concept of the geographic borders of their group. This would be impossible to know for certainty without specifically examining this as part of a comprehensive missions strategy for that group. Furthermore, there might be more castes and tribes than McGavran first assessed because groups that were assumed to be the same based on caste distinction may be divided by a geographic distinction.

Four years after the Lausanne Congress for World Evangelization in 1974, the Committee issued Lausanne Occasional Paper 1 (LOP1), offering a definition of homogeneous units. The committee of prominent mission scholars, primarily from institutions in the United States, defines a homogeneous unit as "a section of society in which all members have some characteristic in common."[14] Recognizing that this definition is "broad and elastic," the committee further explains that "the common bond may be geographical, ethnic, linguistic, social, educational, vocational, or economic, or a combination of several of these and other

11. McGavran, *Ethnic Realities and the Church*, 28.

12. A second significant error might be that he assumes a one-to-one correspondence between ἔθνος and *jati*. It appears troubling to assume that a biblical category can be tightly linked to a category deeply rooted in Vedic religion. Further assessment of this point is outside the bounds of this book, but it does deserve further investigation.

13. McLeod, *History of India*, 123–27. The Indian system of federalism established at the time of India's independence is largely a variation of the British imperial system with similar divisions.

14. LOP1. Of thirty-nine participants and consultants involved in LOP1, all but two are associated with mission organizations or institutions of higher education in the United States. Fifteen are affiliated with Fuller Theological Seminary.

factors."[15] The common bonds identified by the group are a good sample of potential factors by which people groups divide themselves. However, it is unclear what role Scripture played in determining these categories.

Scripture appears to play a minimal role in establishing the definition of homogeneous units from both McGavran and LOP1. Initially, McGavran appeals to Scripture regarding his definition of a "people" only in asserting that his definition corresponds to the scriptural concept of the nations. He declares, "The Greek word translated 'nation' in the English Bible means exactly 'people' in the sense in which we are using that term."[16] In later works, McGavran makes no appeal to Scripture in defining homogeneous units, but he does emphasize the linguistic or cultural divisions above all others.[17]

LOP1 appeals to Scripture in several instances but primarily in responding to whether the homogeneous unit principle leads to divisions in the church. LOP1 largely adopts McGavran's definition of homogeneous units. As a result, the committee does not consider the scriptural foundation of homogeneous units. The potential common bonds listed in LOP1 are helpful, and many of them may be supported by Scripture. However, the starting point for the definition of homogeneous units appears to derive from the social sciences rather than Scripture.[18]

People Groups

Several scholars and groups have proposed definitions of people groups. The first attempt at a unified definition came from the Lausanne Working Group specifically dedicated to developing a definition that could be broadly accepted throughout the field of missiology. While broad

---

15. LOP1.
16. McGavran, *Bridges of God*, 13.
17. McGavran, *Understanding Church Growth* (3rd ed.), 69–70.
18. Hiebert, "Social Sciences and Missions," 192. Hiebert observes, "Social anthropology has had a profound impact on missions in recent years. The major impact of sociology and social anthropology on mission thinking was through the writings of Donald McGavran, Allen Tippett and the Church Growth School. McGavran showed how social dynamics play a major role in the growth and organization of the church. He introduced such concepts as homogeneous groups, people movements, social receptivity/resistance, and social barriers into the mission literature. The results have been a major paradigm shift in modern mission strategizing."

consensus existed and the definition continues to be relevant for missiologists, modifications and adjustments have been proposed.

Lausanne Definition

Ed Dayton, reporting the conclusions of the Lausanne Committee, defines a people group as "a significantly large sociological grouping of individuals who perceive themselves to have a common affinity for one another. From the viewpoint of evangelization this is the largest possible group within which the gospel can spread without encountering barriers of understanding or acceptance."[19] Dayton does not expound on what specifically constitutes "barriers of understanding or acceptance," but the definition indicates that these barriers are primarily sociological rather than based on biblical-theological categories. He does admit that the boundaries may consist of a variety of factors but that some barriers are more important than others. He indicates, "Some [people groups] are ethnolinguistic, such as tribes or language groups. These will be able to incorporate a church of their own. Others are more diverse and complex, such as occupational groups or people in special situations, such as refugees. They may be incorporated in churches of a larger societal group."[20] Dayton reports that the Lausanne Committee found ethnolinguistic groups to be the most important barrier to understanding or acceptance of the gospel. Without question, ethnicity and linguistic divisions are significant barriers, but Scripture does not limit divisions among the nations to ethnicity and language.[21]

The Lausanne definition constitutes the first official definition of people groups from which all others depart. The definition is primarily, even exclusively, sociological. Any later attempts made to give the definition a biblical-theological footing are misordered. For theologically conservative evangelical Christians, Scripture must form the foundation for missiology. Wan asserts, "Scripture is to be the basis and guide of Christian faith and practice. It is axiomatic for evangelical Protestants based on the conviction of '*sola scriptura*.'"[22] Wan argues that evangelical

19. Dayton, "Reaching the Unreached Peoples," 32–33.

20. Dayton, "Reaching the Unreached Peoples," 33.

21. The geographic component was addressed in chapters 2 and 3 of this book. Daniel Block further proposes theological and political factors in national identity. Block, "Foundations of National Identity; Block, *Gods of the Nations*.

22. Wan, "Importance and Significance of Missiological Research."

missiologists fail to give Scripture the place of honor that it is given in other realms of theology when biblical support is sought after the definition is already established from other disciplines. While calling the Lausanne definition of people groups "unbiblical" would be inappropriate, the definition takes sociology as its starting point rather than Scripture, which results in a definition that falls short of the fullness and complexity of the biblical-theological categories associated with national identity.

Despite the lack of foundation on biblical theology, the Lausanne definition does seek to identify people groups according to their emic systems, as indicated by the clause "grouping of individuals who perceive themselves to have common affinity for one another." Regarding this particular aspect, the problem is not as much in the definition as in the application of the definition. Dayton lists six stages to reaching an unreached people group.[23] The process begins when a people group is reported as unreached. Someone then verifies both that the people group is actually distinct from other groups and that they are unreached. Third, Dayton suggests that adequate research must be done so that a Christian outside of the people group can make a decision to attempt to reach it. An individual or missions agency may then make a commitment to reach the people group. Fifth, sufficient resources must be secured. Finally, initial field work begins. This method, as significant a contribution as it was, falls short in that it does not encourage ongoing research conducted by field personnel to gain deeper insight into the emic systems that may reveal further divisions or that previous divisions were etically imposed accidentally. Anecdotally, this has created some unexpected problems with church planting strategies among some people groups.[24]

---

23. Dayton, "Reaching the Unreached Peoples," 34.

24. I encountered this problem while engaging the Sherpa people of the Himalayas. The Sherpa are listed as one people group on people group lists. However, a significant barrier was discovered between the Sherpa who lived above and below the town of Lukla. The barriers were geographic, socioeconomic, and perhaps linguistic to a degree. Christians who lived below Lukla were reluctant to evangelize and plant churches among the Sherpa who lived in the area in Lukla and above. When recordings of Bible stories told by "lower" Sherpa were played, "upper" Sherpa were either unable or unwilling to understand the stories, and some openly mocked the speakers. The conclusion that the Sherpa were a single people group based only on ethnicity and language resulted in strategy decisions that proved ineffective.

David Barrett—World Christian Encyclopedia

David Barrett's *World Christian Encyclopedia* was revolutionary not because it was the first undertaking of its kind, but due to the scope and depth of the project.[25] Barrett's research codified definitions and established a methodology for conducting people group research on a global scale. The first edition took twelve years from inception to publication.[26] Another nineteen years passed before the second edition was published with the purpose of describing "empirical Christianity—those facts about the world Christian movement that are measurable."[27] Barrett seeks to examine the various peoples or people groups of the world with the primary categories of race, language, and culture, which are broadly referred to within the category of "ethnolinguistic."[28]

Barrett's only documented support from Scripture for his definition of ethnolinguistic people groups comes from the seven fourfold formulas found in the book of Revelation (5:9; 7:9; 10:11; 11:9; 13:7; 14:6; 17:15).[29] Barrett amalgamates the various terms into his single "ethnolinguistic" category, which he defines as "that group which speaks the language shown as its first or primary or cultural or official language."[30] However,

---

25. The *World Christian Encyclopedia* was preceded by five editions of the *World Christian Handbook*: 1st ed., eds. Grubb and Bingle (1949); 2nd ed. (1952); 3rd ed. (1957); 4th ed., eds. Coxill and Grubb (1962); 5th ed. (1968). See Jaffarian, "World Christian Encyclopedia," 31.

26. D. Barrett, ed., *World Christian Encyclopedia*, v.

27. Barrett et al., eds., *World Christian Encyclopedia* (2nd ed.), 1:vi. The focus here is on Barrett's definition of people groups as it relates to the biblical category of "the nations." However, others have criticized the reduction of Christianity and especially Christian missions to measurable facts. Engel, "Great Commission Advertising Campaign," 21–23; Engel and Dyrness, *Changing the Mind of Missions*; Escobar, "Movement Divided," 7–13; Escobar, "Managerial Missiology"; Escobar, *Time for Mission*; Wan, *Diaspora Missiology*.

28. Barrett et al., *World Christian Encyclopedia* (2nd ed.), 2:15–16.

29. Barrett et al., *World Christian Encyclopedia* (2nd ed.), 2:15. Barrett uses Matt 28:19 as his launching point, but he spends the majority of the single paragraph dedicated to biblical evidence addressing the terms used in the four-fold formulas. Barrett also does not discuss the context of these verses. Only the first two are positive assessments in that they describe John's vision. The other five instances of the four-fold formulae are either in the context of judgment or a pronouncement of judgment. For further analysis of these verses, see Bauckham, *Climax of Prophecy*, 326–37; Hays, *From Every People and Nation*, 193–99; Schnabel, "Early Christian Mission and Christian Identity," 369–86.

30. Barrett et al., *World Christian Encyclopedia* (2nd ed.), 2:16. The third edition

Barrett's brief treatment of the biblical terms does not sufficiently account for the complexity of the Greek terms or the Old Testament background of the fourfold formulas.

Barrett reduces the various terms used in the seven verses in Revelation to three categories: ethnic, cultural, and linguistic. He asserts that "nation" is an ethnic term, "people" is a cultural term, "tongue" is a linguistic term, and "tribe" is an ethnocultural term.[31] Apart from the relatively simple connotation of "tongue" with languages, Barrett's summary treatment of these terms overlooks their complexity and context.

Barrett contends that "nation" (ἔθνος) is an ethnic term. Generally speaking, this is not inaccurate but lacks some of the nuance that exists in the semantic range. The plural form that occurs in the New Testament (ἔθνη) is used elsewhere in Greek literature to refer to non-Greek nations.[32] However, the term is not so easily reduced to one component. While the ethnic component is important, perhaps even primary, there is difficultly separating ethnicity from other factors, such as political and geographical. The geographic component was addressed extensively in chapter 2, but one example of the political aspect of ἔθνος can be found in Jesus' interaction with Pilate in John 18:33–36. Pontius Pilate asks Jesus

---

(2020) of *World Christian Encyclopedia* omits this section likely due to a significant shift in methodology. The third edition "highlights the most salient points about religious belonging around the world." Johnson and Zurlo further explain, "Given the advent of the internet, it was unnecessary to present certain kinds of data from the second edition, such as extensive demographic information on countries and long lists of cities, languages and peoples." Johnson and Zurno focus on analyzing religions and especially Christian denominations within geopolitical countries. They do not completely ignore the concept of "peoples." They explain, "Individual Christians have distinct ethnic identities, speak identifiable languages and make their homes in specific geographic locations." They do not, however, engage in any analysis of peoples, nor do they present a scriptural defense of their definition. Becky Yang Hsu offers a striking insight in the foreword stating, "But the first step is admitting that these categories, which refer vaguely to geographic areas (with race and ethnicity as a subtext) and historical events, do not tell us much about how people actually see the world from their own point of view." Johnson and Zurlo, *World Christian Encyclopedia* (3rd ed.), xi, 30; Hsu, "Foreword," xiv.

31. Barrett et al., *World Christian Encyclopedia* (2nd ed.), 2:15. He acknowledges that other terms used do not fit neatly into these three categories. He claims that "multitudes" refers to the demographic aspect, and "kings" includes the ideas of nationality, citizenship, and subject status.

32. Silva, "ἔθνος," *NIDNTTE*, 2:89. Aristotle, *Pol.* 1324b10. Schmidt emphasizes the ethnic concept of the term but hedges this description by calling it the most general term used to describe a people. Schmidt, "'Ἔθνος in the NT," *TDNT*, 2:369.

whether or not he is king of the Jews (Σὺ εἶ ὁ βασιλεὺς τῶν Ἰουδαίων; John 18:33). Jesus answers, "Do you say this of your own accord, or did others say it to you about me?" (John 18:34). Pilate responds to this in John 18:35, "Am I a Jew? Your own nation [τὸ ἔθνος τὸ σὸν] and the chief priests have delivered you over to me. What have you done?" Jesus's answer to Pilate's question is shocking not only because of the immediate context of confrontation, but also because Jesus does not respond how one might expect him to respond based exclusively on an ethnolinguistic approach. "Jesus answered, 'My kingdom [Ἡ βασιλεία ἡ ἐμὴ] is not of this world'" (John 18:36). Jesus responds with political terms where one would expect to find him responding with ethnic terms. If Barret is correct that ἔθνος is always an ethnic term, then Jesus' answer is confusing in a modern context, and it would have made even less sense to Pilate. Pilate apparently intends a political meaning in his use of ἔθνος and Jesus responds with appropriate terminology.

Barrett asserts that "people" (λαός) is a cultural term, and he is again partially correct, but reducing this term to one aspect cannot be supported by the lexical evidence. Silva observes that in a majority of instances λαός refers to "a large number of human beings united by their ethnic, cultural, and/or political identity."[33] Λαός also carries more specific and more general meanings. The Septuagint almost always uses λαός to translate the Hebrew term עַם.[34] The term is frequently paired with the Lord in reference to the Israelites as the Lord's people (λαός κυρίου; עַם־יהוה), and over three hundred times λαός occurs with a personal pronoun (ὁ λαός μου) frequently spoken by God (e.g., Ex 8:22; 17:6; 2 Chr 7:14; Ps 81:11; Hos 4:6; Mic 2:8). In some cases, the singular form λαός may be used to refer to Israel in contrast to the pagan ἔθνη.[35] However, λαός tends to be used in a broader sense, referring to a crowd of people without reference to their ethnicity or culture.[36] The Old Testament provides some insight into the New Testament use of λαός, but Barrett's reduction of the word to a "cultural term" alone cannot be supported.

33. Silva, "λαός," NIDNTTE, 3:89. See also Strathmann, "λαός," TDNT, 4:33.

34. "Apart from some 40 instances, the Heb. is always עַם." Strathmann, "λαός," TDNT, 4:32.

35. Silva, "λαός," NIDNTTE, 3:92. Silva cites Matt 4:23; 26:5; 27:64 as examples of this contrast. The context suggests that these passages refer only to Jewish people. However, there is no contrast occurring in these passages. The use of the singular form in these verses seems to have a more general reference.

36. Silva, "λαός," NIDNTTE, 3:91.

Barret makes another unsupported assertion that "multitudes" (ὄχλος) in Rev 17:15 "illustrates the demographic aspect."[37] First, Barrett offers no indication of precisely what he means by "demographic aspect." Barrett defines "demographic" as "Relating to the dynamic balance of a population."[38] The definition does little to clarify the matter apart from the fact that it relates to an analysis of population groups.

Second, Barrett gives no evidence or indication of how ὄχλος is a demographic term. The lemma is used 174 times in the New Testament (all except four instances are located in the Gospels and Acts), and almost always refers to a general crowd of people without any reference to the crowd's constitution. In a few instances, the composition of the crowd is mentioned, such as a crowd of tax collectors (Luke 5:29) and a large group of priests (Acts 6:7).[39] Silva observes, however, that apart from these few specific instances, "what almost always seems to be in view is an unorganized crowd of people not formed or characterized by any specific background or custom."[40] If a demographic aspect may be derived at all from ὄχλος, it can be found in the contrast between the multitudes of people and the ruling classes, such as the Pharisees and scribes (John 7:49).[41] Silva observes that in this context ὄχλος probably takes on the nuance of the Hebrew phrase עַם הָאָרֶץ or "people of the land."[42]

Barrett's treatment of "tribe" (φυλή) is similarly oversimplified. Barrett asserts, "Another term, 'tribe,' (an ethnocultural term, often with the

---

37. D. Barrett, *World Christian Encyclopedia* (1st ed.), 107; Barrett et al., *World Christian Encyclopedia* (2nd ed.), 2:15.

38. Barrett et al., *World Christian Encyclopedia* (2nd ed.), 2:658.

39. Silva, "ὄχλος," NIDNTTE, 3:581.

40. Silva, "ὄχλος," NIDNTTE, 3:581.

41. Bultmann, *Gospel of John*, 310–11. Bultmann argues, "The curse [the Pharisees] pronounce on the people who do not know the law, shows where they, and consequently where the world also, find their security: in the Law. Yet the ὄχλος is made uneasy by Jesus' words, and in the ὄχλος there are believers—however much they may waver—whereas the official authorities, on the whole, remain unshaken; this but serves to illustrate that it is among those who, according to the world's standards, are the most questionable, that we may in the first place expect to find a readiness to receive the world of the Revealer."

42. Silva, "ὄχλος," NIDNTTE, 3:582. Oppenheimer explains that during the intertestamental period that social stratification occurred. He writes "[The social stratification's] basic principle was the study and knowledge of the Torah, with the talmid ḥakham, learned in the Torah, accorded the highest status, and the 'am ha-aretz, ignorant of the Torah and lacking any desire to engage in its study, assigned to the lowest rank in society." Oppenheimer, *'Am Ha-Aretz*, 18.

connotation of colour or skin pigmentation) occurs in 5 of the lists."[43] It is possible that there are some instances where skin color could be related to φυλή in that the term originally referred "a group of people bound together by common descent."[44] However, Silva explains that over time "this biological aspect receded into the background."[45] The term was expanded to include an administrative aspect in addition to family, clan, and peoples aspects.[46] While Rev 7:9 uses φυλή in a broad universal sense (i.e., all the tribes of the earth), Rev 7:4–8 refers to all the tribes of Israel (πάσης φυλῆς υἱῶν Ἰσραήλ), which does not have any reference to skin color. A great deal of caution must be exercised when evaluating the terms that Barrett singles out, but his summary treatment does not allow for the nuance required to address the terms in either their immediate context or the context of the broader metanarrative.

Barrett only addresses geography in the most cursory way. He includes geography as an aspect of culture but does not reflect on how geography and other elements of culture can also influence the development of culture.[47] Throughout the entire first edition and both volumes of the second edition, geography is only addressed in the broadest and most general terms, primarily at a geopolitical level or what Barrett describes as "ethnic culture areas."[48] Overall, Barrett's definition lacks scriptural

43. D. Barrett, *World Christian Encyclopedia* (1st ed.), 107; Barrett et al., *World Christian Encyclopedia* (2nd ed.), 2:15.

44. Silva, "φυλή," *NIDNTTE*, 4:626.

45. Silva, "φυλή," *NIDNTTE*, 4:626.

46. Silva, "φυλή," *NIDNTTE*, 4:626–27.

47. D. Barrett, *World Christian Encyclopedia* (1st ed.), 108; Barrett et al., *World Christian Encyclopedia* (2nd ed.), 2:16. Barrett defines a culture as "a group of people who do things together in a patterned way: sharing beliefs and customs with a worldview at the centre, together with values and standards of judgment and conduct, common institutions, a common language with shared proverbs, myths, folk-tales and arts, a common history, and common land or territory."

48. Barrett's lack of emphasis on geography is mystifying since the *Encyclopaedia Britannica* article whence he derives the "ethnic culture areas" describes the role that geography can play on influencing and conditioning culture. Rohan-Csermak contends, "In Europe, as in other areas of the world, geography is merely a conditioning and not a determining factor in cultural evolution; this is reflected by the fact that its major cultural areas do not correspond with its main topographical divisions. Not one of the large, more or less isolated geographical divisions—the British Isles or the Scandinavian, Iberia, or Balkan peninsulas, for example—is culturally homogeneous, for any tendency toward such cultural polarization has been negated by numerous other influences, including linguistic, religious, and political expansions and repeated technical and social revolutions." Rohan-Csermak, "European Peoples and Cultures," 1121.

support, and even the scriptural support that he references is oversimplified and misapplied.[49]

International Mission Board (IMB)

The International Mission Board of the Southern Baptist Convention (IMB) operated for most of its history along a geopolitical model, appointing missionaries to countries.[50] In 1998, Jerry Rankin announced a radical shift in global strategy and structure, explaining, "The entire organization is in the midst of a strategic shift from a long-standing geo-political focus, such as assigning personnel to countries, states, provinces, and similar political entities, to a Great Commission focus on ethno-linguistic peoples."[51] The IMB gradually shifted further away from considering geography as a significant aspect of people group divisions when, twelve years later, the agency shifted from geographic regions to affinity groups, which focused more on ethnic relationships despite geographic locations. Rankin, presenting to the Southern Baptist Convention annual meeting in 2010, reported, "Most significant among the changes being implemented is the move from a geographic configuration of overseas strategies to nine global affinity groups. This is a natural progression of the people group focus over the past decade as many of the remaining unengaged ethnic language groups are located outside the region of their ethnic and cultural origins."[52]

---

49. In addition to the weak scriptural basis for Barrett's definition, the encyclopedia is inconsistent in its definition. The second edition provides a different definition in each of the two volumes. The first volume defines a "people" as "A significantly large grouping of individuals who perceive themselves to have a common affinity for one another because of their shared language, religion, ethnicity, residence, occupation, class or caste, situation, etc. or combination of these. The statistical unit 'people' in this Encyclopedia always refers to a people, or part thereof, in one single country." Barrett et al., *World Christian Encyclopedia* (2nd ed.), 1:29. The second volume defines a "people" as "(1) A collection of persons who are linked by a common past or a common culture, or who have a common affinity for one another. (2) An ethno-linguistic people or ethnolinguistic sub-family." Barrett et al., *World Christian Encyclopedia* (2nd ed.), 2:670.
50. Crawley, *Global Mission*, 238–39; Estep, *Whole Gospel—Whole World*.
51. Rankin, "International Mission Board Report" (1998), 169.
52. Rankin, "International Mission Board Report" (2010), 174.

Throughout all of the strategic shifts, increasing emphasis has been placed almost exclusively on ethnolinguistic distinctions.

Orville Boyd Jenkins provides the IMB's definition of people groups, contending that "A 'people group' is an *ethnolinguistic group* with a common self-identity that is shared by the various members ... Language is a primary and dominant identifying factor of a people group."[53] Jenkins does allow for a variety of other factors to influence people group distinctions, such as common history, customs, family, clan identities, marriage rules and practices, and age-grades.[54] Where linguistic factors are not inherently determining, such as with monolingual enemies, Jenkins urges, "Various ethnic factors must be considered in addition to language for a full ethno-linguistic profile."[55] However, geography is still relegated to a secondary role. Regarding the role that location plays in distinguishing people groups, Jenkins contends, "All persons and every ethnic group speak a language and live in identifiable locations. Thus, a people group description includes *at least one language and at least one location*."[56] The clarification offered here appears to offer a moderate amount of influence to geographical factors until the people group data is analyzed.

The frequently updated "Global Status of Evangelical Christianity" report uses 31 categories to analyze each of the 11,946 people groups that the IMB has identified.[57] Some of these categories are informative rather than defining factors.[58] Excluding the informative categories, the report still includes 23 categories used to determine people group distinctions. Of these remaining categories, nine of them are related to geography, but three of these may be eliminated as duplicate data in different formatting.[59]

---

53. Jenkins, "What Is a People Group?" Italics original. The IMB is reviewing its definition of people groups to make corrections and identify gaps in the definition and strategy. At the time of publication, a formal definition has not been approved, but this definition will likely be a significant improvement over Jenkins's exclusive emphasis on ethnolinguistic distinctives. Geisler, personal correspondence, September 20, 2021.

54. Jenkins, "What Is a People Group?"

55. Jenkins, "What Is a People Group?"

56. Jenkins, "What Is a People Group?" Italics original.

57. IMB Global Research, *Global Status of Evangelical Christianity* (October 2021).

58. Included in these informative categories are PEID (a numerical identifier code), population, whether certain gospel resources are available, physical exertion required to live among a people group, freedom index, government restrictions index, social hostilities index, U.S. Department of State threat level, and the status of their engagement by evangelical Christians.

59. GENC and FIPS are other codes for the country, and FIPS of Origin is a code

The remaining geographic categories consist of continent, subcontinent, country, country of origin, latitude, and longitude. These categories are helpful, and they do demonstrate some willingness to take geography into account. However, these categories do not indicate that geography is a determining factor in distinguishing people groups. In some ways, the geographic categories seem to be more descriptive than determinative. The continent and subcontinent categories are far too large to allow for meaningful analysis. The country category is helpful in that it offers a narrower set of boundaries, but in large countries such as Canada, Russia, China, Brazil, India, Algeria, Democratic Republic of the Congo, Nigeria, and Chad, a narrower set of boundaries would be necessary for geography to be a meaningfully distinguishing category. The country of origin category may be helpful in identifying and distinguishing diaspora people groups, but to what degree a people's country of origin is the determining factor in their identity is also influenced by other factors, such as their length of time away from their country of origin and whether they are first-, second-, or later-generation immigrants.[60]

The last geographic categories of latitude and longitude can be helpful in that they are remarkably precise—in many cases offering coordinates down to the fifth or sixth decimal, which corresponds to an area of roughly two square meters or 0.01 square meters, respectively. Two major problems arise from the use of latitude and longitude in this manner. First, The overly precise nature of the coordinates gives a false sense of certainty regarding the precise location of each people group. Latitude and longitude are provided for every people group with no indication about the certainty of this data. Second, the use of the latitude and longitude coordinate system is an etic categorization limited in usefulness. While useful for plotting the 11,935 identified people groups on a map, longitude and latitude coordinates communicate nothing about how a people group sees its own geographic boundaries.

The major area where we see geography integrated into people group analysis is in graphical polygons on maps. These polygons originated as visualizations for location of languages and the status of evangelization among people groups, but, over about fifteen years, the polygons developed into an attempt to map geographical locations of people groups.

---

for country of origin.

60. For a study of the various issues related to diaspora missions, see Wan, *Diaspora Missiology*.

The polygons are derived from a combination of descriptive field reports, *Ethnologue* data, and ethnographic sources.[61]

Despite these admirable efforts, the current polygon approach exhibits some significant weaknesses. First, the accuracy of the polygons is questionable. The IMB has described only 20 percent of the polygons with "high confidence," indicating that they have been locally verified. However, attempting to locally verify every boundary is a daunting task, and the IMB is taking steps to modify methodology that will hopefully increase the accuracy of geographic data. Second, the polygon approach to geography seems to suggest a monodirectional relationship between a people group and geography. In other words, the people group is defined independently from geography and then the people group is simply placed on a map. This analytical approach seems to indicate that the potential for geography to play a defining role in a people group's identity has been overlooked. Furthermore, while identifying accurate boundaries is a helpful start, a people group's geography includes far more than boundaries.[62]

Joshua Project

Joshua Project, a ministry of Frontier Ventures, describes itself as "a research initiative seeking to highlight the ethnic people groups of the world with the fewest followers of Christ."[63] Joshua Project explains that they "seek to answer the questions that result from the Great Commission's call to make disciples among every nation or people group."[64] These questions include: "Who are the ethnic peoples of the world? Which people groups still need initial church-planting in their midst? What ministry resources are available to reach the least-reached?"[65] Only the first question will be addressed directly in this study.

Joshua Project takes the Lausanne definition as its starting point for defining the ethnic peoples of the world. Rather than reducing the criteria

---

61. Geisler, personal correspondence, September 13, 2021.

62. For example, different types of boundaries and the importance of cultural, religious, and other kinds of centers. See chapter 5 for more information.

63. "Joshua Project," 2021 (https://joshuaproject.net/about/details).

64. "Joshua Project," 2021 (https://joshuaproject.net/about/details). Throughout the articles and documents produced by Joshua Project, the terms "nation" and "people group" are used interchangeably.

65. "Joshua Project," 2019 (https://joshuaproject.net/about/details).

to focus primarily on one particular barrier, Joshua Project distinguishes people groups by the highest barrier to understanding or acceptance of the gospel. Whichever barrier is determined to be the more significant barrier to the spread of the gospel is the barrier used to establish the boundaries of that people group. Joshua Project explains,

> If understandability is the most important barrier, then a linguistic, or an ethno-linguistic, approach is used. With this approach, one people group doesn't speak more than one language (apart from occasional bi-lingual individuals), although more than one people group may speak a given language if cultural or dialect differences warrant. In most of the world, this is the approach Joshua Project uses... If the cultural / relationship barrier is the greatest barrier (as it often is in South Asia), then we treat caste/tribe as the first criterion for separation. With this approach, one people group may speak more than one language. And as with the first approach, one language may be spoken by more than one people group.[66]

This approach is utilized to facilitate church planting. In order to accomplish this goal, Joshua Project chooses to focus on only one aspect to simplify the divisions among the nations as much as possible serving field church planters. If both factors, barriers of understanding and cultural barriers, were integrated, Joshua Project suggests that the result would be overwhelming. They explain, "If we strictly defined 'people group' this way in India, all individuals in each people group would speak the same language and would be in the same caste or tribe. Easily done, but what would it lead to? We would immediately create potentially over 20,000 people groups in India alone."[67] The desire to create a manageable picture for the field missionaries and church planters drives their methodology.

Despite their willingness to embrace a variety of boundaries, the methodology employed to differentiate nations is unsatisfactory.[68] First, Joshua Project does not ground its definitions in Scripture. The Lausanne definition is adopted, but where the categories within the Lausanne

---

66. "What Is a People Group?" (https://joshuaproject.net/resources/articles/what_is_a_people_group).

67. "What Is a People Group?" (https://joshuaproject.net/resources/articles/what_is_a_people_group).

68. Joshua Project specifically lists caste, religious tradition, location, and common histories and legends as examples of types of cultural or relational barriers to gospel acceptance. "What Is a People Group?" (https://joshuaproject.net/resources/articles/what_is_a_people_group).

definition are clarified, Scripture is never referenced for support of the categories. Additionally, references to Scripture are noticeably absent in their discussion of people groups, the number of people groups, and even their list of organizational distinctives.[69]

Second, Joshua Project's desire to create a manageable situation for church planters is admirable, but simplicity for its own sake is insufficient as a goal. They do not oversimplify to the extent of the ethnolinguistic lists, but they freely confess to simplifying the picture for church planting purposes. Limitations to comprehension of divisions is an inherent problem when blending various barriers, but an artificially simplified picture fails to recognize the interplay among the various factors that result in the self-identity of people groups. Joshua Project emphasizes the highest barrier, but this approach can result in minimizing other factors that influence and are influenced by the highest barrier. Geography will not always be the highest barrier, but geography almost always plays a factor in the self-identity of a nation. James Jordan asserts, "A common geographical location is almost always necessary for a body of people to consider itself a nation."[70] The ubiquity of the geographical aspect does not automatically elevate it to the primary factor in every circumstance. However, Joshua Project's methodology overlooks the influence of geography on national identity unless it is the primary factor. Based on these two weaknesses, a different methodology is required.

John Piper: Let the Nations Be Glad!

John Piper offers one of the most comprehensive examinations of the New Testament use of ἔθνος. Piper argues, "God's call for missions in Scripture *cannot* be defined in terms of crossing cultures to maximize the total number of individuals saved. Rather, God's will for missions is that every people group be reached with the testimony of Christ and that a people be called out for his name from all the nations."[71] He further asserts that "nations" does not refer to political states, but rather "its biblical meaning has to do with an ethnic group that may or may not have

---

69. Joshua Projects lists its distinctives as strategic, effective, comprehensive, neutral, grassroots, and openhanded. "Joshua Project," 2019 (https://joshuaproject.net/about/details).

70. Jordan, *Christendom and the Nations*, 6. Jordan admits that there are exceptions, but they are rare and almost no examples of this exist in the world today.

71. Piper, *Let the Nations Be Glad*, 179.

What Is a People Group?

political dimensions."[72] The two aspects of his argument—that ἔθνη in Matt 28:19 refers to groups rather than individuals and that these groups are ethnic in nature—deserve separate consideration.

Piper references the 1982 Lausanne definition of "people groups," but he reflects, "We should be aware that this definition was developed not merely on the basis of biblical teaching about the specific nature of people groups but also on the basis of what would help missionaries identify and reach various groups."[73] Observing that the 1982 Lausanne definition is not exclusively based on biblical criteria, Piper embarks to understand the scope of the command to make disciples of πάντα τὰ ἔθνη in Matt 28:19. He indicates and asks, "My aim is to test the people-group focus by the Scriptures. Is the missionary mandate of the Bible (1) a command to reach as many individuals as possible, or (2) a command to reach all the 'fields,' or (3) a command to reach all the 'people groups' of the world, as the Bible defines people groups?"[74] Piper, quoting numerous biblical references and citing many more, demonstrates that the singular form (ἔθνος) "very naturally and normally carried a corporate meaning in reference to people in groups."[75] Piper further asserts that these are ethnic groups, but the verses cited do not clearly demonstrate that these are necessarily exclusively ethnic groups, but this will be addressed further below. Piper also reviews the various uses for the plural form (ἔθνη), which he asserts "can refer either to an ethnic group or simply to Gentile individuals who may not make up an ethnic group."[76] Piper once again demonstrates the corporate nature of many instances of ἔθνη, but does not directly address how he arrives at "ethnic groups" in these cases. At this point, he confidently concludes,

> The singular use of *ethnos* in the New Testament always refers to a people group. The plural use of *ethnos* sometimes must be a people group and sometimes must refer to Gentile individuals but usually can go either way. The phrase *panta ta ethnē* must refer to Gentile individuals only once but must refer to people

72. Piper, *Let the Nations Be Glad*, 179 n. 2.
73. Piper, *Let the Nations Be Glad*, 181.
74. Piper, *Let the Nations Be Glad*, 181. Piper does not explicitly define "fields" unless he is referring to the strategy focusing exclusively on geopolitical nations that Ralph Winter addressed in his presentation at the Lausanne Congress for World Evangelization. Piper, *Let the Nations Be Glad*, 179–80.
75. Piper, *Let the Nations Be Glad*, 184.
76. Piper, *Let the Nations Be Glad*, 184–85.

groups nine times. The remaining eight uses may refer to people groups. The combination of these results suggests that the meaning of *panta ta ethnē* leans heavily in the direction of "all the nations (people groups)."[77]

Overwhelmingly, the New Testament use of ἔθνος in its singular and plural forms refers to groups rather than individuals.

Piper regularly uses "people group" and "ethnic group" interchangeably without a clear explanation regarding how he is arriving at an exclusively ethnic concept of people groups. Early in his chapter, he cites Ralph Winter, who indicates, "I'm afraid that all our exultation about the fact that every *country* of the world has been penetrated has allowed many to suppose that every *culture* has by now been penetrated."[78] Piper explains Winter's insight, asserting, "In spite of the fact that every country of the world has been penetrated with the gospel, four out of five non-Christians are still cut off from the gospel because the barriers are cultural and linguistic, not geographic."[79] Piper unnecessarily equates Winter's challenge to think beyond countries as a complete rejection of the idea that geography plays any role in the biblical definition of the nations. Winter attempted to integrate geography into his "unimax groups." While a "country" in Winter's argument refers to a geopolitical entity, this does not necessarily mean that geography by itself is not a valid aspect of identifying the nations.

Furthermore, Piper rejects several categories from the 1982 Lausanne definition without much explanation. He asserts, "I agree with those who say that the biblical concept of 'peoples' or 'nations' cannot be stretched to include individuals grouped on the basis of things such as occupation, residence, or handicaps."[80] However, a few pages later he explains, "The reason that *panta ta ethnē* is such an important phrase is that *ethnē*, when translated as 'nations,' sounds like a political or geographic

---

77. Piper, *Let the Nations Be Glad*, 189.

78. Winter, "New Macedonia," 353; Piper, *Let the Nations Be Glad*, 180.

79. Piper, *Let the Nations Be Glad*, 180.

80. Piper, *Let the Nations Be Glad*, 181. Some push these categories too far, such as Ed Stetzer making the bold claim that the population segment living in multihousing communities "constitutes the largest unreached people group in North America." Stetzer, *Planting Missional Churches*, 10. However, there is some legitimacy to these categories, such as that those who are deaf who necessarily must use a different language. Even though deaf people are the same ethnicity as those around them, they remain culturally distant from them.

What Is a People Group?

grouping. That is its most common English usage. But this is not what the Greek means, nor does the English always mean this. For example, we say the Cherokee nation or the Sioux nation, which means something like 'people with a unifying ethnic identity.'"[81] Piper is partially correct in that "the Cherokee nation or the Sioux nation" is probably closer in meaning to the biblical use of ἔθνη. His example, however, does more to disprove his argument than to prove it. The Cherokee and Sioux certainly have an ethnic identity, but to reduce the Cherokee and Sioux to nothing more than an ethnic identity overlooks their inherently tight connection to the land on which they dwelled and currently do dwell.[82]

Piper's assertion that ἔθνη has an exclusively ethnic meaning is further weakened by one of his examples. He translates 1 Cor 12:2 as "You know that when you were *pagans*, you were led astray to mute idols."[83] He rightfully suggests that "It would not make sense to say, 'When you were nations'" in this verse.[84] The context of 1 Cor 12:2 is clearly religious in nature since Paul's point is that the ἔθνη were once engaged in idolatrous worship. This one example alone suggests that insisting ἔθνη has a purely ethnic semantic domain is insufficient.

Piper comes close to making an argument for something like an ethnic understanding of ἔθνη in his treatment of Gen 12:3. He observes, "In [Gen] 12:3 and 28:14, the Hebrew phrase for 'all the families' (*kol mishpehot*) is rendered in the Greek Old Testament by *pasai hai phylai*.

---

81. Piper, *Let the Nations Be Glad*, 183.

82. Corduan, in his treatment of Native American religion, observes that there is a generally accepted geographic distribution of Native American cultures. He identifies six major regional groupings. Corduan, *Neighboring Faiths*, 238. The reason why one might consider the Cherokee or Sioux nation primarily in ethnic terms without reference to geography is that the Cherokee were removed from their traditional territories. Smithers relates that "the Cherokee were becoming a dispersed people during the latter half of the eighteenth century and this dispersal was occurring on a geographic scale that seemed unprecedented to them. The language of nationalism therefore became a useful rhetorical device that enabled an increasingly diasporic population to locate a cultural and political 'home,' helping Cherokee people to keep their sacred fires burning and imagine an identity that was deeply rooted in history, language, tradition." Smithers, *Cherokee Diaspora*, 29. Piper further overlooks that at one point the Cherokee and Sioux were politically autonomous and continue to exercise semi-autonomous authority within their demarcated geographic territory. However, addressing the political component of national identity is outside the scope of this book.

83. Piper, *Let the Nations Be Glad*, 185. Many English translations (e.g., CSB, ESV, LEB, NASB, and NRSV) also translate ἔθνη as "pagans" in this passage.

84. Piper, *Let the Nations Be Glad*, 185.

The word *phylai* means 'tribes' in most contexts. But *mishpahah* can be and usually is something smaller than a tribe."[85] He further observes, "The other three repetitions of this Abrahamic promise in Genesis use the phrase 'all the nations' (Hebrew: *kol goye*), which the Septuagint translates with the familiar *panta ta ethnē* in each case (18:18; 22:18; 26:4)."[86] He concludes, "This again strongly suggests that the term *panta ta ethnē* in missionary contexts refers to people groups rather than to Gentile individuals."[87] Piper again convincingly shows that πάντα τὰ ἔθνη refers to groups rather than individuals, but his argument falls considerably short of proving that these groups refer exclusively to ethnic groups.

First, Piper does not observe the intricate connection between Gen 12:3 and the fourfold formulas of Gen 10:5; 20; 31, where מִשְׁפָּחֹת and גּוֹיֵ are used together. Most likely, the use of מִשְׁפָּחֹת in Gen 12:3 and גּוֹיֵ in Gen 18:18; 22:18; 26:4 all refer in summary to the divisions of humanity from Genesis 10.[88] While מִשְׁפָּחָה and גּוֹי and φυλή and ἔθνος have some semantic overlap, the words are not identical. Piper shows this in one of his own examples as he references Ps 22:27, which refers to "all the families of the nations" (כָּל־מִשְׁפְּחוֹת גּוֹיִם; πᾶσαι αἱ πατριαὶ τῶν ἐθνῶν).[89] Piper does not convincingly argue that Gen 12:3 provides evidence that πάντα τὰ ἔθνη in Matt 28:19 exclusively refers to ethnic groups.

Piper further attempts to derive an argument for ethnic people groups from Paul's description of his own missionary endeavors in Rom 15:18–21. Piper concludes that Paul's assertion that he has fulfilled the gospel from Jerusalem and around to Illyricum means, "Paul's conception of the *missionary task* is not merely the winning of more and more people to Christ (which he could have done very efficiently in these familiar regions) but the reaching of more and more peoples or nations. His focus was not primarily on new geographic areas. Rather, he was gripped by the vision of unreached peoples."[90] Piper is deeply inconsistent in his treatment of this passage and he seems to misinterpret the geographic references. As mentioned in chapter 3, Paul uses geographic designators rather than ethnic designators in Rom 15:19. Additionally, when Paul

---

85. Piper, *Let the Nations Be Glad*, 190.

86. Piper, *Let the Nations Be Glad*, 190.

87. Piper, *Let the Nations Be Glad*, 190.

88. See chapter 2 for treatment of the Table of Nations in Genesis 10.

89. Piper, *Let the Nations Be Glad*, 192. Further weakening Piper's connection between φυλή and ἔθνος is that the LXX translates מִשְׁפָּחוֹת as πατριά rather than φυλή.

90. Piper, *Let the Nations Be Glad*, 203.

relates what it means to have fulfilled the gospel and his future plans, he again uses geographic references. Paul expresses that he "no longer has place in this region" (μηκέτι τόπον ἔχων ἐν τοῖς κλίμασι τούτοις), where both τόπος and κλίμα are terms that refer primarily to geographic regions.[91] Paul also indicates that his intention is to travel to the Roman province of Spain (Σπανία). There are no ethnic designators in these verses from which to derive Piper's conclusion. Furthermore, Piper identifies the geographic references in Rom 15:18-21 as he writes, "[Paul] says he *has fulfilled the gospel* in the whole region. In fact, he goes so far as to say in Romans 15:23-24, 'But now, since I no longer have any room to work in these regions ... I hope to see you in passing as I go to Spain.' This is astonishing! How can he say not only that he has fulfilled the gospel in that region but also that he has no more room for work?"[92] Piper's conclusion that Paul's focus was not primarily on a new geographic area does not follow from the evidence in Rom 15:18-24, where Paul again describes his task in geographic terms.[93]

John 11:52 records John's theological reflection on the unlikely prophecy of the high priest Caiaphas, who insisted that it was to the advantage of the Pharisees that one man should die for the people (λαός) rather than the whole nation (ἔθνος) perish (John 11:50). John indicates that Jesus would not only die for the nation but also gather together the children of God who are scattered. Piper emphasizes, "The 'children of God' will be found as widely scattered as there are *peoples* of the earth."[94] Certainly, Piper is correct, but, again, God's children being scattered among the peoples of the earth does not negate the emphasis on geography inherent to the meaning of "scattered" (διασκορπίζω) and "gather" (συνάγω).[95] God's children scattered among the nations without question are scattered among various people groups, but they are also scattered among many lands in which those people groups live. John 11:52 does

---

91. Silva, "Τόπος," *NIDNTTE*, 4:500; Köster, "Τόπος," *TDNT*, 8:187-208; LSJ, 960.

92. Piper, *Let the Nations Be Glad*, 202-3.

93. Snodgrass observes, "Apparently, Paul's conception of the apostolic mission in a given locality included a prospective finish-line, when the apostolic worker could conceivably say, as Paul did, that 'I no longer have any room for work in these regions' (Rom 15:23)." Snodgrass, "To Teach Others Also," 46.

94. Piper, *Let the Nations Be Glad*, 206.

95. John may possibly be referring to the scattered and gathered motif identified in Ezekiel 2.

not provide evidence of an exclusively ethnic denotation of the ἔθνη of Matt 28:18–20.

Piper acknowledges the geographic description of the Great Commission in Acts 1:8, but he downplays the references to geography to once again refocus attention on ethnic groups. He explains, "This commission [in Acts 1:8] suggests that getting to all the unreached areas (if not explicitly people groups) is the special task of missions. There is a pressure to keep moving, not just to unconverted individuals nearby but also to places beyond, even to the end of the world."[96] Piper struggles to avoid the geographic terminology intricately woven into Acts 1:8, but he continues, "Not only that, but the phrase 'end of the earth' is sometimes in the Old Testament closely associated with all the peoples of the earth."[97] Piper is correct to say this, as was demonstrated by the numerous examples of "land" as a metonymy of subject for "nations" in chapter 2. However, to disregard the geography as nothing more than a reference to the peoples does not fairly consider either the considerable Old Testament evidence or the plain meaning and context of Acts 1:8. Additionally, Piper does not acknowledge the common observation that Acts 1:8 serves as a geographic table of contents for the entire book of Acts and that Luke-Acts as a whole has more of a geographic focus than the other gospels.[98]

Piper attempts to define a people group, but he confesses that a precise definition is extremely difficult and perhaps impossible. He indicates, "What we have found, in fact, is that a precise definition is probably not possible to give on the basis of what God has chosen to reveal in the Bible. God probably did not intend for us to use a precise definition of people groups."[99] Piper further observes, "There are biblical pointers to the nature of a people group."[100] He examines the fourfold formula of Rev 5:9 as evidence: "By your blood you ransomed people for God from every tribe and language and people and nation." Once again, Piper's analysis is not incorrect, but it is incomplete. Piper acknowledges that none of the four terms in Rev 5:9 (φυλή, γλῶσσα, λαός, and ἔθνος) will reveal a precise definition of people groups.[101] However, insisting that the people groups referenced

---

96. Piper, *Let the Nations Be Glad*, 209.

97. Piper, *Let the Nations Be Glad*, 209.

98. Köstenberger and Alexander, *Salvation*, 121; Schnabel, *Acts*, 78–79; Keener, *Acts*, 1:697; Bruce, *Book of Acts*, 36–37; G. Osborne, *Acts*, 23; Bock, *Luke*, 1:29.

99. Piper, *Let the Nations Be Glad*, 209.

100. Piper, *Let the Nations Be Glad*, 209.

101. Piper, *Let the Nations Be Glad*, 214.

in Matt 28:19 and Rev 5:9 can be described as ethnic groups overlooks the complexity of these groups, which Piper correctly acknowledges.

Piper, it seems, derives his definition of ἔθνος almost entirely from Schmidt.¹⁰² Schmidt asserts, "ἔθνος is the most general and therefore the weakest of these terms (λαός, γλῶσσα, and φυλή), having simply an ethnographical sense and denoting the natural cohesion of a people in general."¹⁰³ Based on Schmidt's assertion, Piper concludes, "Thus, *panta ta ethnē* would be the most suitable term for including the others, which is in fact what we find in Revelation 22:2. Here *ethnē* refers to all the people in the new earth, including the 'languages' and 'peoples' and 'tribes.' So *panta ta ethnē* is probably the simplest way of giving a summary designation not only to the larger but also the smaller groupings."¹⁰⁴ While it is possible that ἐθνῶν in Rev 22:2 is an abbreviated way of referring to the repetitions of the various fourfold formulas in the book of Revelation, the full context of Rev 5:9 expands far beyond Revelation. Bauckham observes, "In Revelation 5:9–10 . . . John is interpreting Exodus 19:5–6, the well-known statement of the Sinai covenant constituting Israel as God's chosen people."¹⁰⁵ If Bauckham's analysis is correct, Exod 19:5 sets "from all the peoples" (מִכָּל־הָעַמִּים) in contrast with the assertion that "all the earth" (כָּל־הָאָרֶץ) belongs to the Lord. Far from being the "weakest" of the four terms in Rev 5:9, ἔθνος is a complex term that cannot be reduced to any one aspect.

Piper provides an excellent defense that πάντα τὰ ἔθνη in Matt 28:19 refers to groups rather than merely individuals. The missionary task of Matt 28:18–20 is certainly to make disciples of all the nations and not just to make disciples of as many individuals as possible no matter where they are located. Piper's assertion that these groups are exclusively ethnic in nature lacks support in the evidence he presents, and he frequently presents evidence that undermines his conclusion. It is, perhaps, possible that Piper is using "ethnic" in a technical sense with a broader definition, but if he is using such a definition, he does not clearly indicate that he is doing so. It is insufficient and reductionistic to assert that we must go to the peoples rather than to the places. Changing geographic location alone does not qualify as engaging in missions. Relocating to a place with no

---

102. Schmidt, "Ἔθνος in the NT," *TDNT*, 2:369–72; Piper, *Let the Nations Be Glad*, 215.

103. Schmidt, "Ἔθνος in the NT," *TDNT*, 2:369; Piper, *Let the Nations Be Glad*, 215.

104. Piper, *Let the Nations Be Glad*, 215.

105. Bauckham, *Climax of Prophecy*, 327.

people, such as uninhabited peaks in the Himalayas, the desolate dunes of the Sahara, or uninhabited volcanic islands in the South Pacific, means it is impossible to make disciples, which cannot be considered missions. However, it is equally impossible to go to a people who do not live in a place. Missions is about going to the peoples in the places where they live. These categories cannot be separated from one another.[106]

Unimax Peoples

Ralph Winter distinguishes "unimax people" from other people group concepts. While part of the 1982 Lausanne definition adopted his language, Winter preferred the term "unimax" to describe the kind of people group intended by the 1982 definition as opposed to ethnolinguistic or sociological peoples.[107] Winter also emphasized a more qualitative approach than the quantitative approach advocated by C. Peter Wagner and Ed Dayton.[108] According to Winter, "[A] unimax people is the maximum sized group sufficiently unified to be the target of a single people movement to Christ, where 'unified' refers to the fact that there are no significant barriers of either understanding or acceptance to stop the spread of the gospel."[109] Winter recognized that since the adoption of the 1982 Lausanne definition, the term "unreached peoples" had become synonymous with ethnolinguistic peoples.[110] He intentionally avoided using "unreached peoples" to avoid confusion.

The concept of unimax peoples was a development from Winter's previous model, which employed the terms "megasphere,"

---

106. Bauckham observes that "Geography is a massively important feature of people's experience of life. It is a key ingredient in the particularity of human experience. The places where we live affect who we are, and to a large extent it has been geography that has made possible the rich diversity of human cultures and societies that globalization now threatens." Bauckham, *Bible and Mission*, 55.

107. Datema, "Defining 'Unreached,'" 54.

108. Datema, "People Group Paradigm."

109. Winter and Koch, "Finishing the Task," 535.

110. Winter defines an ethnolinguistic people as "an ethnic group distinguished by its self-identity with traditions of common descent, history, customs and language." Winter identifies the primary benefit of the ethnolinguistic distinction as raising awareness among the body of Christ about lostness around the world, stimulating prayer, and mobilizing the church to engage in global mission, but the category did not sufficiently take into account all of the potential divisions that could arise among people groups. Winter and Koch, "Finishing the Task," 534–35.

What Is a People Group?

"macrosphere," "minisphere," and "microsphere." A unimax people corresponds with a minisphere people.[111] Winter identifies the divisions that result in unimax groups, explaining,

> While language is often a primary means by which a person understands his or her cultural identity, we must consider other factors that keep people separate. Religion, class distinctions, education, political and ideological convictions, historical enmity between clans or tribes, customs and behaviors, etc., all have potential to develop strong sociocultural boundaries within ethnolinguistic clusters of unimax peoples.[112]

Winter does not provide a biblical defense of all of these categories, but he does contend that a unimax/minisphere people corresponds to the biblical definition of "the nations."

Winter indicates that biblical "nation" boundaries are defined by "race, language, culture, religion, vocation, etc."[113] Winter's biblical defense consists of a summary treatment of three biblical terms. First, Winter observes that ἔθνος is variously translated as "nation," "ethnic unit," "people," "heathen," or "Gentiles."[114] He explains, "In no case does it refer to a country as we think of a political unit today. A more correct usage would be as in the phrase 'the Cherokee nation,' referring to the tribe of American Indians known as the Cherokee."[115] He also contends that "the wording [Jesus] chose [in Matt 24:14] (the Greek word *ethne*) points to the ethnicities, the languages and the extended families which constitute the peoples of the earth."[116] Winter offers no further defense, exegesis, or analysis of ἔθνος.

Winter also briefly interacts with two Hebrew terms. He asserts that עַם "refers to a people, a single race or tribe, or to a specific family of mankind."[117] In defense of this position, Winter references Deut 4:6 and 28:17. The second Hebrew term addressed is מִשְׁפָּחָה, which Winter

---

111. Winter, "Frontier Mission Vision," 62–63; Datema, "People Group Paradigm."
112. Winter and Koch, "Finishing the Task," 535–36.
113. Winter, "Frontier Mission Vision," 72.
114. Winter, "Frontier Mission Vision," 69.
115. Winter, "Frontier Mission Vision," 69. See footnote 82 above for treatment of the example of the Cherokee nation.
116. Winter and Koch, "Finishing the Task," 533.
117. Winter, "Frontier Mission Vision," 69.

maintains "is mainly used to refer to family kindred or relatives."[118] Winter references Gen 12:3 as an example of מִשְׁפָּחָה in the context of all the families of the earth being blessed in Abraham. He concludes, "The concept of 'country' or a politically defined nation is totally absent in both of these cases. The fact that not countries, but rather ethnic units or people groups is what is implied is made even more pointed when in a number of places (e.g. Rev. 5:9, 10:11, etc.) not only is the word 'nation' used, but it is further spelled out as 'peoples, tribes, tongues, kindred.'"[119] While Winter's analysis of these terms is not inaccurate, his analysis is incomplete in that he overlooks other terms related to a scriptural definition of "nations."

Winter's primary purpose in his analysis of the three biblical terms is to push against the idea that the biblical "nation" is equivalent to the present-day concept of a country or geopolitical state. However, as previously stated, the rejection of geopolitical entities as the "nations" of Scripture does not necessitate overlooking geography as a significant factor in a scriptural understanding of the nations. Winter does not completely ignore geographical matters, though. First, he does acknowledge that in some instances a unimax people may be geographically identifiable. He observes, "Jungle tribes and other small, geographically remote peoples are almost always single unimax peoples."[120] This is a helpful concession but does not take into account how geography may play a significant role in larger and less-remote people groups.

Second, his concept of incorporability seems to take a geographical component into account, but in a way that is not entirely clear. Winter defines "incorporability" as "the live opportunity to be incorporated into a vital Christian fellowship representing that group's cultural tradition."[121] The primary question for Winter is: "Are the members of a given group *incorporable* in a culturally relevant congregation accessible to them?"[122] While the primary factor is still cultural relevance, Winter does take into account that the church must be physically present in a given area that is accessible to a group of people in order to consider that group reached. Despite the acknowledgment of geography as a minor category in the distinction among people groups, Winter's unimax peoples falls short of

---

118. Winter, "Frontier Mission Vision," 69.
119. Winter, "Frontier Mission Vision," 69.
120. Winter and Koch, "Finishing the Task," 535.
121. Winter, *Penetrating the Last Frontiers*, 33.
122. Winter, *Penetrating the Last Frontiers*, 33.

taking into account the full scope of scriptural evidence supporting geography as a significant category in distinguishing the nations and does not fully consider geography from an emic perspective.

Ethnic Solidarities (ESOLs)

Mark Kreitzer proposes the use of the term "ethnic solidarity" to describe the scriptural nations. He defines an ethnic solidarity (ESOL) as "*relatively intermarried (endogamous) groups of families of similar religion, custom, language and geo-history who define themselves in respect to the Other, that is dissimilar groups in the ever-changing internal and external contexts throughout time.*"[123] Kreitzer develops ESOLs primarily as an alternative to homogeneous units.[124] He also contrasts ESOLs with various sociological theories of ethnicity such as primordialism, neo-primordialism, instrumentalism, and social constructionism.[125] ESOLs consist of five common characteristics: common geography or land, common language, common descent, generally a common sociopolitical ordering, and multiple generations descending from putative ancestors.[126]

Several elements of Kreitzer's proposal are valuable in the pursuit of a biblical-theological understanding of the nations. First, Kreitzer incorporates geography into his definition of ESOL. Kreitzer takes the Table of Nations (Gen 10:1–32) as his launching point and identifies "land" (אֶרֶץ) as one of the repeated phrases to describe the distinctions between the peoples listed.[127] He emphasizes the mandate given to Adam and Noah to "multiply, fill the land of their sojourn with their seed, and exercise dominion over it, under Yahweh's Suzerainty . . . If a people do not fill their land with children, possessing and cultivating the land, and exercising just dominion over it (e.g., Prv 29:4), Yahweh will drive them out."[128] He further observes that there is a connection between the people and the land in Scripture. He observes, "It is clear in biblical ethics that the land belongs individually and collectively to the ethno-native

---

123. Kreitzer, *Concept of Ethnicity in the Bible*, 98. Italics original.
124. Kreitzer, *Concept of Ethnicity in the Bible*, 4.
125. Kreitzer, *Concept of Ethnicity in the Bible*, 24–32.
126. Kreitzer, *Concept of Ethnicity in the Bible*, 140.
127. Kreitzer, *Concept of Ethnicity in the Bible*, 205.
128. Kreitzer, *Concept of Ethnicity in the Bible*, 205.

citizens (אֶזְרָח)."[129] The connection between land and people continues into the New Testament as Kreitzer cites Paul's reference to Deut 32:8 in his speech at the Aeropagus (Acts 17:26).[130] Emphasizing the connection between the scriptural nations and their land is an essential first step to developing a biblical theology of the nations. While the treatment needs to be more robust than what Kreitzer provides, he offers a preliminary analysis that can be expanded and developed further.

Second, Kreitzer emphasizes the emic perspective in his development of ESOLs. His Trinitarian creationist view upholds the emic and etic distinction. He expounds, "Each cultural-lingual meaning system must be understood within its own context."[131] He does recognize limits but does insist that a researcher can develop an emic understanding of both one's own and other cultures.[132] Presumably, the emphasis on developing an emic understanding would apply to geographical locations and boundaries as well, but Kreitzer does not address this matter directly. He does address questions about how multiethnic states such as Nigeria, Ethiopia, South Africa, and Kenya handle geographic boundaries between ESOLs, and how larger national states with majority ethnic groups relate to other ethnic groups that are not easily absorbed, and he offers critiques of apartheid ideology in the United States and South Africa.[133] If geography is an essential element of the scriptural nations, then a plan is needed to begin developing an emic understanding of geography among various people groups.

The third valuable contribution that Kreitzer makes is that he applies his ESOL concept to missions. His study is not an abstract treatment of ethnicity. Instead, he works toward implementing ESOLs within a missions framework.[134] His focus in his application, however, is primarily upon urging Christians to push beyond monoethnic communities. He contends that God's people united as a "third race" of humanity

> is a sign that a socially unifying new age is breaking into the present evil, socially divisive age. In effect, history is moving towards an individualism, which mandates that each person

---

129. Kreitzer, *Concept of Ethnicity in the Bible*, 206
130. Kreitzer, *Concept of Ethnicity in the Bible*, 208.
131. Kreitzer, *Concept of Ethnicity in the Bible*, 67.
132. Kreitzer, *Concept of Ethnicity in the Bible*, 67.
133. Kreitzer, *Concept of Ethnicity in the Bible*, 209–10, 419–20.
134. Kreitzer, *Concept of Ethnicity in the Bible*, 416–19.

What Is a People Group?

must now break free from the old creation's ethnically (class and gender) divided groups, that once served as the basic building block of human society and of the world community.[135]

He does not specify what role geography plays in his application to missions apart from acknowledging that "God providentially gives to each people its own inheritance of land and allots to each its times on the earth (Acts 17:26–27; Dt 32:8–9)."[136]

Despite the overall value of Kreitzer's proposal, some weaknesses exist in his work. First, in building his definition of ESOLs, he subordinates geography and other elements of a scriptural concept of the nations to ethnicity. This is not problematic in itself since he also incorporates classic elements of ethnicity (e.g., common descent) into his definition, but he does not explicate how the various factors interact with one another. He addresses how geography informs ethnic identity but does not explore how ethnic identity might also affect perceptions of geography.[137] Second, he does not interact with concepts of people groups that developed after McGavran and Wagner's homogeneous units. He does not reference the Lausanne definition of people groups, David Barrett's variation, or any of Ralph Winter's concepts.[138] This leaves a significant gap in Kreitzer's work, which ultimately, by itself, does not discredit Kreitzer's proposal, but does leave it somewhat weakened.

Attempts to Incorporate Geography

At least two contemporary missiological strategies have intentionally attempted to incorporate geography into their methodology. The first, Project 4K, is a novel attempt by Youth with a Mission (YWAM) to divide the world into Omega Zones, which blend the ethnolinguistic people group approach with geographical territories. The second is Roman Catholic missiology, which has long utilized a geographic missions strategy and continues to place preeminence on a geographical approach in the post-Vatican II era. Post-Vatican II Roman Catholics continue to have a significantly different soteriology than evangelicals. Vatican II holds to a

---

135. Kreitzer, *Concept of Ethnicity in the Bible*, 417.
136. Kreitzer, *Concept of Ethnicity in the Bible*, 416.
137. Kreitzer, *Concept of Ethnicity in the Bible*, 140.
138. Kreitzer does cite Winter, but exclusively in his discussion regarding the nature of Israel's mission to the nations. Kreitzer, *Concept of Ethnicity in the Bible*, 171.

soteriology that is strongly related to the presence of the church through which grace flows to people.[139] The emphasis is more on the physical presence of the church rather than, as evangelicals would insist, that presence is required for proclamation so that all may have an opportunity to respond to the good news of Jesus Christ (Rom 10:14–15). Even so, the post-Vatican II Roman Catholic emphasis on geography is one of the few methods that explicitly seeks to use geography as a major category which requires evaluation.

Project 4K

The purpose of Project 4K is "to break the world into little bite-sized pieces so that we as a mission can target people's needs better."[140] Ron Boehme describes the four concepts upon which Project 4K is built. He explains, "First, it is of vital importance to have a biblical worldview that understands the importance of fulfilling the Great Commission. Second is the call of all Christians to actively participate in taking the gospel to all people, to all places, and to all spheres of all societies . . . The third part is determining 'where we are not.'"[141] He concludes, "Finally, the Project 4K map contains a new approach to the use of geography. Population limits are used to reorganize existing civil divisions into a unified system of areas called Omega Zones."[142] Omega Zones are the innovative part of Project 4K. Training material for the project explains that "An Omega Zone is really just a geographic area that already exists, for example: state, province, county, district, etc."[143] By pairing the geographic data with people group data from the World Christian Database, Project 4K establishes the appropriate size of an Omega Zone based upon people's

---

139. *Lumen Gentium*, 1. "Since the Church is in Christ like a sacrament or as a sign and instrument both of very closely knit union with God and the unity of the whole human race, it desires now to unfold more fully to the faithful of the Church and to the whole world its own inner nature and universal mission."

140. *4K Workbook*. Project 4K is listed as the preferred strategy of YWAM on their website. The Nanning Covenant contains the statement: "We covenant with the Lord to follow him into the vision of Project 4K as our next challenge as a mission, and deeply desire his blessings for a new surge of apostolic pioneering." "Nanning Covenant" (August 30, 2002).

141. Boehme, *Fourth Wave*, 145.

142. Boehme, *Fourth Wave*, 145.

143. *4K Workbook*.

access to the gospel in that territory.[144] As a result, an Omega Zone can vary drastically in size and population from the entire country of Central African Republic (240,535 square miles with a population of 5.7 million) to the state of Washington (71,362 square miles with a population of 7.5 million) to the Nepali district of Tanahu (569 square miles with a population of 323,000).[145]

The attempt made by Project 4K to integrate geography into a missiological method is commendable. The project sees geography as an essential component of fulfilling the Great Commission. However, the attempt falls short on at least three counts. First, the project divides the world into an even 4,000 Omega Zones. The stated purpose of this is that 4,000 is a manageable number. Boehme contends that "A church of 4,000 could 'engage' the whole world, in some form, by every member adopting an Omega Zone. A small congregation could target one or a number of Omega Zones for concentrated intercessions and outreach." While churches and individual Christians should certainly be encouraged to pray for the entire world, it begs credulity that the world can be so simply divided into an even 4,000 geographic zones.

Second, the geographic zones used in Project 4K are simply the civil boundaries that already exist. There is no attempt to discover the emic geographic boundaries among peoples in an area. In some instances, either the civil boundaries have been adopted by the people as influential geographic boundaries or the civil boundaries are identical to the ones that a people had already perceived as the barrier between them and others. However, this cannot be assumed and is certainly not true in every case. Further, there does not seem to be any mechanism for adjusting or modifying the Omega Zones if clarifying information is discovered by field personnel.

Finally, Project 4K's approach to integrating geography leaves itself open to committing the same errors of the past that led to Ralph Winter's criticism at the Lausanne Congress and his presentation of hidden

---

144. *4K Workbook*.

145. Boehme, *Fourth Wave*, 145. The variations in size and population are at least partially based on the zone's access to the gospel. Boehme explains, "In an area where the gospel is not available (World A), the population is limited to 3 million per zone . . . In an area where the gospel is partially available (World B), the population is limited to 6 million per zone . . . In an area where the gospel is readily available (World C), the population is limited to 9 million per zone."

peoples.[146] Applying the broad brush of World A, B, and C categories to such large areas creates a significant risk of overlooking smaller people groups within the Omega Zone. In the effort to create a manageable missions strategy, Project 4K has artificially simplified the task. While the missionary task should not be unnecessarily complicated, artificially simplifying the task is equally unacceptable. The world is extremely complex. Missionaries, missiologists, and all Christians must work to understand its complex divisions and distinctions. This will mean missions workers and researchers must broaden their horizon rather than creating a manageable system into which the peoples of the world are squeezed.

Roman Catholic Missions Strategy

Roman Catholic missions have emphasized geography from its beginning. The diocese system originated as an administrative method in the late Roman Empire.[147] As such, the Roman Catholic approach to missions has an inherent geographic emphasis that arose in a particular context and originally was emic in its perception of geographical boundaries. This gadually changed as the Roman Church spread outside of the old Roman Empire to people groups and lands more culturally and geographically distant.[148]

The Second Ecumenical Council of the Vatican (Vatican II), held between 1962 and 1965, was a significant shift in the missiological method and strategy of the Roman Catholic Church. One of the emphases of Vatican II was a reform in missionary method. *Ad Gentes* explains this emphasis: "The pilgrim Church is missionary by her very nature, since

---

146. Winter, *Penetrating the Last Frontiers*, 11. Winter defines "hidden peoples" as "individuals and groups of people who, whether geographically near or far from Christian outreach, are sufficiently different linguistically, socially, economically, or culturally so that they are simply not realistic candidates for membership in existing Christian churches. They are 'hidden' or isolated by an invisible but significant caste or class barrier." See also Winter, "Highest Priority," 213–25.

147. Jones, *Later Roman Empire*, 875. Jones explains, "The church in the ecclesiastical organization normally corresponded to the city in the secular administrative scheme. This was only natural, since the city was the unit not only of government but of social life."

148. Latourette, *History of the Expansion of Christianity*, 2:225–26, 265. Latourette records attempts made by Nestorians to adapt the hierarchical system in Persia with limited success. However, the Roman church persisted in using the same structures in all places.

it is from the mission of the Son and the mission of the Holy Spirit that she draws her origin, in accordance with the decree of God the Father."[149] *Nostra Aetate* further expounds, "In our time, when day by day mankind is being drawn closer together, and the ties between different peoples are becoming stronger, the Church examines more closely her relationship to non-Christian religions."[150] Suso Brechter observes, "No Council has ever so consciously emphasized and so insistently expounded the Church's pastoral work of salvation and its worldwide missionary function as Vatican II."[151]

The primary document addressing missionary practice in the Roman Catholic Church does not address any reform in the geographic approach. Instead, it seems to redefine the nature of missions while upholding the traditional geographic method. *Ad Gentes* explains,

> "Missions" is the term usually given to those particular undertakings by which the heralds of the Gospel, sent out by the Church and going forth into the whole world, carry out the task of preaching the Gospel and planting the Church among peoples or groups who do not yet believe in Christ. These undertakings are brought to completion by missionary activity and are mostly exercised in certain territories recognized by the Holy See. The proper purpose of this missionary activity is evangelization, and the planting of the Church among those peoples and groups where it has not yet taken root.[152]

The emphasis on "certain territories recognized by the Holy See" is asserted in official decrees of the Roman Catholic Church and reasserted in the 1983 revision of canon law.

---

149. *Ad Gentes*, 2.

150. *Nostra Aetate*, 1.

151. Brechter, "Decree on Church's Missionary Activity," 87.

152. *Ad Gentes*, 6. Ralph Martin observes, "*Ad Gentes Divinitus* (The Decree on the Church's Missionary Activity) was intended, in the overall evangelization optic of Vatican II, to reinforce and inspire the ongoing traditional missionary activity of the Church, construed as bringing the Gospel and planting the Church in regions where the Gospel may not have been preached nor the Church established to the point of self-sufficiency." Martin, "Ad Gentes," 267. Stephen Bevans also notes that "[Vatican II] was not a council that had as its main purpose the clarification of a doctrine that had come under debate or the condemnation of a dangerous heresy. Rather, John XXIII's reason for calling the council was to help the church preserve and teach Christian doctrine in a more effective way." Bevans and Gros, *Evangelization and Religious Freedom*, 3.

The 1930 volume of *Acta Apostolicae Sedis* includes an instruction regarding Roman Catholic missions carried out under the umbrella of the Sacra Congregatio de Propaganda Fide (Propaganda Fide). The instruction asserts, "Therefore that he is placed to the mission by the church, whether he will be the Vicar or the Apostolic Prefect or even a simple superior, in governing the mission he depends no longer on the Institute but on the Holy See, and is held to deliver an account about the mission to no Institute, but to the Holy See that chose him."[153] The instruction explains that the activity of the Propaganda Fide is ultimately under the direct responsibility of the Holy See.[154] This assertion is reinforced in a second official Roman Catholic document.

Relationes in Territoriis, issued in 1969, seeks to clarify the roles and relationships within the Roman Catholic hierarchy following Vatican II. The exclusive emphasis, as demonstrated by the title, continues to be on geographic territories. The document reasserts that the Holy See is ultimately responsible for directing the missionary activity of the Church with the Propaganda Fide acting on his behalf:

> The Roman Pontiff has full, supreme, and immediate power throughout the whole Church . . . To exercise this supreme power, the Roman pontiff uses the dicasteries of the Roman curia. Thus for all the missions and for all missionary activity only one is the competent dicastery, namely the Sacred Congregation for Evangelization, which is responsible for directing and coordinating this activity and also for distributing the missionaries in various parts of the world according to the more urgent needs.[155]

Vatican II encouraged the church to engage various peoples in more culturally appropriate ways, but the methodology of establishing the church remains an almost exclusively geographic approach.[156]

---

153. *AAS* 22, 112. "Itaque qui missioni ab Ecclesia praeponitur, sive is Vicarius fuerit sive Praefectus Apostolicus vel etiam simplex Superior, in gubernanda missione non iam ab Instituto sed a Sancta Sede dependet, et de ea non Instituto rationem reddere tenetur, sed Sanctae Sedi, quae eum elegit."

154. The Holy See refers not only to the pope but also to "the Secretariat of State, the Council for the Public Affairs of the Church, and other institutes of the Roman Curia." Canon Law 361.

155. Catholic Church, "Relationis in Territoriis," 636, 638.

156. Bevans observes, "In many ways, *Relationes in Territoriis* (the substance of which is repeated in the 1983 Code of Canon Law) opens a new era in the missionary life of the church. For so many years mission was almost totally in the hands of the foreign missionary, and up until our own day that has meant persons from the more

The 1983 revision to Roman Catholic canon law further solidifies the geographic nature of Roman Catholic missions. Canon law explicitly affirms that "The Roman Pontiff and the college of bishops have the supreme direction and coordination of endeavors and actions which belong to missionary work and missionary cooperation."[157] It further explains,

> The Church accomplished the specifically missionary action which implants the Church among peoples or groups where it has not yet taken root especially by sending heralds of the gospel until the young churches are established fully, that is, when they are provided with the proper resources and sufficient means to be able to carry out the work of evangelization themselves.[158]

Raphael Moya expounds the application of this section of code, explaining, "The Roman Pontiff takes care of the problems of missionary activity generally through the Sacred Congregation for the Evangelization of Peoples or the *Propaganda Fide* (can. 360). It has a quasi universal competence over the Church and missionary activity, with the exception of a few other questions that depend on other Dicasteries (S.C. for the Doctrine of the Faith; S.C. of Religious, etc.)."[159] By contrast, the role of the Collegio Episcoporum (College of Bishops) is limited to the completed work of drafting and approving the various Vatican II documents, namely, *Ad Gentes* and *Lumen Gentium*.[160]

The Roman Catholic Church has unquestionably embraced a geographic approach, nearly to the exclusion of all other factors, and this seems to be driven by their soteriological claim that the physical presence of the Roman Catholic Church serves as a means of grace.[161] Post-Vatican II adjustments have sought to embrace the various cultural distinctives

---

affluent and often arrogant West and North. While the day of the foreign missionary is a long way from being over . . . , and while still in many place the *jus commissionis* remains very much in force, in most of the Catholic world it can be said that 'the responsibility of running the local Church, of determining diocesan policy should be in the hands of the local bishop and his local clergy. The missionary should offer himself to the Local Church to serve where he is needed. Only in this way can the Local Church begin to stand on its own feet and gradually come of age.'" Bevans and Gros, *Evangelization and Religious Freedom*, 83; Vilanova, "Intercession (1963–1964)," 347–490.

157. Canon Law, 782 §1.
158. Canon Law, 786.
159. Moya, "New Code of Canon Law," 171.
160. Moya, "New Code of Canon Law," 171.
161. *Lumen Gentium*, 1.

within those territories, but the overall emphasis remains on geography. The emphasis, however, does not arise from reliance on the scriptural role that geography plays in distinguishing the nations but rather originates in the final centuries of the Western Roman Empire. This approach can only be described as etic at best. Attempts to contextualize the Catholic Church and missionary strategy have had some impact, but the emphasis placed on the outside establishment and direction of Roman Catholic mission territories cannot be ignored and seems likely to continue for the foreseeable future.[162]

Recent Evangelical Attempts to Address New Developments in People Group Thinking

In recent years, questions regarding the definition of unreached people groups have reignited a discussion that has implications for how people groups or nations ought to be properly understood as well. Zane Pratt observes, "The people group theme is common in the Bible, both in the Old Testament and the New. However, as we read the missionary accounts of the Book of Acts, we also notice a clear focus on unreached places."[163] David Platt more critically challenges the traditional definition of unreached people groups, proposing an alternative definition: "Unreached peoples and places are those among whom Christ is largely unknown and the church is relatively insufficient to make Christ known in its broader population without outside help."[164] Platt's emphasis in the article is to

---

162. Schreiter, *Constructing Local Theologies*; Bevans, *Models of Contextual Theology*. The Roman Catholic Church is again in the midst of a massive shift in mission strategy that could impact how missions are governed globally. Inés San Martín reports that a forthcoming document entitled *Praedicate Evangelium* may establish a "super dicastery" for evangelization by merging the Congregation for the Evangelization of Peoples or *Propaganda Fide* and the Pontifical Council for the Promotion of the New Evangelization, which was established in 2010 to confront secularization in Western countries. The document's release has been delayed numerous times. Due to the long precedent and establishment of canon law, apart from a radical reorganization of the entire Roman Catholic Church, shifting away from the current exclusive geographic emphasis seems unlikely. Martín, "New Vatican Document"; Condon, "Analysis."

163. Pratt, "Here's What We Mean."

164. Platt, "Rethinking Unreached People Groups." The traditional definition of unreached people groups that Platt cites is from peoplegroups.org. "A people group is considered unreached when there is no indigenous community of believing Christians able to engage this people group with church planting. Technically speaking, the percentage of evangelical Christians in this people group is less than 2 percent."

push against both an arbitrary 2-percent threshold to call a people group "reached" and stress that "recognizing the unreached in terms of particular *places* has a unique bearing on church planting. As missionaries go and make disciples in places where multiple people groups exist, our aim is not to plant churches just among a particular people group; our aim is to plant churches in a particular place."[165] These two articles raise important points for defining unreached peoples and confronting a misapplied homogeneous unit principle, but neither article addresses how geography more fundamentally factors into perceptions of national identity. They are attempting to add geography to missions strategy alongside ethnolinguistic factors, but do not present them in a way that shows how they intricately connect with one another.

Brad Roderick and Joseph Gordy, in outlining their proposal for a "sustainable engagement continuum," suggest, "A better determination [for reached] would be if believers from the people group are actively participating in a reproducing church planting strategy that radiates throughout the people group geographically and sociologically."[166] Geography does not seem to play a significant factor in their strategy until Phase Four, where they assert, "According to Acts 1:8, Christ's commission calls for the disciples to take the gospel to those living in close proximity to them—in Jerusalem and Judea. Jerusalem and Judea represent people and places where the disciples already have access, both culturally and geographically."[167] Roderick and Gordy are not addressing fundamental issues of carefully defining the nations, although they do indicate that more research ought to be pursued.[168] The primary focus for Roderick and Gordy is to refute a false dichotomy between breadth and depth in missions strategy.[169] The emphasis on place in their strategy is beneficial,

---

However, peoplegroups.org currently simply states that "An Unreached People Group is a people group in which less than 2% of the population are Evangelical Christians." "Frequently Asked Questions" (https://peoplegroups.org/Understand.aspx). The traditional definition of unreached people groups from the Lausanne Working Group closely resembles Platt's proposed definition: "A people group among which there is no indigenous community of believing Christians with adequate numbers and resources to evangelize this people group without outside (cross-cultural) assistance." Dayton, "Reaching the Unreached Peoples," 33.

165. Platt, "Rethinking Unreached People Groups."
166. Roderick and Gordy, "Every People Group, Every Place," 73.
167. Roderick and Gordy, "Every People Group, Every Place," 75.
168. Roderick and Gordy, "Every People Group, Every Place," 73.
169. Roderick and Gordy, "Every People Group, Every Place," 80.

but geography must be considered alongside other factors at the front of the strategy rather than in the middle.

Darren Carlson and Elliot Clark challenged the entire concept of unreached people groups, arguing, "The most significant issue with defining *panta ta ethne* as 'ethnolinguistic people groups' is simple: to do so adopts a modern anthropological definition over a biblical-theological one."[170] Their criticism that a lack of biblical-theological discussion exists regarding a proper understanding of the nations is accurate. They further explain, "While the authors of Scripture could conceive of nations in geographic, cultural, or linguistic categories, we believe they weren't first and foremost thinking of *ethne* in terms of a 20th-century designation of either nation-states or people groups. Instead, the first-century Jewish followers of Jesus would have operated primarily with a biblical-theological understanding of *ethne*, derived from Scripture itself."[171] However, it is an overstatement to suggest that the concepts of unreached people groups and people groups in general are unbiblical. The ἔθνη may not be equivalent to ethnolinguistic people groups, but ethnolinguistic factors cannot be dismissed or ignored any more than geography. The terminology is less important than the definitions and the foundation of the definition. Carlson and Clark are correct to push for an emphasis on biblical-theological foundations for the nations, but rejecting the categories completely cannot be supported by Scripture. Additionally, Carlson and Clark do not offer an alternative solution for developing missions strategy. Without an alternative approach, it seems better to accept the categories and explore a biblical-theological foundation for the categories and redefine them accordingly.

Conclusion

"People group" is an important category in missions strategy. The development of the concept was a significant step to effectively make disciples of the various groups of the world. While alternative terminology has been offered by some, such as "unimax group" and "ethnic solidarity," the term "people group" is a sufficient term that should be retained. However, after carefully evaluating and analyzing several different definitions, strategies, and methodologies, no completely satisfying result

---

170. Carlson and Clark, "3 Words That Changed Missions Strategy."
171. Carlson and Clark, "3 Words That Changed Missions Strategy."

was discovered. The need for a definition of the nations derived primarily from biblical theology must be established. In addition to a biblical-theological definition, implementing the strategy must take into account an emic geographic perspective.

5

Emics and Etics
A Proposal for Discovering Emic Geography and Developing Contextual Missions Strategy

MANY OF THE PROBLEMS that missionaries encounter result from them being cultural outsiders. Misunderstanding, miscommunication, and false assumptions frustrate missionaries attempting to communicate the good news of Jesus Christ and make disciples. As a missionary learns a language and begins the slow process of acculturation, some of the challenges may diminish, but some aspects of the culture may also remain unclear or confusing. While other approaches to missions strategy have sought to identify nations through certain conceptions of ethnicity or language, geography has remained an overlooked or misunderstood characteristic. This chapter will begin by examining the distinction between emic and etic methods of analysis. Special interest will be given to developing contextually relevant missions strategy as it relates to emic understandings of geography. Sociological paradigms that seek to define and describe the nations will be surveyed with an interest in identifying aspects of sociological theory that may prove helpful in further analysis. Finally, this chapter will conclude with a proposal designed to help missionaries begin research and analysis toward discovering emic geography within comprehensive emic systems.

Emic and Etic Distinctions

Etic and emic systems are both essential and important, fulfilling crucial functions for missionaries and missiological researchers. For the development of proper contextual missions strategy, however, emic geographic categories must be discovered. This section will describe the meaning of the terms "etic" and "emic" from Kenneth Pike's linguistic theory, emphasizing the importance of using etic and emic analysis for the correct purposes. This section will then discuss how the discovery of emic geography can assist in developing effective missions strategies with a biblical-theological foundation while remaining contextually relevant.

Origin and Meaning of the Terms

The terms "etic" and "emic" were coined by Kenneth Pike, linguist and the first president of the Summer Institute of Linguistics, and he expounds on the significance of both theories in his work *Language in Relation to a Unified Theory of the Structure of Human Behavior*.[1] He explains, "The etic viewpoint studies behavior as from outside of a particular system, and as an essential initial approach to an alien system. The emic viewpoint results from studying behavior as from inside the system."[2] The etic perspective, he clarifies, examines all languages and cultures at one time in a comparative sense.[3] The emic perspective only examines one culture and language at a time.[4] Both of these perspectives are necessary in the study of linguistics, according to Pike. However, the application of the emic and etic perspectives have significant implications beyond linguistics. However, before addressing the broader implications, a summary of Pike's explanation of the differences between emic and etic perspectives would be helpful.

First, Pike explains that etic classifications are those that are available prior to conducting research while emic classifications are discovered through research. He asserts, "Regardless of how much training one has however, emic units of a language must be determined during the

---

1. Pike, *Language in Relation*, 37. The terms "emic" and "etic" derive from the words "phonetic" and "phonemic."
2. Pike, *Language in Relation*, 37.
3. Pike, *Language in Relation*, 37.
4. Pike, *Language in Relation*, 37.

analysis of that language; they must be discovered, not predicted."[5] The emphasis here is that emic categories are discovered within a given culture only after research and analysis of a given language and culture have been conducted, which is Pike's second characteristic. Pike further states,

> [T]he present volume is written from the point of view that emic systems and emic units of these systems are in some sense to be discovered by the analyst, not created by him. Etic systems, on the other hand, are assumed to be classifications created by the analyst—constructs for the handling of the comparative data, or for the handling of data before its emic ordering can be ascertained.[6]

A missionary or Bible translator who assumes knowledge of linguistic or cultural categories is bound to make critical errors.[7]

Pike's third characteristic is that etic descriptions or analyses are conducted from an outsider perspective using criteria that are external to the system while emic descriptions rely exclusively on criteria from within the system.[8] Fourth, Pike explains, "An etic system may be set up by criteria or 'logical' plan whose relevance is external to the system being studied. The discovery or setting up on the emic system requires the inclusion of criteria relevant to the internal functioning of the system itself."[9] An etic system has relevance for the external research but may or may not correspond to the emic system being studied. An emic system is internally coherent and relevant to itself even when an outside observer may not necessarily comprehend the system's internal coherency.

Fifth, Pike explains that the etic criteria are "absolute" in the sense that they are directly measurable. He contrasts, "Emic criteria are relative to the internal characteristics of the system, and can be usefully described

---

5. Pike, *Language in Relation*, 37.
6. Pike, *Language in Relation*, 55.
7. Richard, "Some Observations," 246. One example of this is in several of William Carey's translations of Scripture in South Asia where he assumed a one-to-one correlation with English words. Richard observes, "Carey placed an undue focus on words in his translation work. Modern linguistics has demonstrated that words vary in meaning according to contexts, as do even sentences, so the central units in communication are sentences and paragraphs. But Carey assumed that words were central and that words in one language have counterparts in other languages, which convey the same meaning."
8. Pike, *Language in Relation*, 38.
9. Pike, *Language in Relation*, 38.

or measured relative to each other."[10] Pike's sixth characteristic is that the etic view does not necessarily see the entire system as a whole but often views individual parts apart from its larger setting. He indicates that the emic view "insists that every unit be seen as somehow distributed and functioning within a larger structural unit or setting, in a hierarchy of units and hierarchy of settings as units."[11] Pike illustrates,

> [I]n an emic approach, the analyst might describe the structural functioning of a particular car as a whole, and might include charts showing the parts of the whole car as they function in relation one to another; in an etic approach he might describe the elements one at a time as they are found in a stock room, where bolts, screws, rims, fenders and complex parts, such as generators and motors from various models and makes of cars, have been systematically "filed" according to general criteria.[12]

In a context where a missionary is developing missions strategy, seeking the emic perspective will not isolate certain elements of the culture but rather work to see how the entire system works together as a whole. To use Pike's illustration, the novice auto mechanic might not understand exactly how a spark plug and a lug nut are related, but knowing that they are part of the same system is essential. In the same way, a missionary may not initially understand precisely how language, geography, ethnicity, religion, and other cultural elements are part of the same system, but knowing that they are part of the same system will help them begin to ask the right questions.

Pike's seventh characteristic is that etic units can be objectively measured and distinguished from one another. Emic units, however, can only be differentiated subjectively. Pike expresses, "Units are different emically only when they elicit different responses from people acting within the system."[13] Where an outsider may see one people group united by language, ethnicity, and religion, the emic reality may be that a river, a ridge, a village, or a road may constitute an inviolable barrier to the spread of the gospel. A difference such as this cannot be easily measured objectively but can only be discovered based on how cultural insiders respond to such barriers. Similarly, where an outsider may see etic barriers, and

---

10. Pike, *Language in Relation*, 38.
11. Pike, *Language in Relation*, 38.
12. Pike, *Language in Relation*, 39.
13. Pike, *Language in Relation*, 38.

even attempt to divide people groups based along ethnic lines, the emic response might not support such a division, or at least as clean a division as some missiological researchers would like to assert.

The eighth characteristic of emic and etic systems relates to the availability of data. Pike asserts that etic data is available early in analysis and with only partial information. Pike contrasts, "[E]mic criteria require a knowledge of the total system to which they are relative and from which they ultimately draw their significance."[14] In other words, emic data only completely makes sense when it is viewed as part of the whole system whereas etic data can be isolated from the system and examined independently from the system. Pike relates an amusing story about attempting to teach cricket players how to play baseball and the frustration he felt when the players did not immediately run upon hitting the ball.[15] The cricket players, familiar with the rules of cricket, in which a player would be allowed to continue to bat if they choose not to run when it is deemed not safe to do so, could not comprehend why Pike was frantically yelling at them to run. Only by understanding the system of baseball as a whole—that the batter will actually be out if he does not run, and running toward base even when the chances seemed slim is the only option available—would they understand Pike's instructions.

Pike, with his ninth characteristic, concludes, "Hence, etic data provide access into the system—the starting point of analysis. They give tentative results, tentative units. The final analysis or presentation, however, would be in emic units."[16] Far from suggesting that the etic is not essential, Pike indicates that each person necessarily starts from an etic perspective. The emic and etic perspectives are not a strict dichotomy. Pike observes, "Each observer will also have some bias in terms of the behavior events most familiar to him—those which are emic in his own activity. These he tends to take as his point of departure, as his norms, so that cultural background may affect an etic report."[17] Pike indicates that training can help lessen these differences, but that each observation will always invariably begin from an etic perspective.[18]

14. Pike, *Language in Relation*, 38.
15. Pike, *Language in Relation*, 51.
16. Pike, *Language in Relation*, 38.
17. Pike, *Language in Relation*, 46.
18. Pike, *Language in Relation*, 41. Pike explains that even for a person who had been working in one dialect and moves to a very similar dialect, the first transcription of that dialect is an etic one even if some of the elements of the transcription end up

Pike emphasizes that it is essential to use the right approach in order to achieve the desired results. He strongly cautions against ignoring the etic-emic distinction and further warns against using at etic description when an emic description is required. He quotes Sapir to clarify his warning, saying,

> It is impossible to say what an individual is doing unless we have tacitly accepted the essentially arbitrary modes of interpretation that social tradition is constantly suggesting to us from the very moment of our birth. Let anyone who doubts this try the experiment of making a painstaking report of the actions of a group of natives engaged in some form of activity, say religious, to which he has not the cultural key. If he is a skillful writer, he may succeed in giving a picturesque account of what he sees and hears, or thinks he sees and hears, but the chances of his being able to give a relation of what happens in terms that would be intelligible and acceptable to the natives themselves are practically nil. He will be guilty of all manner of distortion. His emphasis will be constantly askew. He will find interesting what the natives take for granted as a casual kind of behavior worthy of no particular comment, and he will utterly fail to observe the crucial turning points in the course of action that give formal significance to the whole in the minds of those who do possess the key to its understanding.[19]

If a missionary seeking to understand a people group is not aware that they must look at all aspects of the culture as a single coherent system, then misunderstandings will ensue. If language or religion are examined from an emic perspective but other matters such as ethnicity, geography, or other social distinctions for which there may be no etic counterpart are overlooked, then the analysis will be incomplete at best and inaccurate at worst.[20]

Pursuing an emic understanding of comprehensive cultural systems has the potential for significant impact on missions strategy. First,

---

being emic units in the final analysis.

19. Sapir, *Selected Writings*, 546–47.

20. An example of this incomplete analysis would be seeing the caste system in isolation from its broader cultural context in Hinduism and South Asian culture. While each culture might have socioeconomic distinctions within it, that does not mean that every culture has a caste system. To make a one-to-one comparison between, for example, distinctions between upper, middle, and lower classes in the West and the differences between Brahmin, Kshatriya, Vaishya, and Sudra castes would be a mischaracterization of both.

pursuing an emic understanding is consistent with other practices already emphasized in missiology. Planting properly contextualized indigenous churches requires that church planters understand the emic systems relevant for church planting including language, how a particular culture views religion, appropriate places for gathering, and a variety of other factors. How a people group views its own geography would certainly assist church planters in knowing how far away one church could be from one another, whether it is two blocks over in a different megacity neighborhood or across the river on the other side of a valley.

Missionaries may also become better at gospel proclamation and disciple making as they work toward a full understanding of the emic system. Not only will they learn which words to use and not to use, but they will learn appropriate methods of gospel proclamation that reduce or eliminate barriers to understanding and acceptance.[21] Seeing how the entire system works together rather than seeing each piece in isolation from the others will likely result in a more culturally holistic gospel proclamation that can take root in the context with less difficulty.

Finally, working to discover emic systems will help reveal the real people group distinctions. The lists of people groups that currently exist seem to work toward revealing emic people group distinctions, but they fall short of fulfilling the goal because the people group lists are inherently an etic construct comparing people groups on a fixed set of criteria. There may be no other way to construct people group lists, which means that the lists may be valuable to some extent in strategy development, but they do not necessarily paint a complete picture. Discovering the emic systems of people groups will help reveal real people group distinctions

---

21. Tucker, *From Jerusalem to Irian Jaya*, 130–39. Adoniram Judson is a positive historical example of someone who embraced such a methodology. His intense study of the Burmese language led to a quality Bible translation. His intentional language study reflects his insight into the broader emic system. Tucker narrates, "From their early days in Rangoon, the Judsons were unhappy with the out-of-the-way location of the mission house. For a short while they moved out of the city, but a fire ravaged their area and drove them back to the secluded mission house. However, their dream of attracting large numbers of people came to fruition through the concept of a *zayat*. A *zayat* was a shelter open to anyone who wanted to rest or to discuss the day's events or to listen to Buddhist lay teachers who often stopped by. It was the place to relax and forget the pressures of the day, and there were many such shelters in Rangoon . . . They attended a religious service at a nearby *zayat* to familiarize themselves with seating patterns and other cultural peculiarities. The concept worked. Almost immediately visitors who would never have come to the mission house began stopping by, and the Judsons entered a new phase of their ministry."

based on their own boundaries rather than unintentionally believing a boundary exists where it does not or denying that a boundary exists where it does. A missionary must discover the actual barriers to the gospel, and then, if possible, discover why those barriers exist.

Emic Geography Leads to Contextual Geography in Missions Strategy

Understanding entire emic systems must be a goal for missionaries. At the same time, the mission of the church is a task based on Scripture, which means that the scope of the missionary task must be defined primarily by Scripture. I have attempted to demonstrate that Scripture considers geography to be an essential aspect of national identity. At the same time, Scripture also depicts nations with an understanding of their own geography in their own cultural context.

One of the polemical points made in the book of Jubilees is that the boundaries of the nations established by God in the descendants of Shem, Ham, and Japheth were permanent and inviolable boundaries.[22] Kugel explains, "In the coming day of judgment, God will punish those who have violated these boundaries and invaded the territory of others."[23] Scott further reveals, "Thus, the Table of Nations—and Israel's central position in it—is seen to have timeless value and eternal validity, even for the second century B. C., when *Jubilees* was written."[24] However, the assertion of the book of Jubilees could not be supported by the Old Testament testimony that indicates that not only do nations rise and fall but also that God is the ultimate cause of such events (Job 12:23). The book of Jubilees is a Jewish example of imposing etic geographical concepts on the world. Therefore, while the Table of Nations is the starting place for understanding a biblical theology of the nations, simply making attempts to figure out the modern equivalents to the seventy or seventy-two nations in Genesis 10 is insufficient for developing missions strategy. However, this approach is precisely what John Walvoord attempts.[25] He traces each genealogy in Genesis 10, endeavoring to orient each nation in its ancient geographic setting, and then, in many cases, he makes a direct

---

22. *Jub.* 9:14–15.
23. Kugel, *Walk through Jubilees*, 81.
24. Scott, *Paul and the Nations*, 16.
25. Walvoord, *Nations, Israel and Church*, 24–40.

correlation with whatever nation-state happens to occupy that territory today, with little consideration regarding the numerous mass migrations of peoples throughout human history.[26] Walvoord's study of the Table of Nations may have some benefit from a historical perspective and for understanding certain Old Testament passages, but it does not provide much benefit to a proper understanding and scope of missions.

All of the people group lists employ some form of geography in grouping peoples, but these normally do not get more specific than a country or a state in some cases.[27] These lists are compiled by researchers conducting comparative research on the spread of the gospel and church planting efforts among people groups all over the world. The lists are inherently etic structures that make them helpful and useful for conducting comparative analysis but far less useful for developing effective missions strategies to make disciples and plant churches among specific people groups. Using any kind of universal method of geographic division among people groups will be etic by definition. Additionally, the most generally available universal method of division is the existing geopolitical boundaries. Global research and comparative analysis help capture broad global trends, but some groups are inevitably overlooked. Overlooking people groups because of etic analysis structures is reminiscent of Ralph Winter raising awareness of "hidden peoples" or those peoples who were culturally distant from believers even if they lived within the same geopolitical country.[28] Winter urged missiologists to not only rediscover "hidden peoples" but also to reevaluate previous approaches to missions strategy which included changes in terminology and methods of contextualization. Regarding the use of contextualization, Winter explains that

> we must understand that mere reevaluation of our message and our theology is not sufficient. We do not merely preach a message which must be made relevant to each new context. The Gospel cannot be disembodied. We not only proclaim a *message*, but carry and extend or modify or create a social *mechanism* which

---

26. Walvoord also does not seem to account for the blending of people groups through warfare, relocation, intermarriage, deportation, emigration, or variety of other factors that can result in entire people groups relocating to a new area.

27. Chapter 4 addresses the limited geographic data on the various lists.

28. Winter, "Highest Priority," 213–25.

is essential as a carrier vehicle for the gospel. The medium is not equitable to the message but is part of it.[29]

When we reevaluate the ways in which we understand and differentiate among the nations to include emic geography, missionaries ought to adopt contextualized geography in a similar way that Paul did in Rom 15:19.[30] Emic geography is part of the context in which the gospel spreads, but rather than carrying the gospel, emic geography is the social mechanism in which disciples are made and churches are established.

Geography is part of a unified system that cannot be isolated from other categories such as language, religion, culture, ethnicity, etc. Seeking to gain an emic understanding of language while neglecting other aspects of the emic system will leave the missionary at a disadvantage, the missions strategy incomplete, and the potential that the gospel will remain unestablished in a given cultural context. Missionaries are discouraged from approaching language learning in ways that assume strict lexical parallels between languages. Language learning always starts with those basic etic comparisons, but to understand the language and communicate the gospel effectively, missionaries must move past the etic constructs and embrace the emic system. Bible translators struggle with such translations as demonstrated by the semantic range of ἔθνος. Ἔθνος is variously translated as "nation," "Gentile," "people," and "pagans."[31] Furthermore, ἔθνος is used in the LXX to translate אֻמָּה, גּוֹי, עַם, and even אֶרֶץ.[32] If language learning is approached in a way that urges the missionary to embrace emic language as quickly as possible in order to communicate the gospel and make disciples, a similar compulsion ought to urge the missionary to understand emic geographic divisions in order

---

29. Winter, *Penetrating the Last Frontiers*, 16.

30. See chapter 3 regarding Paul's use of contextualized geography in his letter to the Roman church.

31. Various English translations will translate ἔθνος differently in some different places, so giving precise references for each rendering in all English translations would be unwieldy. Of the 161 instances of ἔθνος in the New Testament, less than ten are translated as "pagans" (1 Cor 12:2; CSB, ESV, LEB, NASB, NIV, NRSV) and "people" (Matt 21:43; Acts 8:9; CSB, CEB, NASB, NIV, NRSV) with the remainder being translated as "nation" or "Gentile," with slightly more instances being rendered as "Gentile" (CSB, ESV, KJV, LEB, NASB, NIV, NRSV).

32. Of the 699 instances of ἔθνος in the LXX, it translates גּוֹי 459 times, עַם 128 times, אֻמָּה 16 times, אֶרֶץ 3 times, אִי twice, הָמוֹן twice, and the remainder having no Hebrew equivalent.

to understand the maximum potential of one local strategy and where another strategy must be utilized.

Survey and Analysis of Socioanthropological Definitions of the Nations

Having examined the distinction in etic and emic systems and how emic geography helps a missionary to properly contextualize the gospel when making disciples and planting churches, a survey of sociological paradigms that propose an understanding of national identity and the nature of nations may be undertaken. This survey will describe and analyze five different paradigms: primordialism, modernism, perennialism, social-constructionism, and ethno-symbolism. Some insights can be gleaned from each paradigm, but each paradigm has weaknesses as well.

Primordialism

Primordialism views nations as an inherent part of creation. Smith, describing primordialism, records, "[Nations] exist in the first order of time, and lie at the root of subsequent processes and developments."[33] Abbé Siéyès, a student of Rousseau, wrote in his pamphlet *Qu'est-ce que le Tiers Etat?*,

> The Nation exists before all things and is the origin of all. Its will is always legal, it is the law itself... Nations on the earth must be conceived as individuals outside the social bond, or as is said, in the state of nature. The exercise of their will is free and independent of all civil forms. Existing only in the natural order, their will, to have its full effect, only needs to possess the *natural* characteristics of a will. In whatever manner a nation wills, it suffices that it does will; all forms are valid and its will is always the supreme law.[34]

In its original form, the primordial view ascribes the nations with a divine status. In fact, Smith critiques, "Indeed, [nations] share with God the attributes of existing before all things and of originating everything."[35]

---

33. A. Smith, *Nationalism*, 55.

34. Cited in Cobban, *History of Modern France*, 1:165. See also A. Smith, *Nationalism*, 47.

35. A. Smith, *Nationalism*, 55.

However, the primordial view has been refined and nuanced slightly differently in more recent scholarship.

Pierre van den Berghe proposes a form of primordialism called "sociobiology," which focuses on a concept of "inclusive fitness." He defines, "Sociobiology is basically the application of evolutionary theory to behavior, and especially to social behavior. It puts social behavior, including that of our own species, in the context of biological evolution, and in comparative perspective."[36] He further explains, "Sociobiology offers us the best existing answer of why animals stick together: they do so to the extent that it contributes to their individual fitness."[37] Sociobiological primordialism, according to Smith, holds that "nations, ethnic groups and races can be traced to the underlying genetic reproductive drives of individuals and their use of strategies of 'nepotism' and 'inclusive fitness' to maximize their gene pools."[38] Smith identifies a few difficulties with this version of primordialism, including the problem of "generalizing from the level of individual reproductive behaviour to that of collective, and political, action."[39] Smith also regards van den Berghe's position inconsistent because by introducing "cultural signs" he "dilutes the rigour and purity of his reductionist biological account, and suggests a much greater role for cultural and social factors that would necessarily diminish the influence of genetic factors."[40] Walker Connor also observes that sociobiological primordialism falsely assumes the alignment of origin myths and historical reality. He rebuts, "The sense of unique descent, of course, need not, and *in nearly all* cases *will not*, accord with factual history."[41] From a biblical worldview, the assumption of a purely materialistic evolutionary explanation of the nations is inadequate and lends very little assistance in understanding the nations as depicted in Scripture.

A second version of primordialism argues that nations and ethnic groups form based on attachments to the "cultural givens" of society.[42] Geertz bases his version of primordialism on "primordial attachments." He explains,

36. Berghe, "Sociobiology," 327.
37. Berghe, "Sociobiology," 331.
38. A. Smith, *Nationalism*, 55–56.
39. A. Smith, *Nationalism*, 56.
40. A. Smith, *Nationalism*, 56.
41. Connor, *Ethnonationalism*, 202
42. A. Smith, *Nationalism*, 56.

> By a primordial attachment is meant one that stems from the 'givens'—or, more precisely, as culture is inevitably involved in such matters, the assumed 'givens'—of social existence: immediate contiguity and kin connection mainly, but beyond them the givenness that stems from being born into a particular religious community, speaking a particular language, or even a dialect of a language, and following particular social practices. These congruities of blood, speech, custom, and so on, are seen to have an ineffable, and at times overpowering, coerciveness in and of themselves.[43]

Geertz is developing his version of primordialism with an interest in understanding the new states that were emerging in Africa and Asia during the postcolonial era.[44] Geertz sees a tension in the new states, such as India, Ceylon, the Congo, Laos, and Thailand, between "the desire to be recognized as responsible agents whose wishes, acts, hopes, and opinions 'matter,' and the desire to build an efficient, dynamic modern state."[45] He explains, "This tension takes a peculiarly severe and chronic form in the new states, both because of the great extent to which their peoples' sense of self remains bound up in the gross actualities of blood, race, language, locality, religion, or tradition, and because of the steadily accelerating importance in this [the twentieth] century of the sovereign state as a positive instrument for the realization of collective aims."[46] Geertz attempts to adapt the theory for the postcolonial era of new nation-states. He does not see anything intrinsic about the primordial attachments that make them a given but rather that human beings see these ties as givens and, therefore, they exert power over them.[47]

Geertz's version of primordialism does have some positive aspects to it. First, he attempts to see the entire culture of a nation as a unified system. While not always entirely clear how different factors interact with one another, Geertz does acknowledge that national identity is complex and includes assumed blood ties, race (what would likely be called "ethnicity" today), language, region, religion, and cultural customs.[48] Further-

---

43. Geertz, *Interpretation of Cultures*, 259.
44. Geertz, *Interpretation of Cultures*, 255–59.
45. Geertz, *Interpretation of Cultures*, 258.
46. Geertz, *Interpretation of Cultures*, 258. See also Shils, "Political Development in the New States," 265–92.
47. A. Smith, *Nationalism*, 57.
48. Geertz, *Interpretation of Cultures*, 261–63.

more, Geertz observes that in some cases geography plays a significant and even a primary role in distinguishing between nations. He recounts,

> Tonkin, Annam, and Cochin in prepartitioned Vietnam... were opposed almost purely in regional terms, sharing language, culture, race, and so on. The tension between East and West Pakistan (now separated into Bangladesh and Pakistan) involved differences in language and culture too, but the geographic element was of great prominence owing to the territorial discontinuity of the country.[49]

Geertz provides excellent examples that demonstrate the importance of geography related to national identity and even an emic understanding of geography.

The primary flaw in his proposal, however, is the seemingly static nature of the cultural "givens." Geertz seems to leave very little room for cultural change, and even change that arises from intracultural tension. Geertz concludes, "The world of personal identity collectively ratified and publicly expressed is thus an ordered world. The patterns of primordial identification and cleavage within the existing new states are not fluid, shapeless, and infinitely various, but are definitely demarcated and vary in systematic ways."[50] Furthermore, Geertz's conclusion seems to switch to an etic system where he had previously been discussing emic concepts. This switch would run afoul of Sapir's warning above.

Modernism

The modernist understanding of nations is closely connected to the concept of nationalism and is often tied to European romanticism, which led to a revised understanding of nations following the French Revolution and parallel concepts throughout Europe such as the German concept of *Volk*.[51] In perhaps overly simplistic terms, this view sees nationalism as

---

49. Geertz, *Interpretation of Cultures*, 262–63.
50. Geertz, *Interpretation of Cultures*, 268.
51. Hobsbawm, *Nations and Nationalism*, 101. It is not entirely clear why the French Revolution creates the boundary for the modernist view instead of the Treaty of Westphalia in 1648. Admittedly, both were radical shifts in the political, social, and cultural order of Europe. However, it seems that the Treaty of Westphalia served as a foundation for what would culminate in the French Revolution and in German and Italian unification. Kissinger explains, "The Peace of Westphalia became a turning point in the history of nations because the elements it set in place were as

a product of modernity.[52] Hobsbawm insists, "The basic characteristic of the modern nation and everything connected with it is its modernity."[53] Gellner similarly sees nations tightly connected to modernism and, especially, industrialization. He contends that "the age of transition to industrialism was bound, according to our model, also to be an age of nationalism, a period of turbulent readjustment, in which either political boundaries, or cultural ones, or both, were being modified, so as to satisfy the new nationalist imperative which now, for the first time, was making itself felt."[54] The modernist understanding also insists on a close connection between nations and states but does not insist on a direct equivalence, although that option is possible in some instances. However, between the two, the state is favored over the nation. Lord Acton explains that "nationality does not aim either at liberty or prosperity, both of which it sacrifices to the imperative necessity of making the nation the mould and measure of the State."[55] The reason for the subordination of the nation to the state was purely utilitarian. Hobsbawn maintains that "the national heterogeneity of nation-states was accepted, above all, because it seemed clear that small, and especially small and backward, nationalities had everything to gain by merging into greater nations, and making the contributions to humanity through these."[56] This assertion parallels the claim made by John Stuart Mill, who writes, "Experience proves that it is possible for one nationality to merge and be absorbed in another: and when it was originally an inferior and more backward portion of the human race the absorption is greatly to its advantage."[57] Speculatively, it was

---

uncomplicated as they were sweeping. The state, not the empire, dynasty, or religious confession, was affirmed as the building block of European order. The concept of state sovereignty was established. The right of each signatory to choose its own domestic structure and religious orientation free from intervention was affirmed, while novel clauses ensured that minority sects could practice their faith in peace and be free from the prospect of forced conversion. Beyond the immediate needs of the moment, the principles of a system of 'international relations' were taking shape, motivated by the common desire to avoid a recurrence of total war on the Continent." Kissinger, *World Order*, 26–27.

52. A. Smith, *Nationalism*, 50.

53. Hobsbawm, *Nations and Nationalism*, 14.

54. Ernest Gellner, *Nations and Nationalism*, 39.

55. Acton, "Nationality," 37. See also A. Smith, *Nationalism and Modernism*, 9–11.

56. Hobsbawm, *Nations and Nationalism*, 34.

57. Mill, *Utilitarianism, Liberty and Representative Government*, 363. See also Hobsbawm, *Nations and Nationalism*, 34.

via this process that nations and states became generally synonymous in common English, leading to much of the confusion regarding the nations as the object of the Great Commission.[58]

Numerous definitions of nations from modernity exist, but two prominent definitions will be treated here.[59] Gellner limits his definitions to only two, but thorough, points. He asserts, "Two men are of the same nation if and only if they share the same culture, where culture in turn means a system of ideas and signs and associations and ways of behaving and communicating."[60] He further maintains,

> Two men are of the same nation if and only if they *recognize* each other as belonging to the same nation. In other words, *nations maketh man*; nations are the artefacts of men's convictions and loyalties and solidarities. A mere category of persons (say, occupants of a given territory, or speakers of a given language, for example) becomes a nation if and when the members of the category firmly recognize certain mutual rights and duties to each other in virtue of their shared membership of it. It is their recognition, and not the shared attributes, whatever they might be, which separate that category from non-members.[61]

Despite the seemingly emic proposal from Gellner, his definitions and approach are still based on modernist assumptions. Breuilly writes of Gellner's approach, "His anthropology was informed by the view that ideas were a function of social organization. His philosophy was that one could obtain objective knowledge of society by means of empirical and rational procedures."[62] Gellner's underlying philosophy seems to contradict the subjective nature of his second point. The contradiction can be at least partially explained, but not eliminated, by Gellner's insistence that

---

58. Attempting to trace a precise origin to the conflation of the terms "state" and "nation" is outside the bounds of this study, and such an argument may not even be possible. However, more research is required in this area.

59. While not interacting with his definition directly, Hobsbawm asserts that Stalin's definition is probably the best known definition of the nations. Stalin affirms, "A nation is a historically evolved, stable community of language, territory, economic life, and psychological makeup manifested in a community of culture." Stalin, *Marxism and the National Question*, 11. See also Hobsbawm, *Nations and Nationalism*, 5.

60. Gellner, *Nations and Nationalism*, 6.

61. Gellner, *Nations and Nationalism*, 7.

62. Breuilly, "Introduction," xx.

culture, the shared basis for a nation to exist, is established by objective and empirical factors.[63]

While not necessarily supporting this view himself, Hobsbawm records three criteria that were historically held by modernists as necessary for the establishment of a nation.[64] First, modernists insisted that a nation must have a historic association with a current state or one with a fairly lengthy and recent past.[65] Second, nations must possess a "long-established cultural elite, possessing a written national literary and administrative vernacular."[66] A third criterion, Hobsbawm laments, "[I]t must unfortunately be said, was a proven capacity for conquest."[67] These criteria for status as a nation simply affirm the antecedent. The definition describes nineteenth- and twentieth-century European states and is then applied as an objective definition for all nations, where clearly some people groups who would qualify as a nation under biblical criteria would not according to the narrow definition outlined by Hobsbawm.

The most glaring shortcoming of the modernist approach is its reliance on an evolutionary view of nations, distinct from but similar to the primordial understanding. Gellner suggests, "Most of mankind enters the industrial age from the agrarian stage." He continues, "The social organization of agrarian society, however, is not at all favourable to the nationalist principle, to the convergence of political and cultural units, and to the homogeneity and school-transmitted nature of culture within each political unit."[68] An evolutionary approach, as mentioned above, cannot be reconciled with the biblical evidence or with the significant evidence that nations existed, albeit with some different forms and structures in some cases, long before industrialization occurred.

The modernist approach also seeks to not only define a nation strictly on objective characteristics but also insists that the characteristics of

---

63. Gellner, *Nations and Nationalism*, 9. One example of this dynamic is an emphasis on literacy establishing culture. Gellner writes, "Literacy, the establishment of a reasonably permanent and standardized script, means in effect the possibility of culture and cognitive storage and centralization."

64. Hobsbawm is simply describing this view rather than subscribing to it himself. He concludes that the terms "nation" and "nationalism" are "no longer adequate terms to describe, let alone to analyse, the political entities described as such, or even the sentiments once described by these words." Hobsbawm, *Nations and Nationalism*, 192.

65. Hobsbawm, *Nations and Nationalism*, 37.

66. Hobsbawm, *Nations and Nationalism*, 37.

67. Hobsbawm, *Nations and Nationalism*, 38.

68. Gellner, *Nations and Nationalism*, 38–39.

each nation be empirically observable. This seems to be another example of Sapir's warning about attempting to examine emic characteristics with etic categories. At the same time, this does not mean, as Hobsbawm concludes, that the term "nation" becomes useless or inadequate.[69] It is only inadequate if it is examined only with etic categories rather than accounting for the coherent emic systems unique to each nation or people group.

The modernist perspective does contribute one important piece to properly understanding the nations today. Something very significant happened in the seventeenth or eighteenth century regarding the general understanding of nations in Europe, depending on whether one chooses the Treaty of Westphalia or the French Revolution as the starting point. The definition of "nations" shifted dramatically, which led to a shift in how the Great Commission was interpreted and carried out.[70] Knowing that a radical shift occurred relatively recently in history helps to highlight that a course correction is needed in order to establish a scripturally sound missions strategy for making disciples of all nations.

Perennialism

Perennialism is a less-defined model in that it allows for a bit more variety within the category. This view holds that "even if nationalist ideology was recent, nations had always existed in every period of history, and that many nations existed from time immemorial."[71] While it might be possible for a perennialist to hold a primordial view of the nations, this is not absolutely necessary. Renan insists, "Nations are not eternal. They have a beginning and they will have an end."[72] At the same time, there is some overlap with modernism. Hastings defines a nation, writing, "Formed from one or more ethnicities, and normally identified by a literature of its own, [a nation] possesses or claims the right to political identity and autonomy as a people, together with the control of specific territory, comparable to that of biblical Israel and of other independent entities in

---

69. Hobsbawm, *Nations and Nationalism*, 192.

70. An example of the shift in missions strategy that resulted from the modernist shift may be found in Carey, *Enquiry*. Carey's survey of the world makes distinctions primarily on the basis of geopolitical and linguistic divisions. The strategy that Carey proposes involved making the gospel available in every language and in every geopolitical country of his day.

71. A. Smith, *Nationalism*, 53.

72. Renan, *Qu'est-ce qu'une nation?*, 11.

a world thought of as one of nation-states."[73] The only real fundamental characteristic of perennialism is to believe that nations, or some nations, have existed for a long period of time, and that this belief is founded on empirical observation.[74]

Renan, writing originally in 1882, rejects much of the modernist methods of distinguishing between nations. He rebuffs race, language, interests, religious affinity, geography, and military necessities. In short, he asserts, "Nothing material suffices."[75] Instead, Renan semi-spiritualizes nations, insisting, "A nation is a soul, a spiritual principle."[76] Two aspects, which Renan insists are actually the same, comprise this "national soul"— the past and the present. Regarding how these attributes interact with one another, he explains, "One is the possession in common of a rich legacy of memories; the other is present consent, the desire to live together, the desire to continue to invest in the heritage that we have jointly received."[77] Renan's view comes remarkably close to the social-constructionist view described below. However, some significant differences exist arising from Renan's embracing the burgeoning Romanticism of the late eighteenth century. He concludes, "I summarize, Messieurs. Man is a slave neither of his race, his language, his religion, the course of his rivers, nor the direction of his mountain ranges. A great aggregation of men, in sane mind and warm heart, created a moral conscience that calls itself a nation."[78] Yet, at the same time, he persists in calling his proposal an "empirical solution."[79] The apparent contradiction evidenced here is a feature of Romanticism, which simultaneously "favours the concrete over the abstract, variety over uniformity, the infinite over the finite, nature over culture, convention, and artifice, the organic over the mechanical, freedom over constraint, rules and limitations," and "disdains ordinary rationality as a practical makeshift for the earth-bound yielding only a truncated, superficial, and distorted picture of the world as it really is."[80]

---

73. Hastings, *Construction of Nationhood*, 3.
74. A. Smith, *Nationalism*, 54.
75. Renan, *Qu'est-ce qu'une nation?*, 10.
76. Renan, *Qu'est-ce qu'une nation?*, 10.
77. Renan, *Qu'est-ce qu'une nation?*, 10.
78. Renan, *Qu'est-ce qu'une nation?*, 11.
79. Renan, *Qu'est-ce qu'une nation?*, 11.
80. Quinton, "Romanticism, Philosophical," 821–22.

Renan's proposal is overstated likely due to his philosophical presuppositions. While the modernist proposal errs in seeing all aspects of national identity accessible through etic categories, Renan's perennialism errs in seeing the totality of national identity only through an indistinct concept of "national spirit." Renan's proposal could perhaps be seen as an attempt to understand nations through emic categories, but a rejection of everything except a sense of national spirit leaves very little to work with in terms of understanding a nation. In many ways, the uncertainty is reminiscent of the perhaps accurate but not entirely helpful quote from Walter Bagehot: "[W]e know what [a nation] is when you do not ask us, but we cannot very quickly explain or define it."[81] Renan's proposal, while still advancing the conversation, overcorrects from the modernist proposal and leaves very little to work with from a missiological perspective.

Hastings, holding to a slightly different view of perennialism, argues that "ethnicities naturally turn into nations or integral elements within nations at the point when their specific vernacular moves from an oral to written usage to the extent that it is being regularly employed for the production of a literature, and particularly for the translation of the Bible."[82] He insists that England serves as the prototype for this proposal and contends that the writings of Bede serve as the starting point for English national identity.[83] Hastings explains, "In his Northumbrian monastery [Bede] did indeed imagine England: he did it through intensely biblical glasses, but no less through linguistic and ecclesiastical ones, and he did it so convincingly that no dissentient imagining of his country has ever since seemed quite credible."[84] Hastings, in a slightly different way from Renan, overstates the importance of language, and especially of Bible translation, in the formation of national identity. As significant as having a written language may be, and especially having religious literature in a common vernacular, Hastings's proposal is far too narrow in scope to apply to all nations. At best, the proposal could apply to many European nations.

One positive aspect of perennialism is that the paradigm acknowledges that nations rise, fall, and transform. In fact, as much as national

81. Bagehot, *Physics and Politics*, 20–21.
82. Hastings, *Construction of Nationhood*, 12.
83. Hastings, *Construction of Nationhood*, 4, 36.
84. Hastings, *Construction of Nationhood*, 38. Hastings makes a similar argument regarding the role of Martin Luther's translation of the Bible into German having an equally substantial impact on the formation of German nationalism. Hastings, *Construction of Nationhood*, 108–9.

identity is dependent upon a shared culture, a nation may always be transforming even if the change is imperceptibly slow. The rise and fall of nations has at least one significant missiological implication. If the concept of nations is perennial, but individual nations rise, fall, and transform, how can one expect to complete the task of making disciples of all nations? This conundrum is only truly problematic if one assumes that *completion* of the Great Commission is necessary rather than *fulfillment* of the Great Commission, which suggests obedience to God's command rather than a task to be completed.[85] The uncertainty associated with what it means for the Great Commission to be complete also corresponds with Jesus' insistence in Acts 1:7 that it is not for the disciples to know when Jesus will ultimately establish his kingdom.[86] Understanding that nations rise, fall, and transform compels missionaries to constantly evaluate their context and strategies to make certain that proper contextualization is occurring and, correspondingly, the gospel is being communicated accurately and effectively in the process of making disciples.

Social Constructionism

The social-constructionist view swung the pendulum even further from the primordialist view by seeing nations as purely subjective creations. Benedict Anderson is the strongest proponent of this view. Anderson argues, "[A nation] is an imagined political community—and imagined as both inherently limited and sovereign."[87] He explains that a nation is imagined because no nation, regardless of how small or large, will know most of their fellow members, and yet will imagine themselves as part of the same community.[88] He further insists, "The nation is imagined as limited because even the largest of them encompassing perhaps a billion living human beings, has finite, if elastic, boundaries, beyond which lie other nations."[89] Each nation, Anderson argues, is also sovereign "because the concept was born in an age in which Enlightenment and Revolution were destroying the legitimacy of the divinely ordained,

---

85. Silva, "Πληρόω," *NIDNTTE*, 3:787–89.
86. Merkle, "Could Jesus Return at Any Moment?," 280–81.
87. Anderson, *Imagined Communities*, 6.
88. Anderson, *Imagined Communities*, 6.
89. Anderson, *Imagined Communities*, 7.

Emics and Etics 165

hierarchical dynastic realm."[90] The nations, in Anderson's paradigm, should expect to have an internal religious pluralism. Finally, the nation in a social-constructionist view is imagined as a community. Anderson defends this view on the basis that a nation "is always conceived as a deep, horizontal comradeship" regardless of any actual inequality that may exist within it.[91] Kreitzer summarizes, "Ethnicity, according to [the social-constructionist] view, is a mentally imagined community with such imagined common characteristics as a common language and ancestors. No individual in the community can know what others in the community of imagination actually speak, what the common ancestors really were if anything, and so forth. These common characteristics are individually and communally imagined."[92] A nation ends up being little more than an individualistic concept that is assumed to be universalized.

Anderson does not directly address the political aspect of his definition, which has more significance than he lets on in his initial explanation. Anderson identifies the American states that came into existence in the late eighteenth and early nineteenth centuries as exemplars of his proposal. He explains, "All, including the USA, were creole states, formed and led by people who shared a common language and common descent with those against whom they fought. Indeed, it is fair to say that language was never an issue in these early struggles for national liberation."[93] The reason for the formation of new nations in the Americas was, according to Anderson, primarily political. He finds evidence for this understanding in that he sees the increased political restrictions imposed by European governments and "republicanism" as the major reasons for the various revolutions from the American Revolution to the revolutionary movements of Bolívar and San Martín in Peru.[94]

Closely connected with the political aspect, Anderson identifies the importance of a shared language for the establishment of a nation. He contends that "the convergence of capitalism and print technology on the fatal diversity of human language created the possibility of a new form of imagined community, which in its basic morphology set the

90. Anderson, *Imagined Communities*, 7.
91. Anderson, *Imagined Communities*, 7.
92. Kreitzer, *Concept of Ethnicity in the Bible*, 31.
93. Anderson, *Imagined Communities*, 47. He defines "creole" as a "person of (at least theoretically) pure European descent but born in the Americas (and, by later extension, anywhere outside Europe)."
94. Anderson, *Imagined Communities*, 49–51.

stage for the modern nation."[95] He places special emphasis on national print languages—the single language used to communicate news and ideas of interest. He argues that these print languages "created unified fields of exchange and communication below Latin and above the spoken vernaculars."[96] He also insists these languages helped to give the language "fixity" that had been previously lacking.[97] Finally, he contends that the print languages resulted in "languages of power," where those whose dialects were closer to the print language had more advantages than those whose dialect differed.[98]

Anderson strongly rejects the primordialist view but swings the pendulum too far in the opposite direction. His emphasis on the emic aspects of nations would be commendable if it were not the case that he goes beyond the emic to emphasize an individualistic understanding of nations. Kreitzer observes that "social constructionists downplay the essential nature and foundational role of language, territory, and endogamy that Scripture emphasizes."[99] Anderson's proposal argues for such a radical subjectivism and individualism that makes it difficult to see how anyone could share any concept of similarity if each person is unable to exchange ideas with any amount of certainty even in the form of national print languages.

Furthermore, Anderson argues from the particular to the general, and his specific examples provide an inadequate basis for his argument. He primarily—nearly exclusively—focuses on the nation-states that developed in the Americas in the late eighteenth and early nineteenth centuries. While these were formative and influential, these nation-states of the Western Hemisphere cannot account for the varieties of nations that have existed in history and that exist in the world today. Balakrishnan, responding to Anderson, writes, "But there are several ways in which nations are not 'conceived in language.' Throughout the world the boundaries of nation-states and the boundaries of linguistic distributions rarely overlap—many nations share the same language; many states are officially multilingual; in some the most official language is no one's mother

---

95. Anderson, *Imagined Communities*, 46.
96. Anderson, *Imagined Communities*, 44.
97. Anderson, *Imagined Communities*, 44.
98. Anderson, *Imagined Communities*, 45.
99. Kreitzer, *Concept of Ethnicity in the Bible*, 31–32.

tongue."[100] He further critiques, "Language is stressed by Anderson because it defines membership in ways that fundamentally connected to his specific conception of the nation."[101] Additionally, Anderson's emphasis specifically on print language overlooks oral communities, whose primary means of the transmission of ideas and culture is through oral means rather than writing. These communities, according to his definition, would not qualify as nations.

While Anderson's proposal appears to be largely influenced by postmodern epistemology, which leaves little real sense of shared national identity, the social-constructionist position does offer some helpful correction. Kreitzer rightly observes, "This view correctly emphasizes the ever changing and developing collective, social consciousness of a people. Every people, even so-called native peoples, possess an insider-outsider, us-versus-them perspective. Scripture testifies to this in the case of the Israelite tribes."[102] Missiologically, identifying where these boundaries exist is essential, not only from a research perspective, but in order to develop relevant, contextual strategies that take into account the emic barriers of each people group, whether linguistic, ethnic, geographical, religious, socioeconomic, or whatever other perceived barriers there may be. However, contrary to Anderson's argument, this information is accessible to outsiders, even if in a limited way. Similar to the way that linguists work from the phonetic to the phonemic, missionary strategists can move toward an emic understanding of geographic (and other) barriers.

Ethno-Symbolism

Fredrick Barth marks both a paradigm shift among anthropologists and an attempt to find a mediating position among the others. Barth argued that it is "the ethnic boundary that defines the group, not the cultural stuff that it encloses."[103] The essence of Barth's argument is that ethnic boundaries determine culture rather than culture determining ethnic boundaries. While Barth did not develop a comprehensive paradigm of national identity, he represents a fundamental shift in how the concept of national identity was seen. Kreitzer explains, "[T]he focus is upon ethnic

100. Balakrishnan, "National Imagination," 207.
101. Balakrishnan, "National Imagination," 207.
102. Kreitzer, *Concept of Ethnicity in the Bible*, 31.
103. Barth, "Introduction," 15.

boundaries as perceived by insiders (emic perspective). Since Barth, most social scientists seek to understand an emic, self-defining, social discourse that each [ethnic solidarity] uses to distinguish itself from other groups."[104] Barth's argument laid the foundation for later ethnic understandings of nations.

One such paradigm is Anthony Smith's ethno-symbolism. Smith defines a nation as "a named human population sharing an historic territory, common myths and historical memories, a mass, public culture, a common economy and common legal rights and duties for all members."[105] Smith embraces the complex nature of nations. Additionally, different from several other paradigms, he explicitly distinguishes between states and nations. He indicates, "While modern states must legitimate themselves in national and popular terms as the states of particular nations, their content and focus are quite different."[106] The focus of nations, according to Smith, can be divided into external and internal functions.

The external functions of nations relate to the territorial, economic, and political aspects while the internal functions refer to how a nation interacts among itself—namely, methods of socialization of members, development of social bonds by the use of shared symbols and traditions, and a distinct culture that separates them from others.[107] All of these functions deserve separate attention as part of a unified emic system, but this study will focus exclusively on Smith's treatment of the territorial function. He maintains, "Nations, first, define a definite social space within which members must live and work, and demarcate an historic territory that locates a community in time and space."[108] These spaces may also include "sacred centres," which reveal what Smith calls the "moral geography" of the nation.[109] The geographic boundaries and various centers perform two essential functions. First, the boundaries, whether recognized political boundaries or socially defined, differentiate the nation from others. Regarding the development of missions strategy, a missionary would need to identify these boundaries, which may be more difficult depending on what kind of boundaries they are and on

---

104. Kreitzer, *Concept of Ethnicity in the Bible*, 30.
105. A. Smith, *National Identity*, 14.
106. A. Smith, *National Identity*, 15.
107. A. Smith, *National Identity*, 16–17.
108. A. Smith, *National Identity*, 16.
109. A. Smith, *National Identity*, 16.

how forthcoming a people group is regarding these boundaries. If the boundaries are internationally recognized or internally defined political boundaries, then the identification of these boundaries will be fairly easy. However, socially defined emic boundaries may be more difficult to discover. The political boundaries may be accepted as emic boundaries, but one cannot assume this without investigating.

Second, identifying geographic centers provides insight into the unified emic cultural system. Elsewhere, Smith describes the sanctification of certain locations as the "territorialization of memory."[110] He explains, "This term refers to a process by which particular places evoke a series of memories, handed down through persons and events in particular places and through them create a field or zone of powerful and peculiar attachments."[111] Smith sees this dynamic at work in the early history of the United States. He observes,

> Strictly speaking, America was not a promised land in the biblical sense, but it very soon became one for the Puritan settlers, who, having experienced a perilous exodus across the seas, were disposed to create in their minds' eye, at least, an ideal "American Israel" and a "New English Jerusalem" in a vast and fertile country, far superior to the land and social order of England, especially after the Restoration . . . The American Puritans' ideal of the "city on the hill" and their sense of providential guidance, though originally confined to the inner life and social organization of small settlements and towns, came from the early nineteenth century to embrace the vast expanses of the continent. As the western frontier expanded and indigenous populations died from disease or were displaced, the belief in a providential and manifest destiny was extended from the chosen people to the land and landscapes of America.[112]

---

110. A. Smith, *Chosen Peoples*, 134.

111. A. Smith, *Chosen Peoples*, 134. Such centers can be seen vividly in the Philippines from small jungle villages to the various neighborhoods of Manila. Within each community, often in the geographic center, a plaza can be found. Almost uniformly, each of these plazas consist of a basketball court, a large, elevated stage, and a Catholic church. Sometimes the government offices are located in a building adjacent to the plaza, but not necessarily. These plazas were used for various social and religious events. These plazas are the single most important geographic location within a community for the transmission of cultural values. Matejowsky, "Privatization of Public Plazas," 263–300.

112. A. Smith, *Chosen Peoples*, 138.

Similarly, the Old Testament describes the Lord commanding the Israelites to create monuments with the express purpose of communicating to both future generations and outsiders regarding the deeds that the Lord had done (Josh 4:1–24).

Smith also distinguishes between nations and ethnic communities, what he refers to as "*ethnies*." He identifies six characteristics of an *ethnie*: a collective proper name, a myth of common ancestry, shared historical memories, one or more differentiating elements of common culture, an association with a specific "homeland," and a sense of solidarity for significant sectors of the population.[113] By way of clarification, Smith strongly insists, "Such a community must be sharply differentiated from race in the sense of a social group that is held to possess unique hereditary biological traits that allegedly determine the mental attributes of the group . . . But a glance at the above list of ethnic attributes reveals not only their largely cultural and historical content, but also (with the exception of number 4) their strongly subjective components."[114] As with Smith's internal and external functions of a nation, all six characteristics of an *ethnie* deserve consideration, but only an ethnic community's association with a specific homeland can be addressed here.

Every *ethnie*, according to Smith, possesses an emic concept of its historical territory or homeland. He suggests, "Attachments to specific stretches of territory, and to certain places within them, have a mythical and subjective quality. It is the attachments and associations, rather than residence in or possession of the land that matters for ethnic identification. It is where we belong . . . We belong to it, as much as it belongs to us."[115] He further explains that "an *ethnie* may persist, even when long divorced from its homeland, through an intense nostalgia and spiritual attachment."[116] Smith's emphasis on an emically discerned territory belonging to an ethnic community is very similar to the manner in which Scripture depicts the relationship between the nations and their

---

113. A. Smith, *National Identity*, 21.

114. A. Smith, *National Identity*, 21–22.

115. A. Smith, *National Identity*, 22–23. Smith may be overstating here somewhat. It may also be true than an *ethnie*'s territory influences its ethnic identification as well as far as the geography impacts the development of culture. Those people groups living in extreme terrains such as the desert Bedouins of North Africa, the Inuit peoples of the Arctic, or the Sherpas dwelling in the Himalaya Mountains of Nepal have all been influenced by their geography. However, further research regarding how geography may impact culture is required.

116. A. Smith, *National Identity*, 23.

geography. He does, however, slightly overstate his case when he insists that territory becomes less important among diaspora communities. Referring to Jewish people prior to 1948, Smith indicates, "The land of Israel was at times more than a symbol of messianic restoration; groups of Jews made their way there from time to time and founded synagogues. Yet here too the yearning for Zion was often more spiritual than actual, a vision of perfection in a restored land and city."[117] This may be true in some cases and among certain sections of the Jewish *ethnie*, but there certainly were significant exceptions. When Theodor Herzl proposed an alternative Jewish homeland in Uganda at the Sixth Zionist Congress in 1903 as a measure to permit Russian Jews an opportunity to escape fierce pogroms, many delegates to the congress saw it as a betrayal of Zionist principles. Even the Russian delegates walked out on the congress. The Uganda proposal was rejected at the Seventh Zionist Congress in 1905.[118] Herzl reflected, "Palestine is the only land where our people can come to rest."[119] Among other diaspora communities, a sense of homeland remains complex, but not easily reduced to a spiritual or emotional sense. Mishra indicates,

> If the coolie diaspora displays nothing more than an emotional feeling for India, then what precisely is this affect sundered from any thought of a bounded homeland territory? One answer may be that for certain clusters (Trinidadian or Guyanese 'East' Indians, for instance) *milieu effects* such as the dholak, the charpoy or a household deity serve as deterritorialised cultural markers rather than as metonymic signs of an absent geopolitical order... Such contrapuntal readings subvert the straitjacket into which the dual territorial schema inserts diasporic entities; they also open up the possibility of forms of relationship other than the geopolitical or national.[120]

---

117. A. Smith, *National Identity*, 33.

118. Johnson, *History of the Jews*, 401–2.

119. Johnson, *History of the Jews*, 402.

120. Mishra, *Diaspora Criticism*, 30. Mishra is responding to Helweg, who claims, "For non-residents, India is their cultural homeland, but the meaning of India as an ethnic home varies for different groups. For those in East Africa, India is the place of return as for retirement, the home of their kinsmen, the location of their ancestral land, the source of their culture and the reason for the extensive, present-day networks. For others, such as those of indenture origins in Trinidad, India evokes in them an emotional feeling and nothing more." Helweg, "Indian Diaspora," 115.

Mishra's observation emphasizes that seeking an emic understanding of geography is indispensable for properly developing missions strategy, whether among a people group in their own homeland or among diaspora communities. So, while some reforms and adjustments may be necessary for a diaspora community to retain a distinct identity, the sense of belonging to a specific territory remains—whether that territory refers to the country of origin or shifts over time to refer to a specific ethnic enclave within their new context.[121]

While Smith holds that nations and *ethnies* are distinct, he affirms that each nation contains an "ethnic core." He describes, "[Ethnic cores] are fairly cohesive and self-consciously distinctive *ethnies* which form the kernel and basis of states and kingdoms such as the barbarian *regna* of the early medieval era."[122] Identifying these ethnic cores may also aid the development of missions strategy since, Smith writes, "Locating such ethnic cores tells us a good deal about the subsequent shape and character of nations . . . It helps us to answer in large part the question: *who* is the nation? and to some extent: *where* is the nation? That is to say, a state's ethnic core often shapes the character and boundaries of the nation; for it is very often on the basis of such a core that states coalesce to form nations."[123] In Smith's ethno-symbolism, "ethnic" has a broader meaning than is often suggested among those who insist on an ethno-linguistic approach to people groups. "Ethnic" refers to the entire emic system rather than just one component of it. In this regard, Smith's definition of ethnic communities, with its complex constitution, is closer to the way that ἔθνος and גוי are used in Scripture. Smith's proposal also closely parallels the 1982 Lausanne definition of people groups. Even so, caution must be exercised to make sure that biblical categories are determining the categories and terms for the sociological tools. Smith's definition does not appear to be explicitly based on Scripture, but it does align with Scripture in many ways.

Conclusion

This section surveyed various sociological paradigms that seek to present a definition and understanding of nations and national identity.

---

121. A. Smith, *National Identity*, 35–37.
122. A. Smith, *National Identity*, 38–39.
123. A. Smith, *National Identity*, 39.

Primordialism views nations as an inherent part of creation and, at least Geertz's primordialism, understands the culture of nations as a unified system. However, primordialism tends to view nations as static entities. Modernism's understanding of the nations closely connects the rise of nations to the advent of philosophical modernism. Modernist proponents helpfully observe the significant shift in Western thinking regarding the nature of nations in the seventeenth and eighteenth centuries, but insist on relying exclusively on empirically observable (etic) characteristics for distinguishing nations from one another. Perennialists indicate that the concept of nations is a constant, but that specific nations may rise, fall, or change in the course of history. Social constructionists such as Benedict Anderson argue that nations are nothing more than subjective creations or "imagined communities." This paradigm stresses the social aspect of nations in the perceived shared identity, but overemphasizes the individualistic subjective perception of nations , which results in only an apparent shared identity. Anthony Smith's proposed ethno-symbolism, while having some flaws, most closely aligns with the scriptural evidence despite not being explicitly based on biblical theology. Smith properly observes the interdependent system of various characteristics that result in a nation. Smith also emphasizes that identifying "ethnic cores" helps to properly locate the boundaries of an *ethnie*. Having surveyed and evaluated the various sociological approaches and discovering valuable lessons in each paradigm, but finding Smith's ethno-symbolism particularly helpful, a proposal for discovering emic geography will be proffered.

A Proposal for Discovering Emic Geography

Much of the early research and methodology regarding aiding outsiders toward gaining an emic perspective of culture was done in the field of linguistics with application in cultural anthropology, but the study of emic systems has spread broadly to numerous disciplines.[124] Cultural anthropology urges that those studying other cultures or serving as missionaries among other cultures should work toward discovering an

---

124. Headland, "Introduction," 16–24. Headland reports that by 1990, at least 278 articles or books had been written using emic and etic as significant terms. Fields using emic/etic terms include anthropology, psychology, linguistics, ethnography, sociology, medicine, education, archaeology, folklore, and economics. In 2021, a search for books and journal articles on WorldCat for "emic" in the title returns over two thousand results in a wide variety of academic fields.

emic understanding of the culture, but very little guidance is provided to instruct someone precisely how to successfully accomplish this.[125] Regarding practical methodology directly related to missions, some help may be found in the field of linguistics. Direct application of all linguistic principles working toward an emic understanding of language systems may not apply, but some lessons may be gleaned. Pike anticipated such a possible exchange, urging that "there is needed a theory which will not be discontinuous, and which will not cause a severe jar as one passes from non-verbal to verbal activity. There is needed a unified theory, a unified set of terms, and a unified methodology which can start from any kind of complex human activity with various sub-types of activity included, and analyze it without sharp theoretical or methodological discontinuities."[126] Geography and language are different subsystems within the same emic system. The training that Dallas International University provides for Bible translators offers some specific guidance about how to move from etic to emic categories.

Start with Etic Categories

A researcher or missionary has little choice other than to start with the etic categories available to them. In linguistics, training begins with phonetics, particularly a nearly universally applicable phonetic alphabet. Marlett instructs, "Phonetics deals with the physical aspects of the sounds of languages, especially how sounds are articulated and perceived, but not how they are organized. A person trained in phonetics is able to transcribe words from virtually any language."[127] MacMahon defines and describes

---

125. Hiebert, *Anthropological Insights for Missionaries*, 94–97; Kraft, *Christianity in Culture*, 230–31; Eriksen, *Small Places, Large Issues*, 47–48. Hiebert instructs, "When we participate deeply in another culture, we discover that there are different views of reality. We are forced by this to step outside the thought system of our own culture and think in new ways." Kraft describes, "Outside analysts develop a series of categories in terms of which they view and compare the specific data of many cultural systems. They speak of the subsystems (e.g., religion, politics, economics, social structure, worldview, etc.) of culture and illustrate each from their understanding of the content of each subsystem. The insiders may not use these categories at all, since they are not necessarily comparing them with similar practices of other peoples. But analysts need such categories to facilitate their cross-cultural comparisons."

126. Pike, *Language in Relation*, 26.

127. Marlett, *Introduction to Phonological Analysis*, 2. While this text remains unpublished, it is the primary text for Principles of Phonological Analysis at Dallas

phonetic notation, writing, "The term *phonetic notation* refers both to the repertoire of phonetic symbols and diacritics used in the transcription of spoken language, and to the employment of such symbols and diacritics in creating a transcription of pronunciation . . . Phonetic notation focuses exclusively on the articulatory dimension of speech, i.e. the postures and movements of the speech organs."[128] The phonetic analysis of a language is where a person must begin with analysis as there is no other method by which to begin, but this initial etic analysis is gradually refined so that the emic system becomes more clear.[129] Marlett insists, "Successful literacy programs in other languages also depend on similar knowledge of how the sound systems in those languages work—of their phonologies. Our understanding of these systems may begin with phonetics, but it does not end there."[130] Stopping analysis at the level of etic description provides an incomplete or even inaccurate representation of the emic language system.

A similar situation is true of working toward an emic understanding of geography. While no comparable phonetic alphabet exists for geography, it is possible to begin with very broad categories that can be subdivided as necessary. The two broad categories are boundaries and centers. A boundary may be defined as a physical or imaginary geographical barrier that is perceived to divide one people group from another. A center is a geographic location or locations within the perceived territory of a people group that hold particular cultural significance (e.g., religious, historical, economic, political, etc.). In the Old Testament, boundaries

---

International University. This course "provides practice in recognizing the difference between phonetic (etic) and phonological (emic) data through numerous practical exercises." "Dallas International University Fall 2020–Spring 2021 Academic Catalog."

128. MacMahon, "Phonetic Notation,", 821.

129. Pike, *Language in Relation*, 38–39. Pike doubts than an emic description will ever fully replace an etic description, but that should not prevent a person from striving toward as close to an emic description as possible.

130. Marlett, *Phonological Analysis*, 3. Marlett provides an example of this from English writing: "Consider also the words *vain* and *vanity* in English, or the pair *sane* and *sanity*. The first word in each pair has the phonetic vowel (or dipthong) [ej] and the second has the phonetic vowel [æ]. If we were to write the words 'scientifically', then these are the symbols we should use, one might say. But these vowels, be what they may be phonetically, are typically referred to in traditional studies of English as 'long a' and 'short a', and often written as the letter *a* with and without a macron over the letters. This transcription is not phonetic—what does the letter *a* have to do with the phonetic transcript [ej]? However, the names 'long *a*' and 'short *a*' are important in that they point to a systematic correspondence between phonetic sequences which is fundamental to understanding the sound patterns of English."

and centers were incredibly important. Considerable space is dedicated to clearly establishing the territories of the various tribes of Israel (Joshua 13–19). Moving a boundary marker was a serious offense subject to punishment in accordance with the covenant curses, which placed it in the same category as creating idols and dishonoring parents (Deut 19:14; 27:17; Prov 22:28; Hos 5:10). While less explicit, centers also played a major role for Israel. The most obvious center is Jerusalem after David moved the ark of the Lord to Jerusalem (2 Samuel 6) and especially after Solomon constructed the temple as a permanent place of worship (1 Kings 6–8). However, prior to Jerusalem, other centers existed in Israel: cities of refuge in the various tribal territories (Josh 20:1–9), the burial locations of Joshua, Joseph, and Eleazor in Timnath-serah, Shechem, and Gibeah, respectively (Josh 24:29–33), and Shiloh (Josh 18:1; Judg 18:31; 1 Sam 1:3).

The primary function of boundaries is to divide the territory of one people group from another. Boundaries differ in strength and may be as easy to cross as walking to the other side of a street or may require passports, visas, and submitting to a thorough security screening. However, a boundary that is physically easy to cross should not be confused for a boundary that is easy to cross culturally. Boundaries may also be divided into subcategories. Boundaries may exist in the form of natural topographical features such as rivers, ridges, and valleys or artificial topographical features such as streets, highways, and railroad tracks.[131] Boundaries may also exist in the form of imaginary boundaries such as international geopolitical boundaries, internal political boundaries between states, regions, districts, counties, or communities.[132] Imaginary boundaries may also appear completely arbitrary to the etic observer.

---

131. These examples do not exhaust the possible types of natural and artificial topographical features but merely provide a sample from which to begin building etic categories. The point here is to begin with whatever etic categories are available to the observer. This is the case wherever examples are provided through the remainder of this section. Crider specifically identifies "paths," "districts," and "edges," which would be specific examples of boundaries and bounded geographic territories. Crider, "Mapping," 52–56. Crider derives most of his categories from Lynch, *Image of the City*, 46–90.

132. Calling these boundaries "imaginary" does not indicate that the boundaries do actually exist or that the boundaries do not have real influence on a people group. Rather these boundaries are imaginary in the sense that they are invisible lines as opposed to visible topographical features.

The primary purpose of centers is to create, sustain, or sometimes modify the cultural identity of a people group within its perceived territory. Centers may also be divided into at least two subcategories: nodes and hubs. A node is a center where members of a people group congregate for the purpose of sharing and communicating culturally significant events and ideas. Crider indicates, "Nodes are centers of activity, such as plazas, squares, metro stations, parks, business centers, or shopping malls."[133] From a missiological perspective, nodes are important because they are "strategic foci into which the observer can enter."[134] A people group may have numerous nodes or a single node depending on the size of the people groups and the number of individual communities within a people group.

Hubs are a center from which cultural influence emanates out to the surrounding community. Many people do not necessarily need to physically go to a hub for it to exert influence on the community. Examples of hubs may include monuments, government centers, various landmarks, certain districts such as a city's arts district, or high places.[135] A hub exerts cultural influence on the surrounding people group or community even when people are not in the immediate vicinity of the hub because the hub is seen as an important, sometimes integral, component of the cultural identity of the people group—like the hub of a wheel turning the outer rim because it is connected by spokes. A hub and a node may, at times, be the same location, but not in every instance. Even when they are the same location, a node/hub center may fulfill different functions at different times.

---

133. Crider, "Mapping," 53.

134. Lynch, *Image of the City*, 72.

135. Crider, "Mapping," 60–61. Crider relates that "in most cultures, areas with higher physical elevations tend to be assigned some level of importance. 'Sacred' structures are often built in these locations and can have significant influence upon a city's history and culture . . . In nearly every city in the world, the high places are significant historically, culturally, geographically, and spiritually. The very existence of high places says much about the people who built them."

Etic Geographic Categories			
Boundaries		Centers	
Topographical	Imaginary	Nodes	Hubs
Natural	Artificial		

Figure 5.1

Discover Emic Categories

Etic geographic categories establish a beginning framework, but a missionary or researcher must intentionally work to discover emic geographic categories within the cultural framework of a people to whom they wish to proclaim the gospel and among whom they wish to make disciples and plant churches.[136] There are no shortcuts to the hard work necessary to discover emic geographic categories. It is impossible to establish a step-by-step process of discovering emic geography.[137] As opposed to language, emic geographical categories are not easily observable. An outsider may need to carefully watch behavioral patterns and responses to geographic centers and boundaries. Despite the incredible challenges to developing a comprehensive, universally applicable system for discovering emic categories, some general rules and guidelines may be offered.

Recognizing that emic systems exist and they may look remarkably different than what an outside observer expects is an essential first step. The step may appear obvious, but in practice many remain content to see geography through an etic lens only. Once a person observes that there are other viewpoints and other ways of viewing geography, this frees them to begin exploring the emic systems. Until this first step happens, no progress can be made toward discovering emic systems. While the other guidelines below generally can happen nonsequentially, coming to terms with the

---

136. The etic-to-emic process is not limited to only language or geography. Rather, the etic-to-emic process should be done for all aspects of culture and worldview recognizing that each component is part of a unified emic system.

137. The process is somewhat easier in linguistics since language, in many cases, is mechanical, but not in every instance—for example, idioms, colloquialisms, slang, etc. Language is also one of the most obvious and easily observed characteristics of a people group.

existence of emic geographic categories that may differ significantly from those of an outside observer is the gate through which everyone must pass. In other words, a missionary must set aside their ethnocentrism even to begin this process. Hiebert indicates, "The root of ethnocentrism is our human tendency to respond to other people's ways by using our own affective assumptions, and to reinforce these responses with deep feelings of approval or disapproval."[138] Pike further relates, "Each observer will also have some bias in terms of the behavior events most familiar to him—those which are emic in his own activity. These he tends to take as his point of departure, as his norms, so that cultural background may affect an etic report."[139] Failure to identify our ethnocentrism in regard to perceptions of geography will allow us to remain comfortable at an etic level, which may lead to critical errors in developing missions strategy.

Furthermore, missionaries must acknowledge that emic geography exists as part of an entire emic system. This step is nearly as crucial as the first step because even if someone acknowledges that emic geography exists but they do not properly locate geography as part of an entire emic system, the conclusions drawn from observations and research will be flawed and the insights could be inappropriately applied. Stratification of the various emic categories will leave gaps in understanding about the individual categories overall and how they influence one another. Hiebert contends, "The stratigraphic approach leads to a sharp division between science and religion. Science studies the natural world using empirical methods; religion studies the supernatural world using dogma and faith."[140] In addition to creating divisions between science and religion, stratification will also lead to divisions between ethnicity, language, geography, politics, socioeconomics, and anything else that helps distinguish people groups from one another. As an outsider, it may be impossible to completely grasp every detail of an emic system, but even awareness that such interdependent components exist will improve observation and analysis.[141]

138. Hiebert, *Anthropological Insights*, 97.

139. Pike, *Language in Relation*, 46.

140. Hiebert, *Gospel in Human Contexts*, 130.

141. Brody and Sobel, "Systems View of Health and Disease," 88; Hiebert, *Gospel in Human Contexts*, 132–33. Brody and Sobel define, "A system is an organized set of components that is conveniently regarded as a whole consisting of interdependent parts ... Parts of a system are organized and function under the influence of the information flow in the systems." Brody and Sobel do not explicitly cite Pike or use the term "emic," but their analysis serves as an example for how analysis of emic systems may be conducted outside the specific field of linguistics.

Hiebert indicates, "Systems approaches to integration see causality as multidirectional."[142] So as a missionary seeks to discover emic geography, they must also remain aware of the entire interdependent emic system.

Second, working from etic categories, missionaries should begin to refine the categories and establish rules that accurately describe the emic reality to the best of their ability. This step parallels linguistics as it moves from the phonetic to the phonological (emic). Marlett instructs, "Phonological rules account for the exact pronunciation of the morphemes since there is evidence that some phonological information about morphemes is not stored in the lexicon."[143] The goal here is not to create a complex system of rules but rather to "start out with as simple a formulation as possible. Add extra features only as necessary to prevent it from making incorrect claims."[144] These rules may be as simple as approximately identifying the boundary that separates one people group from another or a particular section of a city that represents a cultural center. Informed guesses can be ventured so long as they lead to further investigation and refinement of the rule. At this point, the tentative rules are not yet fully emic in nature, but they represent a step in that direction. Early on, the rules are still primarily governed by etic categories, but as they are refined and modified to reflect the emic system, they represent emic geography more accurately. Obtaining perfect knowledge of the emic system may never be possible for missionaries as finite creatures inseparable from their own cultural context, but every step towards understanding an emic viewpoint regarding geography will aid the missionary in using contextual geography as they develop appropriate missions strategy for a given people group.

A third action in the process is that missionaries must pay attention to how people respond to different boundaries and centers. Subjective behavioral responses constitute a major aspect of emic systems. Pike, explaining his concept of a "behavioreme," writes, "As a first approximation of the meaning of the term behavioreme, we suggest that it be used to label an emic unit of top-focus behavior which is related to its cultural setting in such a way that cultural documentation may be found for its beginning, ending, and purposive elements."[145] A behavioreme is generally

---

142. Hiebert, *Gospel in Human Contexts*, 133.
143. Marlett, *Phonological Analysis*, 54.
144. Marlett, *Phonological Analysis*, 56.
145. Pike, *Language in Relation*, 121.

determined by its context. Meaning cannot be ascribed to a behavior, as with a word, in isolation from its context. Observing how people interact with one another at centers and boundaries can provide insight into the meaning and significance of those geographical locations. One may discover that what appears to be a single center is actually a series of centers fulfilling different functions. For example, the Thamel district of Kathmandu, Nepal might be seen as a single cultural center, but within the district one will find an expatriate enclave, a tourist shopping district, Hindu idols of various size, and two mosques. The various functions overlap within a single district, but separate people groups respond differently to the various centers. Hindus do not attend the mosques, Muslims do not frequent the Hindu idols, and local residents of any people group rarely shop in this district.[146] Similarly, boundaries evoke distinct responses. People on either side of the geopolitical border between India and Pakistan respond differently to one another than different groups of people respond to the geopolitical border between India and Nepal.[147]

A fourth step for a missionary to take is to draw a map of the area in which they are working. Maps available for purchase may help a person get from one location to another, but mass-produced maps are etic by nature. They are created for outsiders. An insider does not need a map. Crider observes, "Mapping is an invaluable skill for all ministries. An outsider wanting to begin ministry in a new place can gain great value from walking the streets and documenting everything observed. People are greatly affected by the places in which they live, and by studying their environment one can learn much."[148] The map, however, is not an emic tool all by itself. By itself, the map represents an etic observation of the environment. Like the categories of boundaries and centers, a map can exist as a visualization of the etic categories that can be refined and adjusted to move towards an emic understanding. As with careful etic analysis of language, some of the etic observations that occur through thoughtful mapping may end up accurately reflecting emic categories. Pike relates, "[I]f a person working in one dialect moves to a very similar neighboring dialect, his first transcription is an etic one, perforce, because he is alien to that dialect, but it may actually be very close to the final emic

---

146. These distinctions were observed through firsthand research conducted by the author while living in Kathmandu, Nepal for several years.

147. Menon, *Performance of Nationalism*, 22–53; Chettri, *Ethnicity and Democracy*, 33–64.

148. Crider, "Mapping," 51.

transcription which he will produce, many of his tentative etic units will turn out to be emic units as well."[149] A map, just as with the other steps, must constantly undergo revision and refinement. Refining the observations will come as a result of increasing in knowledge of the entire emic system, such as through language study, through general acculturation, and through cultural informants.

The final step, which really ought to be done throughout the entire process, is refinement and adjustment. Language study and acculturation will aid a missionary in moving toward an emic understanding of geography, but the best method for refinement is through a trusted partner who may serve as a cultural informant. A cultural informant can answer questions regarding the existence, location, and nature of boundaries and centers. A cultural informant can also clarify, confirm, and correct observations regarding behavioral responses to geographical features. Further, a cultural informant can point out omissions on a map and add depth of understanding about certain features previously observed. Finding a trusted cultural informant may be one of the easiest or the most difficult parts of the entire process based on how forthcoming and transparent individuals are within a given people group. This method parallels how Bible translators look for native speakers to check translations. Additionally, some people are not consciously aware of their own emic systems, and many have not considered the reasons behind certain behaviors. It may be necessary, in the course of building a relationship, to equip a trusted cultural informant with training in etics and emics. The training does not only benefit the missionary but also aids the national partner. This training will assist them to evaluate their own cultural context so that evangelism, disciple making, and church planting are properly contextualized. Training in emics and etics will also equip them and others who receive similar training to function well as cross-cultural missionaries. The refining process is a continuous cycle. Pike describes the continuous nature of emic discovery through a short poem: "See, and know. Know, and be. Be, and do. Do, and see. See, and know."[150]

---

149. Pike, *Language in Relation*, 41–42.
150. Pike, "On the Emics and Etics," 45.

Conclusion

This chapter has reviewed and evaluated various sociological views of the nations, seeking correspondence with a scriptural understanding of the nations especially as it relates to the role that geography plays in national identity. While some lessons resulted from evaluation of every paradigm, Anthony Smith's ethno-symbolism paradigm proved to share the most similarity to a scriptural understanding of the nations and emphasized the importance of geographic and cultural boundaries in understanding national identity. This chapter then presented an etic framework from which to begin analysis of geography in any people group. Boundaries are divided into topographical and imaginary boundaries. Topographical boundaries are further divided into natural and artificial topographical boundaries. Similarly, two types of centers were presented: nodes and hubs. Finally, a process for discovering emic systems was presented, including acknowledgement that emic geographic understandings exist, and that they exist as part of a comprehensive and coherent emic system, begin hypothesizing rules about the existence, location, and nature of various boundaries and centers, observe behavioral responses to boundaries and centers, utilize an intentional mapping process, and seek the help of a partner who serves as a cultural informant to offer corrections and draw attention to omissions. Continuous adjustment and refinement should permeate every step of the discovery process.

6

Conclusion

Summary of Findings

I HAVE ATTEMPTED TO establish a biblical-theological foundation for scriptural missions strategy regarding the geographic element of national identity. I have also evaluated various approaches to missions strategy and sociological models in light of the biblical-theological evidence. The findings of this study have bearing on both biblical theology and on the development and implementation of missions strategy.

Biblical-Theological Findings

This book examined twenty-five verses or passages from Scripture and one section from the book of Jubilees in order to demonstrate that land constitutes a very important aspect of national identity in both the Old and New Testaments. These passages provide a sample of the broader significance of land, especially in the Old Testament. The geographical component, while not the only characteristic or even always the most important characteristic, is one of the most visible and obvious aspects of national identity. The significance of land for national identity is demonstrated by the connection of land to people in creation (Gen 2:4–17), the prominence placed on land in the Table of Nations (Gen 10:5, 20, 31), and that God established geographic boundaries between the nations

(Deut 32:8; Acts 17:26). Furthermore, land and nations are connected intimately so that the land can be used as a metonymy of subject for the nation that dwells in it (Exodus 7–11; 1 Chr 14:17; 2 Chr 7:14; 17:10; 20:29; 36:3; Isa 8:9; 14:26; 37:18; 45:22; Ezek 5:5–6; 12:15; 20:23; 22:15; 29:12; 30:26; 36:19, 24). A national identity could also be gained or lost at least partially based on whether or not a nation possessed land or land was divinely given or taken. Additionally, the authors of the Old and New Testaments use emic geography since the audience shares the same understandings of geography as the authors.

Scripture further shows that perceptions of geography are largely dependent on cultural context. Paul indicates in Rom 15:19, "[S]o that from Jerusalem and all the way around to Illyricum I have fulfilled the ministry of the gospel of Christ" (ὥστε με ἀπὸ Ἰερουσαλὴμ καὶ κύκλῳ μέχρι τοῦ Ἰλλυρικοῦ πεπληρωκέναι τὸ εὐαγγέλιον τοῦ Χριστοῦ). First, Paul utilizes exclusively geographic terms in Rom 15:19. He references Roman provinces rather than ethnic identifiers. Furthermore, his use of κύκλῳ in Rom 15:19 reinforces the geographic emphasis since κύκλῳ tends to be used as a geographic descriptor in both the New Testament and first-century Greek literature. Second, rather than relying on the Jewish geography of his upbringing or the Greek geography of the eastern portion of the Roman Empire, Paul referenced the Roman geography of his audience. He effectively contextualized describing the extent of his missionary activity to a predominantly Roman audience.

Missions Strategy Findings

The development of missions strategy since the middle of the twentieth century has decreasingly emphasized geography, and emic geography specifically has only been considered in a limited way by prominent missions strategists. McGavran's early definition of homogenous units originally included a geographic component, but geography was relegated to a minor factor in later versions.[1] The 1982 Lausanne definition of people groups included emic geography ("a significantly large sociological grouping of individuals who perceive themselves to have a common affinity for one another"), but the methodology suggested for identifying people groups did not effectively lead to the discovery

---

1. McGavran, *Understanding Church Growth*, 85; McGavran, *Understanding Church Growth* (3rd ed.), 69.

of emic geography.[2] Other definitions of people groups that take the 1982 Lausanne definition as their starting point limited the definition to ethnolinguistic categories.[3] Ralph Winter attempted to introduce new terminology ("unimax peoples") with a slightly modified definition, suggesting that "a unimax people is the maximum sized group sufficiently unified to be the target of a single people movement to Christ, where 'unified' refers to the fact that there are no significant barriers of either understanding or acceptance to stop the spread of the gospel."[4] Winter and others who attempt to explain people groups mostly overlook geography as a potentially significant barrier except in rare circumstances such as remote tribal groups.[5] Mark Kreitzer proposes the term "ethnic solidarities" (ESOLs) in place of "people groups," which he defines as "relatively intermarried (endogamous) groups of families of similar religion, custom, language and geo-history who define themselves in respect to the Other, that is dissimilar groups in the ever-changing internal and external contexts throughout time."[6] Kreitzer does attempt to account for geographic boundaries among ESOLs, but he subsumes geography under the category of ethnicity. Furthermore, he does not specify how geographic considerations affect missions strategy.

Despite the emphasis on ethnolinguistic barriers, some have attempted to use geography in their mission strategy. Project 4K attempts to incorporate geography by blending ethnolinguistic people groups and four thousand geopolitical divisions. Their purpose in creating such divisions, however, is to pragmatically make the missionary task more manageable rather than seeking a biblical-theological definition of the nations or attempting to discover emic geographic boundaries.[7] Roman Catholic missiology continues to rely heavily on geography for their missions strategy based on the belief that the physical presence of the Church is a means of grace. In the last few years, several evangelicals have proposed that geography be somehow accounted for in missions strategy, but no known specific strategy proposals have been offered.[8]

2. Dayton, "Reaching the Unreached Peoples," 31–38.

3. Barrett et al., *World Christian Encyclopedia* (2nd ed.), 1:15–16; Jenkins, "What Is a People Group?"; Piper, *Let the Nations Be Glad*, 184–85.

4. Winter and Koch, "Finishing the Task," 535.

5. Winter and Koch, "Finishing the Task," 535.

6. Kreitzer, *Concept of Ethnicity in the Bible*, 98.

7. *4K Workbook*.

8. Pratt, "Here's What We Mean"; Platt, "Rethinking Unreached People Groups";

Kenneth Pike's concept of emic systems forms a foundation for discovering how a people group defines and identifies its own geographical boundaries and centers. Pike defines, "The etic viewpoint studies behavior as from outside of a particular system, and is an essential initial approach to an alien system. The emic viewpoint results from studying behavior as from inside the system."[9] A researcher or missionary will necessarily always begin from an etic perspective, but must always work towards discovering the emic systems to better understand the unique geographic boundaries and centers of the people group. The process of discovering the emic system will assist missionaries and mission researchers to make strategic decisions regarding church planting, discipleship, and evangelism. Several sociological and anthropological definitions of nations have been proposed by scholars. While most of them provide some helpful insight, Anthony Smith's ethno-symbolism most closely aligns with the biblical evidence and accounts for emic geography.[10] Smith observes the existence of interdependent emic systems that help formulate a national identity. One of these emic systems is geographic, and Smith suggests that each nation has various boundaries and centers that fulfill various functions. Additionally, Smith's understanding of "ethnic" closely corresponds to the complex nature of ἔθνη as it is used in Scripture.[11]

Based on the biblical evidence with assistance from Pike's methodology and Smith's model, a process for discovering emic geography begins with the broad etic categories of boundaries and centers. Etic boundaries may be divided into imaginary and topographical boundaries, and topographical boundaries may be further divided into artificial and natural boundaries. A geographical center may be a node where members of a people group congregate for the purpose of sharing and communicating culturally significant events and ideas. Alternatively, a geographical center may be a hub from which cultural influence emanates out to the surrounding community. These etic categories provide a starting point for preliminary analysis, and a missionary or researcher intentionally must then work to discover how geography is understood in the emic system.

Roderick and Gordy, "Every People Group," 71–82; Carlson and Clark, "3 Words That Changed Missions."

9. Pike, *Language in Relation*, 37.
10. A. Smith, *National Identity*, 21–23.
11. A. Smith, *National Identity*, 21–22.

Missions Strategy Steps

First, missionaries must acknowledge that emic systems exist and that the system may be remarkably different than one may first assume. Furthermore, geography is an essential part of every people group's emic system. Second, once research begins, missionaries may establish rules that accurately describe the emic reality to the best of their ability. These rules may be as simple or as complex as required, but they must be continually refined as a missionary gains more understanding of the entire emic system. Third, missionaries must intentionally examine how people respond to different boundaries and centers. Behavior cannot be properly analyzed without comprehending the context in which the behavior occurs. Fourth, a missionary should draw a map of the area, attempting to incorporate the various boundaries and centers with notes regarding their findings. Finally, the process of refining findings should permeate the entire process and continue perpetually as new discoveries are made.

Defining the Nations

The 1982 Lausanne definition continues to serve as the point from which all other people group definitions depart. According to the Lausanne definition, a people group is defined as "a significantly large sociological grouping of individuals who perceive themselves to have a common affinity for one another. From the viewpoint of evangelization this is the largest possible group within which the gospel can spread without encountering barriers of understanding or acceptance."[12] The definition makes several positive contributions that must not be minimized or discarded. First, the 1982 definition does call for an emic understanding of national identity. Many of the problems that have arisen in missions strategy are due to incomplete methods for attaining an emic understanding. Furthermore, while a perfect emic understanding is likely never possible for a cultural outsider, lack of perfect knowledge is not a valid reason to not make every effort to attain knowledge of emic systems to the best of one's ability. Defining people groups according to their self-perception must not be seen as merely an idealistic goal. The efforts required to gain such an understanding are worth the effort in pursuit of fulfilling the divinely given missionary task.

12. Dayton, "Reaching the Unreached Peoples," 32–33.

Second, the original 1982 definition held to a very broad view of what constitutes a barrier to evangelization.[13] The concern that the understanding of barriers in the 1982 definition are too broad is valid. Taken to an extreme, nearly infinite subdivisions could occur. However, the response must not be to ignore, overlook, or minimize potentially legitimate barriers. Missionaries must be equipped and encouraged to work hard to discover the emic barriers to evangelism, discipleship, and church planting.

One primary aspect of the 1982 definition of people groups requires significant modification. The 1982 Lausanne definition emphasizes sociological groupings rather than groups primarily defined by biblical-theological categories. Sociological groupings are not mutually exclusive from the biblical-theological categories, but scriptural definitions must take priority over sociological definitions. A definition of people groups that drives and directs missions strategy must have a strong foundation in Scripture so that a definition will not drift with shifts in sociology that may eventually run counter to scriptural distinctions. Furthermore, ensuring that the definition of people groups is established on biblical-theological categories will reinforce that the missionary task is primarily a biblical-theological task. Additional research is required to clearly identify potentially relevant biblical-theological categories, but Daniel Block argues that language, ethnicity, geography, religion, and politics all had some bearing on national identity in the ancient Near East.[14] At a minimum, these five categories should be included in the people group definition and researched further.

An additional modification could possibly be made regarding the 1982 definition's emphasis on barriers to evangelism. It may be better to say, "From the viewpoint of missions strategy" to account for the full scope of missions, which includes entry, evangelism, discipleship, church planting, and leadership development.

Taking the 1982 Lausanne definition as the starting point and making the modifications based on the findings of this study, a people group may be defined as a grouping of individuals who perceive themselves to have a common affinity for one another based on categories with a biblical-theological foundation, which may include language, ethnicity, geography, religion, political factors, or any combination of these factors.

13. Dayton, "Reaching the Unreached Peoples," 33.
14. Block, "Foundations of National Identity."

From the viewpoint of evangelization, this is the largest possible group within which the gospel can spread without encountering barriers of understanding, acceptance, or transmission.

Implications

My desire throughout this book has been to serve missionaries, missiologists, and missions researchers in the common pursuit of faithfully fulfilling the Great Commission task to which all followers of Christ have been called. The findings are intended to encourage Great Commission laborers to continuously examine definitions and methods to ensure both that all fellow laborers are grounding the task in Scripture and that the discovery process of emic systems are continuously refined. To this end, I am not calling for a completely innovative approach to missions strategy. However, missions strategists and practitioners must make modifications to strategy and practice whenever necessary. Sometimes adjustments are minor while others are remarkably major, denoting a paradigm shift in missions such as the shift from geopolitical nation-states to people groups. The implications for missions strategy based on the my findings are intended to serve as an extension and refinement of the current people group missions strategy. On the one hand, the actual adjustments to strategy are closer to minor than a paradigm shift. Many of the proposed practices parallel methods already in use in other aspects of missions. Cultural acquisition, language learning, and contextualization are already part of the missionary's task. The practices I propose apply many existing strategic methods to the scriptural category of geography as it relates to how a people group distinguishes itself from others. On the other hand, establishing a strong scriptural foundation for the barriers among people groups is a significant implication of this study. As demonstrated by the 1982 Lausanne definition and various other definitions of people groups, biblical-theological categories were rarely considered. A major shift in the way that people groups are understood and defined is essential. People groups must be understood primarily through the lens of biblical theology while using sociology and anthropology as helpful tools once the categories have been established and defined.

Modifying the definition of people groups to include emic geography may increase the number of people groups. More research is necessary to determine the significance of the increase or, in some cases, the decrease in the number of people groups. However, an increase in the number of people groups should not be a significant barrier to accepting the findings presented here. First, one of the primary concerns of missionaries and missions strategists should be to define the missionary task scripturally and accurately. Seeking accuracy in the missionary task will require that missionaries embrace the highly complex nature of people groups and the emic systems in which geographical and other barriers are discovered. The goal is not to overcomplicate or oversimplify missions strategy. The goal is to work diligently toward understanding people groups on their own terms. Embracing the complex nature of people groups will almost certainly create challenges for missions research in general and people group research specifically. The challenges to research, however, are not new. Rather, complex developments in people group research have been eagerly embraced from early in the strategy.

In 1974, the year Ralph Winter delivered his address to the Lausanne Congress, less than two hundred geopolitical countries existed in the world. Since the advent of people group thinking, missionaries have been encouraged to embrace the cultural complexity of people groups. Rather than just celebrating the successes of previous missionaries, Winter called Christians to see the world in a new way. What resulted from the shift to people group thinking was an almost unbelievable increase in distinct people groups, who all potentially required a distinct missions strategy. Today, the number of people groups ranges from approximately twelve thousand to seventeen thousand.[15] Using the lowest figure still indicates a nearly 6,000-percent increase in the scope of missions strategy. While it is impossible to anticipate how many distinct people groups will be identified as a result of this new approach to people group research, that dramatic of an increase is unlikely.

Rather than seeing any increase as a discouragement, the modest potential increase should increase missions urgency and commitment to mobilization. While delivering his paper at the Lausanne Congress, Winter was aware of the immensity of the task he was laying before the attendees. Throughout his presentation, he made the statistics personal. For example, he explains, "I want you to think for a moment about this latter number—2700 million. Do you notice that this is about one million people for each participant in this Congress? (This means that if each of

---

15. "People Groups," 2020 (http://www.peoplegroups.org); "Global Statistics," 2020 (https://joshuaproject.net/people_groups/statistics); Winter and Koch, "Finishing the Task," 541. Winter and Koch estimates twenty-four thousand unimax peoples.

you all had been busy and had won a million people on the way here, we would have been able to disband the Congress!)."[16] Implementing the proposed strategies should also encourage missionaries to diligently, intentionally, and continuously work toward a deeper understanding of the people group among whom they are committed to making disciples. A commitment to ongoing research must not be misunderstood as an end to itself but rather in service to the missionary task.

Personnel are the primary resource necessary for executing any missions strategy. Discovery of emic geographic boundaries may result in more people groups, and the increase, in turn, may result in an increase of missionaries required. However, any potential increase in the need for missionaries should be minimal for two reasons. First, as mentioned above, the increase in distinct people groups may not be a dramatic increase, although the increase is impossible to precisely predict without further research. Second, in many cases, it may be possible for a single missions team or even an individual missionary to work separate strategies where geographic boundaries are weak or where people groups are geographically (and otherwise) distinct from one another but do not exhibit hostility toward one another. In some cases, however, additional missionary personnel will be required especially where geographic boundaries are strong and people groups have historical animosity towards one another.[17]

Far more significant than a potential increase in the number of people groups or in the number of missionaries required, the findings of this study suggest that more churches are necessary to provide people groups with adequate access to the gospel. Missionaries must carefully examine the emically discovered geographic territory of the people group whom they serve and determine, preferably with the assistance and guidance of national Christian partners, how many churches must be planted to sufficiently allow each person access to gospel proclamation and true fellowship with other believers. While identifying a certain percentage of evangelicals within a people group is helpful, this metric alone provides

---

16. Winter, "Highest Priority," 228.

17. An example of where separate missionary personnel might be required is the Burusho people of Hunza Valley in northern Pakistan. Despite speaking the same language (with some dialectal differences) and sharing ethnicity, the Bursho distinguish themselves from one another geographically in addition to religious and socioeconomic distinctions. The strength of the geographic boundaries and the combination of barriers almost certainly require separate missionaries working distinct strategies to reach the three distinct Burusho people groups. Backstrom, "Burushaski," 31–54.

an incomplete picture of the status of evangelical Christianity in a given people group. For example, a certain people group could theoretically have a population that is 20 percent evangelical, but if all of the evangelical Christians live in one village or one neighborhood of a city, then the percentage as an isolated metric could lead to unjustified conclusions. The problem of "hidden peoples" could resurface where missionaries do not strive to discover emic geographic boundaries. This is another instance where effective mapping skills may prove helpful in strategic planning. Identifying not only the location of people groups and their emic geographic boundaries and centers but also the location of churches may visually reveal geographic gaps where strategic church planting is required.

Mapping can be combined with other strategic planning tools to create a comprehensive strategic planning tool for evangelism, discipleship, and church planting endeavors that take into account church health, leadership development, and church multiplication. For example, mapping churches geographically could be combined with generational church tracking and healthy church assessments to identify strategic needs.[18] Placing church health and generational church planting information on a geographic map could assist in making strategic decisions. Leaders and members of a healthy church that is geographically near a church that is still progressing towards maturity could be encouraged to intentionally mentor potential leaders within the maturing church. As churches multiply, and several generational streams form, two or more churches may be planted in relatively close geographic proximity. The two churches could be encouraged to partner together to identify other areas for church planting endeavors, sharing resources, and mutually encouraging and equipping one another. Contrastingly, identifying two churches geographically near one another may raise questions about the presence of two churches. Potentially, two churches may exist because of space limitations for gathering together, but the existence of two or more churches near one another geographically may reveal undiscovered geographic boundaries or other distinctions (e.g., linguistic, ethnic, cultural, political, etc.).

Discovering the emic geography of people groups has the potential for dramatic implications for diaspora missions. Some of the current strategies regarding engaging diaspora peoples focus exclusively on ethnic distinctions. One of the stated reasons for the Southern Baptist

---

18. Shank, "Generational Mapping," 26–30.

International Mission Board's (IMB) shift to affinity groups was to account for ethnolinguistic groups in other geographic territories. Rankin explains, "Once the focus of mission strategies became reaching all peoples, it was a logical step to reorganize in order to reach them wherever they were in the world. It was essential to dispense with a geographic field structure that limited missionaries to a geographic area and assign them to a global affinity group."[19] One strategic decision regarding diaspora missions includes seeking to establish churches in areas where missionaries could proclaim the gospel more openly anticipating, as Rankin explains, "Planting churches among expatriate believers would inevitably allow the gospel to flow through indigenous believers back to relatives and communities in their native countries that were more restrictive and represented a higher threat level to expatriate missionaries."[20] In some scenarios, this strategy may work, but it does not account for emic understandings of geography that may present a significant barrier to successful implementation. First, this strategy assumes that diaspora peoples constitute a single people group that can be reached with a single strategy. In one sense, the assumption is that diaspora peoples share many or all of the cultural affinity with those of the same ethnic background in their country of origin. This may be true in some cases, especially among early first-generation immigrants. However, diaspora communities quickly become extremely complicated as time passes and as subsequent generations emerge in the new geographic and cultural context. Second and third generations may or may not maintain the same attachment to the culture and language of their parents and grandparents, which will possibly reduce the effectiveness of a strategy to reach them if the strategy is developed with assumptions that only apply to first-generation immigrants.

Furthermore, Rankin's strategy proposal contends that the gospel will inevitably bridge back to the homeland. The assumption is that members of the diaspora community perpetually retain the sense that their homeland is somewhere other than where they live. Again, this assumption may be generally true among first-generation immigrants, but it is less certain that the second or third generation would share the sentiment of their homeland being elsewhere. Diaspora communities are remarkably complex and may exhibit unexpected internal social dynamics.

19. Rankin, "Organizing to Reach the Diaspora," 209.
20. Rankin, "Organizing to Reach the Diaspora," 211.

Rubesh insists that "all diasporas acknowledge the idea of the 'old country,' the conception of a linkage, actual or perceived, to a natal land that lays some claim on the community's loyalty and emotions."[21] The strength of this connection to a natal land among second and subsequent generations requires further study. At some point, it seems inevitable that the land in which one dwells exhibits as much or more cultural influence on a person and community. Regardless of when the transition occurs, the implication from the findings in this study is that missionaries must discover the emic geography rather than assume an etic geography among diaspora people groups.

A final implication is that missionaries must be offered at least basic training in emics and etics. Whether this training occurs in preparatory work in Bible college or seminary coursework or within field orientation programs administered by sending agencies, those entrusted with training missionaries and equipping them to effectively make disciples of all nations should help missionaries understand unified emic systems. Pike, explains how emic systems ought to be studied:

> If a language analyst has set up his tape recorder and captured the sounds emitted during [a game being analyzed] he can make good progress on analyzing and describing the first verse . . . But for the second verse the language analyst, as such, is unable to 'make sense' of out of the data . . . Persons using theories and field techniques adequate for describing nonlinguistic behavior, but discontinuous with linguistic theory and practice, would, on the other hand, face problems complementary to those just described for the linguist. Starting with a moving-picture record of the game, with supporting data, the sociologist or anthropologist could give an over-all description of the social situation in which the game occurred and could in detail describe the gestures. Yet except for [general statements], it would be difficult or impossible for him to give for the total event, as a unit, a unified description which—with no change of outlook or procedure—would simultaneously analyze and describe the nonlinguistic behavior as well as the smallest and most intricate elements of linguistic structure.[22]

Similar to how missionaries are trained and equipped with various methods for language and cultural acquisition, missionaries can be trained and

---

21. Rubesh, "Diaspora Distinctives," 72.
22. Pike, *Language in Relation*, 25–26.

equipped with specific tools to discover emic systems, including emic conceptions of geography, to effectively serve and develop missions strategy.

In conclusion to the implications, it is important to reemphasize that the strategy proposed and the implications derived from the findings of this study do not seek to revert to rely on geopolitical organizational structures or divisions unless missionaries discover that geopolitical boundaries correspond to emic geographic boundaries. I have attempted to continue embracing the general principles of existing people group strategies while arguing that the way a people group perceives its own geography frequently influences and is influenced by other elements of national identity.

Suggestions for Further Study

The findings of this study present opportunities for further research. First, geography is only one aspect of national identity. Other facets of national identity as it relates to missions strategy require research. These various aspects include, but may not be limited to, ethnicity, language, religion, and politics. Other factors may be discovered which will require similar treatment. Additionally, even though recent missions literature has focused on ethnicity and language as significant factors by which people groups are distinguished, further research is needed to ground ethnic and linguistic components in biblical theology. There is still much work to do to develop a robust biblical theology of nations in conversation with anthropology and sociology and application to missions strategy.

Diaspora missions, in general, require quite a bit more research, but specifically on how various diaspora communities perceive their geography in relation to their homeland and where ethnic enclaves exist in urban areas. This research is especially important among multigenerational diaspora communities, where attachment to a traditional homeland may or may not continue to hold influence over those born and raised in a different land and culture.

Conclusion

Jesus Christ, the Lord, has commanded all of his followers to make disciples of all nations to the ends of the earth. People and the land in which they live are connected, and, likewise, the commission that the church has been given demands that the disciples of Jesus cross all boundaries in making disciples—linguistic, ethnic, cultural, geographic, etc. Crossing these boundaries and making disciples who will also cross boundaries in faithful obedience to the Great Commission is essential to the church's mission. I have examined one aspect of the Great Commission with the hope that the contents will not only advance scholarship but will also encourage and equip the global church to faithfully obey the Lord by going to the ends of the earth.

Bibliography

4K Workbook. Project 4K, n.d. http://4kworldmap.com.
Acton, Lord. "Nationality." In *Mapping the Nation*, edited by Gopal Balakrishnan, 17–38. London: Verso, 1996.
"Ad Gentes." Second Ecumenical Council of the Vatican, 1965. http://www.vatican.va/archive/hist_councils/ii_vatican_council/documents/vat-ii_decree_19651207_ad-gentes_lt.html.
Agathemerus. "Geographiae Informatio." In *Geographi Graeci Minores*, edited by K. Müller, 2:471–87. Paris: Didot, 1861.
Aitken, Allen P. "שָׁמַע." In *NIDOTTE*, 4:175–81.
Akin, Daniel L, Benjamin L. Merkle, and George G. Robinson. *40 Questions about the Great Commission*. 40 Questions. Grand Rapids: Kregel Academic, 2020.
Aland, Barbara, Kurt Aland, Johannes Karavidopoulos, Carlo M. Martini, and Bruce Metzger, eds. *The Greek New Testament*. 5th ed. Stuttgart: Deutsche Bibelgesellschaft, 2014.
Alexander, Philip S. "Geography and the Bible (Early Jewish)." In *The Anchor Bible Dictionary*, edited by David Noel Freedman, 2:977–88. New York: Doubleday, 1992.
———. "Notes on the 'Imago Mundi' of the Book of Jubilees." *JJS* 33.1 (1982) 197–213.
———. "The Toponymy of the Targumim with Special Reference to the Table of Nations and the Boundaries of the Land of Israel." PhD diss., University of Oxford, 1974.
Alexander, T. Desmond. *Exodus*. Edited by David W. Baker and Gordon J. Wenham. ApOTC. London: Apollos, 2017.
Allen, Leslie C. *Ezekiel 1–19*. Edited by David A. Hubbard and Glenn W. Barker. WBC 28. Dallas: Word, 1994.
———. *Ezekiel 20–48*. Edited by David A. Hubbard and Glenn W. Barker. WBC 29. Waco, TX: Word, 1990.
———. "סבב." In *NIDOTTE*, 3:218–20.

Allen, Roland. *Missionary Methods: St. Paul's or Ours?* London: Robert Scott, 1912.

Allenbach, J., and Centre d'analyse et de documentation patristiques (France). *Biblia Patristica: Index des Citations et Allusions Bibliques dans la Littérature Patristique.* Paris: Editions du Centre national de la recherche scientifique, 1975. http://www.biblindex.mom.fr/.

Anderson, Benedict. *Imagined Communities: Reflections on the Origin and Spread of Nationalism.* Rev. ed. London: Verso, 2016.

Anthes, Rudolf. "Egyptian Theology in the Third Millennium B.C." *Journal of Near Eastern Studies* 18.3 (1959) 169–212.

Appian. *Roman History.* Translated by Horance White. LCL. London: Heinemann; New York: Macmillan, 1913.

———. *Roman History, Volume VI: Civil Wars, Book 5 and Fragments.* Edited by Brian McGing. Translated by Brian McGing. LCL. Cambridge, MA: Harvard University Press, 2020.

Aristotle. *History of Animals, Volume II: Books 4–6.* Translated by A. L. Peck. LCL. Cambridge, MA: Harvard University Press, 1970.

———. *History of Animals, Volume III: Books 7–10.* Translated by D. M. Balme. LCL. Cambridge, MA: Harvard University Press, 1991.

———. *On the Heavens.* Translated by W. K. C. Guthrie. LCL. Cambridge, MA: Harvard University Press, 1939.

———. *Politics.* Translated by H. Rackham. LCL. Cambridge, MA: Harvard University Press, 1932.

Armayor, O. Kimball. "Did Herodotus Ever Go to Egypt?" *Journal of the American Research Center in Egypt* 15 (1978) 59–73.

———. "Did Herodotus Ever Go to the Black Sea?" *Harvard Studies in Classical Philology* 82 (1978) 45–62.

Arnaud, Pascal. "Texte et Carte de Marcus Agrippa: Historiographie et Données Textuelles." *Geographia Antiqua* 16–17 (2007) 73–126.

Aune, David E. *Revelation 1–5.* WBC 52A. Dallas: Word, 1997.

———. *Revelation 6–16.* WBC 52B. Nashville: Thomas Nelson, 1998.

Backstrom, Peter C. "Burushaski." In *Sociological Survey of Northern Pakistan*, vol. 2, *Languages of Northern Areas*, 31–54. Islamabad, Pakistan: National Institute of Pakistan Studies and Summer Institute of Linguistics, 1992.

Bagehot, Walter. *Physics and Politics; or, Thoughts on the Application of the Principles of "Natural Selection" and "Inheritance" to Political Society.* New York: Appleton, 1904.

Bakker, Egbert J., Irene J. F. de Jong, and Hans van Wees, eds. *Brill's Companion to Herodotus.* Leiden: Brill, 2002.

Balakrishnan, Gopal. "The National Imagination." In *Mapping the Nation*, edited by Gopal Balakrishnan, 198–213. London: Verso, 1996.

Barrett, C. K. *A Critical and Exegetical Commentary on the Acts of the Apostles.* Vol. 1. Edinburgh: T. & T. Clark, 2004.

Barrett, David B., ed. *World Christian Encyclopedia: A Comparative Study of Churches and Religions in the Modern World, AD 1900–2000.* Nairobi: Oxford University Press, 1982.

Barrett, David B., George T. Kurian, and Todd M. Johnson, eds. *World Christian Encyclopedia: A Comparative Survey of Churches and Religions in the Modern World.* 2 vols. 2nd ed. Oxford: Oxford University Press, 2001.

Barth, Fredrik. "Introduction." In *Ethnic Groups and Boundaries: The Social Organization of Culture Difference*, edited by Fredrik Barth, 9–38. Long Grove, IL: Waveland, 1969.

Bauckham, Richard. *Bible and Mission: Christian Witness in a Postmodern World.* Milton Keynes: Paternoster; Grand Rapids: Baker Academic, 2003.

———. *The Climax of Prophecy*. Edinburgh: T. & T. Clark, 1993.

Bavinck, J. H. *An Introduction to the Science of Missions*. Translated by David Hugh Freeman. Grand Rapids: Baker, 1960.

Beale, G. K. *The Book of Revelation: A Commentary on the Greek Text.* NIGTC. Grand Rapids: Eerdmans, 1999.

———. *The Temple and the Church's Mission: A Biblical Theology of the Dwelling Place of God*. NSBT 17. Downers Grove, IL: InterVarsity, 2004.

Beekes, R. S. P., and Lucien van Beek. *Etymological Dictionary of Greek*. Leiden Indo-European Etymological Dictionary Series 10. Leiden: Brill, 2010.

Berggren, J. Lennart, and Alexander Jones. *Ptolemy's Geography: An Annotated Translation of the Theoretical Chapters*. Princeto, NJ: Princeton University Press, 2000.

Berghe, Pierre L. van den. "Sociobiology: A New Paradigm for the Behavioral Sciences?" *Social Science Quarterly* 59.2 (1978) 326–32.

Bevans, Stephen B. *Models of Contextual Theology*. Rev. ed. Maryknoll, NY: Orbis, 2002.

Bevans, Stephen B., and Jeffrey Gros. *Evangelization and Religious Freedom: Ad Gentes, Dignitatis Humanae*. Rediscovering Vatican II. New York: Paulist, 2009.

Bird, Michael F. *Romans*. The Story of God Bible Commentary. Grand Rapids: Zondervan, 2016.

Block, Daniel I. *The Book of Ezekiel: Chapters 1–27*. NICOT. Grand Rapids: Eerdmans, 1997.

———. *The Book of Ezekiel: Chapters 28–48*. NICOT. Grand Rapids: Eerdmans, 1998.

———. "The Foundations of National Identity: A Study in Ancient Northwest Semitic Perceptions." PhD diss., University of Liverpool, 1982.

———. *The Gods of the Nations: Studies in Ancient Near Eastern National Theology*. 2nd ed. Grand Rapids: Baker Academic, 2000.

Boatwright, Mary T. "Visualizing Empire in Imperial Rome." In *Aspects of Ancient Institutions and Geography: Studies in Honor of Richard J. A. Talbert*, edited by Lee L. Brice and Daniëlle Slootjes, 235–59. Leiden: Brill, 2015.

Bock, Darrell L. *Acts*. Edited by Robert W. Yarbrough and Robert H. Stein. Baker Exegetical Commentary on the New Testament. Grand Rapids: Baker Academic, 2007.

———. *Luke*, vol. 1, *1:1—9:50*. BECNT. Grand Rapids: Baker Academic, 1994.

———. *Mark*. New Cambridge Bible Commentary. Cambridge: Cambridge University Press, 2015.

Boehme, Ron. *The Fourth Wave: Taking Your Place in the New Era of Missions*. Seattle: YWAM, 2011.

Bovon, François. *Luke 1*. Translated by Christine M. Thomas. Hermeneia. Minneapolis: Fortress, 2002.

Bowers, William Paul. "Studies in Paul's Understanding of His Mission." PhD diss., University of Cambridge, UK, 1977.

Brechter, Suso. "Decree on the Church's Missionary Activity." In *Commentary on the Documents of Vatican II*, edited by Herbert Vorgrimler, translated by Hilda Graef, W. J. O'Hara, and Ronald Walls, 4:87–181. New York: Herder, 1969.

Breuilly, John. "Introduction." In *Nations and Nationalism*, by Ernest Gellner. 2nd ed. Ithaca, NY: Cornell University Press, 2006.

Brewer, Raymond Rush. "Revelation 4:6 and Translations Thereof." *JBL* 71.4 (1952) 227–31.

Briggs, Charles A., and Emilie Grace Briggs. *A Critical and Exegetical Commentary on the Book of Psalms*. Vol. 1. International Critical Commentary. New York: Scribner, 1906.

Brighton, Louis A. *Revelation*. Concordia Commentary. Saint Louis: Concordia, 1999.

Brodersen, Kai. "Mapping Pliny's World: The Achievement of Solinus." *Bulletin of the Institute of Classical Studies* 54.1 (2011) 63–88.

———. *Terra Cognita: Studien Zur Römischen Raumerfassung*. Spudasmata 59. Hildesheim: Olms, 1995.

Brody, Howard, and David S. Sobel. "A Systems View of Health and Disease." In *Ways of Health: Holistic Approaches to Ancient and Contemporary Medicine*, edited by David S. Sobel, 87–104. New York: Harcourt Brace Jovanovich, 1979.

Brown, Francis, S. R. Driver, and Charles A. Briggs. *A Hebrew and English Lexicon of the Old Testament*. Peabody, MA: Hendrickson, 1997.

Bruce, F. F. *The Book of Acts*. Rev ed. NICNT. Grand Rapids: Eerdmans, 1988.

———. *The Epistle to the Galatians: A Commentary on the Greek Text*. NIGTC. Grand Rapids: Eerdmans, 1982.

———. *Paul: Apostle of the Heart Set Free*. Carlisle: Paternoster, 1977.

———. "Paul and Jerusalem." *Tyndale Bulletin* 19 (1968) 3–25.

Brueggemann, Walter. "The Book of Jeremiah: Portrait of the Prophet." In *Interpreting the Prophets*, edited by James Luther Mays and Paul J. Achtemeier, 113–29. Philadelphia: Fortress, 1987.

———. *Genesis*. Edited by James Luther Mays. Atlanta: John Knox, 1982.

Bullinger, E. W. *Figures of Speech Used in the Bible: Explained and Illustrated*. Reprinted 1968. Grand Rapids: Baker, 1898.

Bultmann, Rudolph. *The Gospel of John: A Commentary*. Translated by G. R. Beasley-Murray, R. W. N. Hoare, and J. K. Riches. Philadelphia: Westminster, 1971.

Burchard, Christoph. "Fussnoten zum Neutestamentlichen Griechisch." *ZNW* 61.3–4 (1970) 157–71.

Burge, Gary M. *Jesus and the Land: The New Testament Challenge to "Holy Land" Theology*. Grand Rapids: Baker Academic, 2010.

Cadbury, Henry J. *The Book of Acts in History*. Eugene, OR: Wipf & Stock, 2004.

Caesar. *The Civil Wars*. LCL. London: Heinemann; New York: Macmillan, 1914.

———. *The Gallic War*. Translated by H. J. Edwards. LCL. London: Heinemann; New York: Putnam, 1919.

Carey, William. *An Enquiry into the Obligations of Christians to Use Means for the Conversion of the Heathens in Which the Religious State of the Different Nations of the World, the Success of Former Undertakings, and the Practicability of Further Undertakings Are Considered*. Leicester, 1792.

Carlson, Darren, and Elliot Clark. "The 3 Words That Changed Missions Strategy—and Why We Might Be Wrong." *The Gospel Coalition*, September 11, 2019. https://www.thegospelcoalition.org/article/misleading-words-missions-strategy-unreached-people-groups/.

Carpenter, Eugene. "כרת." In *NIDOTTE*, edited by Willem A. VanGemeren, 2:729–31. Grand Rapids: Zondervan, 1997.

Carrol R., M. Daniel. "פּוּץ." In *NIDOTTE*, edited by Willem A. VanGemeren, 3:585–89. Grand Rapids: Zondervan, 1997.
Carrol R., M. Daniel, and Mark D. Futano. "זָרָה." In *NIDOTTE*, edited by Willem A. VanGemeren, 1:1144–45. Grand Rapids: Zondervan, 1997.
Casson, Lionel. *The Periplus Maris Erythraei*. Princeton, NJ: Princeton University Press, 1989.
Catholic Church. "Relationis in Territoriis: De Relationibus Inter Ordinarios Locorm et Instituta Missionalia." *Enchiridion Della Chiesa Missionaria* 1 (1997) 630–45.
Chan, Alan Kam-Yau, Thomas B. Song, and Michael L. Brown. "רָפָא." In *NIDOTTE*, edited by Willem A. VanGemeren, 3:1162–73. Grand Rapids: Zondervan, 1997.
Chapple, Allan. "Paul and Illyricum." *RTR* 72.1 (2013) 20–35.
Charles, R. H., trans. *The Book of Jubilees or The Little Genesis*. London: A. & C. Black, 1902.
Charles, R. H., ed. *The Book of Jubilees or The Little Genesis: Notes*. London: A. & C. Black, 1902.
Chettri, Mona. *Ethnicity and Democracy in the Eastern Himalayan Borderland: Constructing Democracy*. Amsterdam: Amsterdam University Press, 2017.
Childs, Brevard S. *Isaiah: A Commentary*. Louisville: Westminster John Knox, 2001.
Christidis, A. F. *A History of Ancient Greek: From the Beginnings to Late Antiquity*. Cambridge: Cambridge University Press, 2007.
Clarke, E. J., trans. *Targum Pseudo-Jonathan: Deuteronomy: Translated with Notes*. Aramaic Bible 5B. Collegeville, MN: Liturgical, 1998.
Clarke, Katherine. *Between Geography and History: Hellenistic Constructions of the Roman World*. Oxford: Clarendon, 1999.
Clement of Alexandria. "The Stromata, or Miscellanies." In *Fathers of the Second Century: Hermas, Tatian, Athenagoras, Theophilus, and Clement of Alexandria (Entire)*, edited by Alexander Roberts, James Donaldson, and A. Cleveland Coxe, 299–568. Ante-Nicene Fathers 2. Buffalo, NY: Christian Literature Company, 1885.
Clements, Ronald E. "Isaiah 45:20–25." *Interpretation* 40.4 (1986) 392–97.
———. "גּוֹי." In *TDOT*, 9:426–30. Grand Rapids: Eerdmans, 1998.
Cobban, Alfred. *A History of Modern France*, vol. 1, *Old Régime and Revolution, 1715–1799*. Middlesex, UK: Penguin, 1976.
Collins, Adela Yarbro. *Mark: A Commentary*. Hermeneia. Minneapolis: Fortress, 2007.
Columella. *On Agriculture, Volume II: Books 5–9*. Translated by E. S. Forster and Edward H. Heffner. LCL. Cambridge, MA: Harvard University Press, 1954.
Condon, Ed. "Analysis: New Vatican Constitution to Centralize Power in State Secretariat." *Catholic News Agency*, July 2, 2019. https://www.catholicnewsagency.com/news/analysis-new-vatican-constitution-to-centralize-power-in-state-secretariat-15873.
Connolly, R. Hugh. *Didascalia Apostolorum: The Syriac Version Translated and Accompanied by the Verona Latin Fragments*. Oxford: Clarendon, 1929.
Connor, Walker. *Ethnonationalism: The Quest for Understanding*. Princeton, NY: Princeton University Press, 1994.
Connors, Catherine. "Eratosthenes, Strabo, and the Geographer's Gaze." *Pacific Coast Philology* 46.2 (2011) 139–52.
Cooke, G. A. *A Critical and Exegetical Commentary on the Book of Ezekiel*. International Critical Commentary. Edinburgh: T. & T. Clark, 1936.
Cooper, Sr., Lamar Eugene. *Ezekiel*. NAC. Nashville: Broadman & Holman, 1994.

Corduan, Winfried. *Neighboring Faiths: A Christian Introduction to World Religions.* 2nd ed. Downers Grove, IL: IVP Academic, 2012.

Coxill, H. Wakelin, and Kenneth Grubb, eds. *World Christian Handbook.* 4th ed. London: World Dominion, 1962.

———, eds. *World Christian Handbook.* 5th ed. London: World Dominion, 1968.

Craigie, Peter C. *The Book of Deuteronomy.* NICOT. Grand Rapids: Eerdmans, 1976.

Cranfield, C. E. B. *The Epistle to the Romans.* Vol. 1. International Critical and Exegetical Commentary. Edinburgh: T. & T. Clark, 1980.

Crawley, Winston. *Global Mission: A Story to Tell: An Interpretation of Southern Baptist Foreign Missions.* Nashville: Broadman, 1985.

Crider, Caleb. "Mapping." In *Tradecraft or the Church on Mission*, by Caleb Crider, Larry McCrary, Rodney Calfee, and Wade Stephens, 51–66. Portland, OR: Urban Loft, 2013.

Crook, J. A. "Augustus: Power, Authority, Achievement." In *The Cambridge Ancient History*, edited by Alan Bowman, Edward Champlin, and Andrew Lintott, 10:113–97. 2nd ed. Cambridge: Cambridge University Press, 1996.

Crüsemann, Frank. "Die Eigenständigkeit der Urgeschichte: Ein Beitrag zur Diskussion um den »Jahwisten«." In *Die Botschaft und die Boten: Festschrift für Hans Walter Wolff Zum 70. Geburtstag*, edited by Jörg Jeremias and Lothar Perlitt, 11–29. Neukirchen-Vluyn: Neukirchener, 1981.

"Dallas International University Fall 2020–Spring 2021 Academic Catalog." https://www.diu.edu/documents/diu-current-cat-2021.pdf.

Danker, Frederick William, Walter Bauer, W. F. Arndt, and F. W. Gingrich, eds. "'Έθνος.'" In *A Greek-English Lexicon of the New Testament and Other Early Christian Literature*, 276. 3rd ed. Chicago: University of Chicago Press, 2000.

Datema, Dave. "Defining 'Unreached': A Short History." *IJFM* 33.2 (2016) 45–71.

———. "The People Group Paradigm in 2020: Relevant for Today, Relic from the Past or Something in Between?" Webinar, Missio Nexus, January 9, 2020. https://missionexus.org/the-people-group-paradigm-in-2020/.

Dayton, Edward R. "Reaching the Unreached Peoples: Guidelines and Definitions for Those Concerned with World Evangelization." *IJFM* 2.1 (1985) 31–38.

Delitzsch, Franz. *Isaiah.* Translated by James Martin. Commentary on the Old Testament 7. Peabody, MA: Hendrickson, 1996

———. *A New Commentary on Genesis.* Translated by Sophia Taylor. Vol. 1. Minneapolis: Klock, 1978.

Dempster, Stephen G. *Dominion and Dynasty: A Theology of the Hebrew Bible.* Downers Grove, IL: InterVarsity, 2003.

Dever, Mark. "The Church." In *A Theology for the Church*, edited by Daniel L. Akin, 603–68. Rev. ed. Nashville: Broadman & Holman, 2014.

Di Berardino, Angelo. "The Historical Geography of Asia Minor at the Time of Paul and Thecla: The Roman Provinces and the Means of Communication." *Augustinianum* 57.2 (2017) 341–70.

Dibelius, Martin. *Studies in the Acts of the Apostles.* Edited by Heinrich Greeven. London: SCM, 1956.

Dietrich, Manfried, Oswald Loretz, and Joaquin Sanmartin, eds. *The Cuneiform Alphabetic Texts from Ugarit, Ras Ibn Hani and Other Places.* 2nd ed. Münster: Ugarit, 1995.

Dilke, O. A. W. *Greek and Roman Maps.* Ithaca, NY: Cornell University Press, 1985.

Dillard, Raymond B. *2 Chronicles.* WBC 15. Waco, TX: Word, 1987.

Donaldson, Terence L. "'The Field God Has Assigned': Geography and Mission in Paul." In *Religious Rivalries in the Early Roman Empire and the Rise of Christianity*, edited by Leif E. Vaage, 109–37. Studies in Christianity and Judaism /Études sur le Christianisme et le Judaïsmejudaisme. Waterloo, ON: Wilfrid Laurier University Press, 2006.

———. "Nations." In *The New Interpreter's Dictionary of the Bible*, edited by Katharine Doob Sakenfeld. 4:231–38. Nashville: Abingdon, 2009.

Dreytza, Manfred. "יָד." In *NIDOTTE*, edited by Willem A. VanGemeren, 2:402–5. Grand Rapids: Zondervan, 1997.

Dueck, Daniela. "The Date and Method of Composition of Strabo's 'Geography.'" *Hermes* 127.4 (1999) 467–78.

———. *Strabo of Amasia: A Greek Man of Letters in Augustan Rome*. London: Routledge, 2000.

Dunn, James D. G. *Romans 1–8*. WBC 38A. Dallas: Word, 1988.

Dunstan, William E. *Ancient Rome*. Lanham, MD: Rowman and Littlefield, 2011.

Edwards, James. *The Gospel According to Luke*. Pillar New Testament Commentary. Grand Rapids: Eerdmans, 2015.

———. *The Gospel According to Mark*. Pillar New Testament Commentary. Grand Rapids, Leicester: Eerdmans, Apollos, 2001.

Eichrodt, Walther. *Ezekiel: A Commentary*. Translated by Cosslett Quin. Philadelphia: Westminster, 1970.

———. *Theology of the Old Testament*. Translated by J. A. Baker. Vol. 2. Philadelphia: Westminster, 1967.

Elvers, Karl-Ludwig. "Strabo." In *BNP*, edited by Hubert Cancik, Helmuth Schneider, and Christine F. Salazar, 13:866–69. Leiden: Brill, 2008.

Engel, James F. "The Great Commission Advertising Campaign: Misuse of the Mass Media in World Evangelization." *Transformation* 9.4 (1992) 21–23.

Engel, James F., and William A. Dyrness. *Changing the Mind of Missions: Where Have We Gone Wrong?* Downers Grove, IL: InterVarsity, 2000.

Eriksen, Thomas Hylland. *Small Places, Large Issues: An Introduction to Cultural and Social Anthropology*. 4th ed. London: Pluto, 2015.

Escobar, Samuel. "Managerial Missiology." In *Dictionary of Mission Theology: Evangelical Foundations*. Downers Grove, IL: InterVarsity, 2007.

———. "A Movement Divided: Three Approaches to World Evangelization Stand in Tension with One Another." *Transformation* 8.4 (1991) 7–13.

———. *A Time for Mission*. Carlisle: Langham Global Library, 2013.

Estep, William R. *Whole Gospel—Whole World: The Foreign Mission Board of the Southern Baptist Convention 1845–1995*. Nashville: Broadman & Holman, 1994.

Eusebius. *Eusebi Chronicorum Liber Prior*. Edited by Alfred Schoene. Berlin: Weidmann, 1875.

Evans, Craig A. "Paul and the Pagans." In *Paul: Jew, Greek, and Roman*, edited by Stanley E. Porter, Pauline Studies 5, 117–39. Leiden: Brill, 2008.

Feldman, Louis H. "'Hellenizations' in Josephus' Portrayal of Man's Decline." In *Religions in Antiquity: Essays in Memory of Erwin Ramsdell Goodenough*, edited by Jacob Neusner, 336–53. Eugene, OR: Wipf & Stock, 2004.

Filson, Floyd V. "The Journey Motif in Luke-Acts." In *Apostolic History and the Gospel: Biblical and Historical Essays Presented to F. F. Bruce on His 60th Birthday*, edited by W. Ward Gasque and Ralph P. Martin, 68–77. Exeter: Paternoster, 1970.

Fitzmyer, Joseph A. "Languages of Palestine in the First Century AD." *Catholic Biblical Quarterly* 32.4 (1970) 501–31.

———. *Romans: A New Translation with Introduction and Commentary*. AB 33. New York: Doubleday, 1993.

Flemming, Dean. *Contextualization in the New Testament: Patterns for Theology and Mission*. Downers Grove, IL: IVP Academic, 2005.

Forbes, Greg W. *1 Peter*. Edited by Andreas J. Köstenberger and Robert W. Yarbrough. Exegetical Guide to the Greek New Testament. Nashville: B&H Academic, 2014.

France, R. T. *The Gospel of Mark: A Commentary on the Greek Text*. NIGTC. Grand Rapids: Eerdmans, 2002.

Fredriksen, Paula. *Paul: The Pagans' Apostle*. New Haven, CT: Yale University Press, 2017.

"Frequently Asked Questions." 2020. https://peoplegroups.org/Understand.aspx.

Frontinus. *The Strategems and the Aquaducts of Rome*. Translated by Charles E. Bennett. LCL. London: Heinemann; New York: Putnam, 1925.

Garcia-López, F. "סבב." In *TDOT*, 10:126–38. Grand Rapids: Eerdmans, 1999.

Gardner, Jane F. "The 'Gallic Menace' in Caesar's Propaganda." *Greece and Rome* 30.2 (1983) 181–89.

Geertz, Clifford. "'From the Native's Point of View': On the Nature of Anthropological Understanding." *Bulletin of the American Academy of Arts and Sciences* 28.1 (1974) 26–45.

———. *The Interpretation of Cultures: Selected Essays*. New York: Basic, 1973.

Gellner, Ernest. *Nations and Nationalism*. 2nd ed. Ithaca, NY: Cornell University Press, 2006.

Geus, Klaus. "Claudius Ptolemy on Egypt and East Africa." In *The Ptolemies, the Sea, and the Nile: Studies in Waterborne Power*, edited by Kostas Buraselis, Mary Stefanou, and Dorothy J. Thompson, 218–31. Cambridge: Cambridge University Press, 2013.

Geyser, Albert S. "Un Essai d'Explication de Rom 15:19." *NTS* 6.2 (1960) 156–59.

"Global Statistics." 2020. https://joshuaproject.net/people_groups/statistics.

Goldsworthy, Adrian. "'Instinctive Genius': The Depiction of Caesar the General." In *Julius Caesar as Artful Reporter: The War Commentaries as Political Instruments*, edited by Kathryn Welch and Anton Powell, 193–220. London: Duckworth, 1998.

Gould, John P. A. "Herodotus." In *The Oxford Classical Dictionary*, edited by Simon Hornblower and Antony Spawforth, 696–98. 3rd ed. Oxford: Oxford University Press, 1996.

Grant, Robert M. "Early Christian Geography." *Vigiliae Christianae* 46.2 (1992) 105–11.

Griffin, Miriam, "Nerva to Hadrian." In *The Cambridge Ancient History: Volume XI: The High Empire, A.D. 70–192*, edited by Alan K. Bowman, Peter Garnsey, and Dominic Rathbone, 84–131. Cambridge: Cambridge University, 2000.

Grisanti, Michael A. "אֲדָמָה." In *NIDOTTE*, 1:269–74.

Grubb, Kenneth George, and E. J. Bingle, eds. *World Christian Handbook*. London: World Dominion, 1949.

———, eds. *World Christian Handbook*. 2nd ed. London: World Dominion, 1952.

———, eds. *World Christian Handbook*. 3rd ed. London: World Dominion, 1957.

Grudem, Wayne A. *1 Peter*. Tyndale New Testament Commentary. Downers Grove, IL: IVP Academic, 1988.

Guelich, Robert A. *Mark 1–8:26*. WBC 34A. Dallas: Word, 1989.

Hahn, Ferdinand. *Mission in the New Testament*. Studies in Biblical Theology 47. Naperville, IL: Allenson, 1965.

Hamilton, Victor P. "אָדָם." In *NIDOTTE*, 1:262–66.

Harley, J. B. "The Map and the Development of the History of Cartography." In *The History of Cartography*, edited by J. B. Harley and David Woodward, 1:1–42. Chicago: University of Chicago Press, 1987.

Harley, J. B., David Woodward, and Germaine Aujac. "The Foundations of Theoretical Cartography in Archaic and Classical Greece." In *The History of Cartography*, 1:130–47. Chicago: University of Chicago Press, 1987.

———. "The Growth of an Empirical Cartography in Hellenistic Greece." In *The History of Cartography*, 1:148–60. Chicago: University of Chicago Press, 1987.

Harrill, J. Albert. *Paul the Apostle: His Life and Legacy in Their Roman Context*. Cambridge: Cambridge University Press, 2012.

Hart, George. *The Routledge Dictionary of Egyptian Gods and Goddesses*. 2nd ed. London: Routledge, 2005.

Hastings, Adrian. *The Construction of Nationhood: Ethnicity, Religion and Nationalism*. Cambridge: Cambridge University Press, 1997.

Hawkins, J. D. "The Neo-Hittite States in Syria and Anatolia." In *The Cambridge Ancient History: Volume III, Part I: The Prehistory of the Balkans; and the Middle East and the Aegean World, Tenth to Eighth Centuries B.C.*, edited by John Boardman, I. E. S. Edwards, N. G. L. Hammond, and E. Sollberger, 2nd ed, 372–441. Cambridge: Cambridge University Press, 1982.

Hays, J. Daniel. *From Every People and Nation: A Biblical Theology of Race*. NSBT 14. Downers Grove, IL: InterVarsity, 2003.

Headland, Thomas N. "Introduction: A Dialogue between Kenneth Pike and Marvin Harris on Emics and Etics." In *Emics and Etics: The Insider/Outsider Debate*, edited by Thomas N. Headland, Kenneth L. Pike, and Marvin Harris, 13–27. Newbury Park, CA: Sage, 1990.

Heidegger, Martin. *Hebel der Hausfreund*. Pfullingen: Neske, 1957.

Helweg, Arthur W. "The Indian Diaspora: Influence on International Relations." In *Modern Diasporas in International Politics*, edited by Gabriel Sheffer, 117–29. London: Croom Helm, 1986.

Hengel, Martin. *Acts and the History of Earliest Christianity*. 1st Fortress Press ed. Minneapolis: Fortress, 1980.

———. "Der Vorchristliche Paulus." In *Paulus und das Antike Judentum*, edited by Martin Hengel and Ulrich Heckel, 177–293. WUNT 58. Tübingen: Mohr Siebeck, 1991.

Hengel, Martin, and Anna Maria Schwemer. *Paul between Damascus and Antioch: The Unknown Years*. Louisville: Westminster John Knox, 1997.

Herodotus. *The History of Herodotus*. Translated by George Rawlinson. Chicago: University of Chicago Press, 1952.

Hiebert, Paul G. *Anthropological Insights for Missionaries*. Grand Rapids: Baker Academic, 1985.

———. *The Gospel in Human Contexts: Anthropological Explorations for Contemporary Missions*. Grand Rapids: Baker Academic, 2009.

———. "The Social Sciences and Missions: Applying the Message." In *Missiology and the Social Sciences*, edited by Edward Rommen and Gary Corwin, 184–213. Evangelical Missiological Society Series 4 Pasadena, CA: William Carey Library, 1996.

Hild, Friedrich. "Tarsus." In *BNP*, 14:155–56.
Hill, Andrew E. "אָפֵס." In *NIDOTTE*, 1:481–82.
Hobbs, T. R. *2 Kings*. WBC 13. Waco, TX: Word, 1985.
Hobsbawm, E. J. *Nations and Nationalism since 1780: Programme, Myth, Reality*. 2nd ed. Cambridge: Cambridge University Press, 1990.
Homer. *Iliad, Volume II: Books 13–24*. Translated by A. T. Murray and William F. Wyatt. LCL. Cambridge, MA: Harvard University Press, 1925.
———. *Odyssey*. Translated by A. T. Murray and George E. Dimock. 2 vols. LCL. Cambridge, MA: Harvard University Press, 1919.
Hummel, Horace D. *Ezekiel 1–20*. Saint Louis: Concordia, 2005.
Hunt, Arthur. "2000 Years of Map Making." *Geography* 85.1 (2000) 3–14.
IMB (International Mission Board). *Foundations*. Richmond, VA: International Mission Board of the Southern Baptist Convention, 2021.
IMB (International Mission Board) Global Research. *Global Status of Evangelical Christianity: Listing of People Groups*. International Mission Board of the Southern Baptist Convention, October 2021. https://grd.imb.org/wp-content/uploads/documents/gsec-files/2021-10_GSEC_Listing_of_People_Groups.xls.
Jacob, Christian. "Toward a Cultural History of Cartography." *Imago Mundi* 48 (1996) 191–98.
Jacoby, Felix. *Die Fragmente der Griechiscen Historiker*. Vol. 1. Leiden: Brill, 1957.
Jaffarian, E Michael. "The *World Christian Encyclopedia*, First (1982) and Second (Forthcoming) Editions." *Missiology* 27.1 (1999) 31–34.
James, Edward Boucher. "Illyricum." In *Dictionary of Greek and Roman Geography*, edited by William Smith, 2:35–39. Boston: Little, Brown, 1857.
Japhet, Sara. *I & II Chronicles: A Commentary*. Old Testament Library. Louisville: Westminster John Knox, 1993.
Jenkins, Orville Boyd. "What Is a People Group?" 2004. https://grd.imb.org/people-group/.
Jewett, Robert. *Romans: A Commentary*. Hermeneia. Minneapolis: Fortress, 2007.
Johnson, Paul. *A History of the Jews*. New York: Harper, 1987.
Johnson, Todd M., and Gina A. Zurlo. *World Christian Encyclopedia*. 3rd ed. Edinburgh: Edinburgh University, 2020.
Johnstone, William. *1 and 2 Chronicles*, vol. 1, *1 Chronicles 1—2 Chronicles 9: Israel's Place among the Nations*. Journal for the Study of the Old Testament Supplement Series 253. Sheffield: Sheffield Academic, 1997.
Jones, A. H. M. *The Later Roman Empire 284–602: A Social Economic and Administrative Survey*. Vol. 2. Norman, OK: University of Oklahoma Press, 1964.
Jordan, James B. *Christendom and the Nations*. West Monore, LA: Theopolis, 2018.
"Joshua Project." https://joshuaproject.net/about/details.
Kaiser, Walter C., Jr. "Exodus." In *Genesis–Leviticus*, edited by Tremper Longman III and David E. Garland, 333–562. EBC. Rev. ed .Grand Rapids: Zondervan, 2008.
Kaiser, Otto. *Isaiah 1–12: A Commentary*. Translated by John Bowden. 2nd ed. Philadelphia: Westminster, 1983.
———. *Isaiah 13–39: A Commentary*. Translated by R. A. Wilson. Philadelphia: Westminster, 1974.
Keener, Craig S. *Acts: An Exegetical Commentary*. Vol. 2. Grand Rapids: Baker Academic, 2014.
———. *Acts: An Exegetical Commentary*. Vol. 3. Grand Rapids: Baker Academic, 2014.

Keil, C. F. *The Pentateuch*. Peabody, MA: Hendrickson, 1996.
Kim, Hyun Chul Paul. *Reading Isaiah: A Literary and Theological Commentary*. Macon, GA: Smyth & Helwys, 2016.
Kissinger, Henry. *World Order*. New York: Penguin, 2014.
Klein, George L., and Gordon H. Matties. "כָּנָף." In *NIDOTTE*, 2:670–71
Knox, John. "Romans 15:14–33 and Paul's Conception of His Apostolic Mission." *JBL* 83.1 (1964) 1–11.
Koehler, Ludwid, and Walter Baumgartner. *The Hebrew and Aramaic Lexicon of the Old Testament*. Edited by Walter Baumgartner and Johann Jakob Stamm. Translated by M. E. J. Richardson. Rev. ed. Leiden: Brill, 1994.
Koelsch, William A. "Squinting Back at Strabo." *Geographical Review* 94.4 (2004) 502–18.
Köstenberger, Andreas J., and T. Desmond Alexander. *Salvation to the Ends of the Earth: A Biblical Theology of Mission*. 2nd ed. NSBT 11. Downers Grove, IL: InterVarsity, 2020.
Kraft, Charles H. *Christianity in Culture: A Study in Biblical Theologizing in Cross-Cultural Perspective*. Rev. ed. Maryknoll, NY: Orbis, 2005.
Kreitzer, Mark R. *The Concept of Ethnicity in the Bible: A Theological Analysis*. Lewiston, NY: Edwin Mellen, 2008.
Kruse, Colin G. *Paul's Letter to the Romans*. Pillar New Testament Commentary. Grand Rapids: Eerdmans, 2012.
Kugel, James L. *A Walk Through Jubilees: Studies in the Book of Jubilees and the World of Its Creation*. Supplements to the Journal for the Study of Judaism 156. Leiden: Brill, 2012.
Latourette, Kenneth Scott. *A History of the Expansion of Christianity*, vol. 2, *The Thousand Years of Uncertainty: A.D. 500–A.D. 1500*. New York: Harper, 1938.
Lausanne Movement. "The Pasadena Consultation: Homogeneous Unit Principle." LOP 1. June 2, 1977. https://www.lausanne.org/content/lop/lop-1.
Liddell, Henry George, Robert Scott, and Henry Stuart Jones. *A Greek-English Lexicon*. Revised and supplemented. Oxford: Clarendon, 1996.
Lindheim, Sara H. "Pomona's Pomarium: The 'Mapping Impulse' in Metamorphoses 14 (and 9)." *Transactions of the American Philological Association (1974–)* 140.1 (2010) 163–94.
Lipiński, E. "נָחַל." In *TDOT*, 9:319–35.
Longenecker, Richard N. *The Epistle of the Romans: A Commentary on the Greek Text*. NIGTC. Grand Rapids: Eerdmans, 2016.
Lucan. *The Civil War: Books I–X (Pharsalia)*. Translated by J. D. Duff. LCL. London: Heinemann; Cambridge, MA: Harvard University Press, 1962.
Lynch, Kevin. *The Image of the City*. Cambridge, MA: MIT Press, 1960.
Maass, Fritz. "אָדָם." In *TDOT*, 1:75–87.
Mabie, Frederick J. "1 and 2 Chronicles." In *1 Chronicles–Job*, 23–336. EBC. Rev. ed. Grand Rapids: Zondervan, 2010.
———. "2 Chronicles." In *Zondervan Illustrated Bible Backgrounds Commentary: Volume 3*, edited by John H. Walton, 287–393. Grand Rapids: Zondervan, 2009.
———. "Geographical Extent of Israel." In *Dictionary of the Old Testament: Historical Books*, edited by Bill T. Arnold and H. G. M. Williamson, 316–28. Downers Grove, IL: IVP Academic, 2005.
MacMahon, Michael K. C. "Phonetic Notation." In *The World's Writing Systems*, edited by Peter T. Daniels and William Bright, 821–46. Oxford: Oxford University Press, 1996.

Magda, Ksenija. *Paul's Territoriality and Mission Strategy: Searching for the Geographical Awareness Paradigm behind Romans*. WUNT 266. Tübingen: Mohr Siebeck, 2009.

Marcus, Joel. *Mark 1–8: A New Translation with Introduction and Commentary*. AB. New York: Doubleday, 2000.

Marlett, Stephen. *An Introduction to Phonological Analysis*. Unpublished, 2001.

Marshall, I. Howard. "Acts." In *Commentary on the New Testament Use of the Old Testament*, edited by G. K. Beale and D. A. Carson, 513–606. Grand Rapids: Baker Academic, 2007.

———. *The Gospel of Luke*. NIGTC. Grand Rapids: Eerdmans, 1978.

Martín, Inés San. "New Vatican Document to Put Evangelization ahead of Doctrine." *Crux*, April 22, 2019. https://cruxnow.com/vatican/2019/04/new-vatican-document-to-put-evangelization-ahead-of-doctrine/.

Martin, Ralph. "Ad Gentes." In *The Reception of Vatican II*, edited by Matthew L. Lamb and Matthew Levering, 266–91. Oxford: Oxford University Press, 2017.

Masʿūdī, ʿAlī ibn al-Ḥusayn al-. *Al-Masʿūdī's Kitāb al-Tanbīh Wa l-Išrāf = Kitab al-Tanbih Wa-al-Išraf*. Edited by M. J. de Goeje. Leiden: Brill, 2014.

Matejowsky, Ty. "The Privatization of Public Plazas in the Philippines: Three Cases from Pangasinan." *Philippine Quarterly of Culture and Society* 28.3 (2000) 263–300.

Matties, Gordon H. "גבל." In *NIDOTTE*, 1:802–4.

Matties, Gordon H., and Tremper Longman III. "קָצָה." In *NIDOTTE*, 3:959–60.

Mazar, Benjamin. *The Early Biblical Period: Historical Studies*. Edited by Shmuel Ahituv and Baruch A. Levine. Jerusalem: Israel Exploraition Society, 1986.

McGavran, Donald A. *The Bridges of God: A Study in the Strategy of Missions*. Eugene, OR: Wipf & Stock, 2005.

———. *Ethnic Realities and the Church: Lessons from India*. Pasadena, CA: William Carey Library, 1979.

———. *Understanding Church Growth*. Grand Rapids: Eerdmans, 1970.

———. *Understanding Church Growth*. Edited by C. Peter Wagner. 3rd ed. Grand Rapids: Eerdmans, 1990.

McLeod, John. *The History of India*. Westport, CT: Greenwood, 2002.

McRay, John. *Archaeology and the New Testament*. Grand Rapids: Baker Academic, 1991.

Menon, Jisha. *The Performance of Nationalism: India, Pakistan, and the Memory of Partition*. Cambridge: Cambridge University Press, 2013.

Merkle, Benjamin L. "Could Jesus Return at Any Moment?: Rethinking the Imminence of the Second Coming." *Trinity Journal* 26.2 (2005) 279–92.

Merrill, Eugene H. "יָצָא." In *NIDOTTE*, 2:498–500.

Mill, John Stuart. *Utilitarianism, Liberty and Representative Government*. London: J. M. Dent, 1910.

Mishra, Sudesh. *Diaspora Criticism*. Edinburgh: Edinburgh University Press, 2006.

Moffitt, John F. "Medieval Mappaemundi and Ptolemy's Chorographia." *Gesta* 32.1 (1993) 59–68.

Mommsen, Theodor. *C. Iulii Solini: Collectanea Rerum Memorabilium*. 2nd ed. Berlin: Berolinum, 1895.

Montanari, Franco. *The Brill Dictionary of Ancient Greek*. Leiden: Brill, 2015.

Moo, Douglas J. *The Epistle to the Romans*. 2nd ed. NICNT. Grand Rapids: Eerdmans, 2018.

Morris, Leon. *The Epistle to the Romans*. Leicester: Apollos, 1988.

Mostowlansky, Till, and Andrea Rota. "A Matter of Perspective? Disentangling the Emic-Etic Debate in the Scientific Study of Religions." *Method and Theory in the Study of Religion* 28.4/5, special issue (2016) 317–36.

Motyer, J. Alec. *The Prophecy of Isaiah: An Introduction and Commentary.* Downers Grove, IL: IVP Academic, 1993.

Mounce, Robert H. *The Book of Revelation.* NICOT. Grand Rapids: Eerdmans, 1977.

Moya, Raphael. "The New Code of Canon Law and the Missions." *East Asian Pastoral Institute* 22.2 (1985) 164–79.

Murphy, Trevor. *Pliny the Elder's Natural History: The Empire in the Encyclopedia.* Oxford: Oxford University Press, 2004.

Murphy-O'Connor, Jerome. *Paul: A Critical Life.* Oxford: Oxford University Press, 1997.

―――. *St. Paul's Corinth: Texts and Archaeology.* 3rd ed. Collegeville, MN: Liturgical, 2002.

"The Nanning Covenant." August 30, 2002. https://www.ywam.org/about-us/nanning-covenant/.

Nel, Philip J. "מֶלֶךְ." In *NIDOTTE*, 2:956–65.

Nicolet, Claude. *Space, Geography, and Politics in the Early Roman Empire.* Ann Arbor: University of Michigan Press, 1991.

"Nostra Aetate." Second Ecumenical Council of the Vatican, 1965. http://www.vatican.va/archive/hist_councils/ii_vatican_council/documents/vat-ii_decl_19651028_nostra-aetate_lt.html.

Olivier, J. P. J. "סָלַח." In *NIDOTTE*, 3:259–64.

Olley, John W. *Ezekiel: A Commentary Based on Iezekiēl in Codex Vaticanus.* Leiden: Brill, 2009.

Olshausen, Eckart. *Einführung in die Historische Geographie der Alten Welt.* Darmstadt: Wissenschaftliche Buchgesellschaft, 1991.

Oppenheimer, Aharon. *The 'Am Ha-Aretz: A Study in the Social History of the Jewish People in the Hellenistic-Roman Period.* Translated by I. H. Levine. Leiden: Brill, 1977.

Osborne, Grant R. *Acts: Verse by Verse.* Osborn New Testament Commentaries. Bellingham, WA: Lexham, 2019.

Osborne, William. "Nations, Table of." In *Dictionary of the Old Testament: Pentateuch*, edited by T. Desmond Alexander and David W. Baker, 588–96. Downers Grove, IL: InterVarsity, 2003.

Oswalt, John N. *The Book of Isaiah: Chapters 1–39.* NICOT. Grand Rapids: Eerdmans, 1986.

―――. *The Book of Isaiah: Chapters 40–66.* NICOT. Grand Rapids: Eerdmans, 1998.

Ottosson, Magnus. "אֶרֶץ." In *TDOT*, 1:388–405.

―――. "גְּבוּל." In *TDOT*, 2:361–66.

Paassen, Christiaan van. *The Classical Tradition of Geography.* Groningen: J. B. Wolters, 1957.

Parks, S. Kent. "What Happened to People Group Thinking?". https://joshuaproject.net/resources/articles/what_happened_to_people_group_thinking.

Paul, Shalom M. *Isaiah 40–66: Translation and Commentary.* Eerdmans Critical Commentary. Grand Rapids: Eerdmans, 2012.

"People Groups." http://www.peoplegroups.org.

Peters, George. *A Biblical Theology of Missions.* Chicago: Moody, 1972.

Peterson, David G. *The Acts of the Apostles*. Grand Rapids: Eerdmans, 2009.
Philo. "De Praemiis et Poenis et de Exsecrationibus." In *Philonis Alexandrini Opera Quae Supersunt*, edited by L. Cohn, 5:336–76. Berlin: Reimer, 1906.
———. "Legatio Ad Gaium." In *Philonis Alexandrini Opera Quae Supersunt*, edited by L. Cohn and S. Reiter, 6:155–223. Berlin: Reimer, 1915.
Pike, Kenneth L. *Language in Relation to a Unified Theory of the Structure of Human Behavior*. 2nd rev. ed. The Hague: Mouton, 1967.
———. "On the Emics and Etics of Pike and Harris." In *Emics and Etics: The Insider/Outsider Debate*, edited by Thomas N. Headland, Kenneth L. Pike, and Marvin Harris, 28–47. Newbury Park, CA: Sage, 1990.
Piper, John. *Let the Nations Be Glad: The Supremacy of God in Missions*. 3rd ed. Grand Rapids: Baker Academic, 2010.
Platt, David. "Rethinking Unreached People Groups: Why Place Still Matters in Global Missions." *Desiring God*, February 13, 2019. https://www.desiringgod.org/articles/rethinking-unreached-peoples.
Pliny. *Natural History*. Translated by H. Rackham. 10 vols. LCL. London: Heinemann; Cambrdge, MA: Harvard University Press, 1961.
Plöger, Josef. "אֲדָמָה." In *TDNT*, 1:88–98.
Podossinov, Alexander V. "Introduction." In *The Periphery of the Classical World in Ancient Geography and Cartography*, 1–5. Colloquia Antiqua 12. Leuven: Peeters, 2014.
Pogorzelski, Randall J. "Orbis Romanus: Lucan and the Limits of the Roman World." *Transactions of the American Philological Association (1974–)* 141.1 (2011) 143–70.
Pompeo, Flavia. "Dative." In *Encyclopedia of Ancient Greek Language and Linguistics*, edited by Georgios K. Giannakis, 1:414–17. Leiden: Brill, 2014.
Porter, Stanley E. *The Apostle Paul: His Life, Thought, and Letters*. Grand Rapids: Eerdmans, 2016.
———. "Did Paul Speak Latin?" In *Paul: Jew, Greek, and Roman*, edited by Stanley E. Porter, 289–308. Pauline Studies 5. Leiden: Brill, 2008.
———. "Paul as Jew, Greek, and Roman: An Introduction." In *Paul: Jew, Greek, and Roman*, edited by Stanley E. Porter, 1–6. Pauline Studies 5. Leiden: Brill, 2008.
Pratt, Zane. "Here's What We Mean by Unreached Peoples and Places." International Mission Board, November 22, 2016. https://www.imb.org/2016/11/22/what-do-we-mean-by-unreached-peoples-and-places/.
Prontera, Francesco. "Centre et Périphérie dans les Mappemondes Grecques." In *The Periphery of the Classical World in Ancient Geography and Cartography*, 13–29. Colloquia Antiqua 12. Leuven: Peeters, 2014.
———. "Timosthenes and Eratosthenes: Sea Routes and Hellenistic Geography." In *The Ptolemies, the Sea, and the Nile: Studies in Waterborne Power*, edited by Kostas Buraselis, Mary Stefanou, and Dorothy J. Thompson, 207–17. Cambridge: Cambridge University Press, 2013.
Propp, William H. *Exodus 1–18*. AB2. New York: Doubleday, 1999.
Pseudo-Dionysius. *On the Heavenly Hierarchy*. n.d.
Purcell, Nicholas. "Geography." In *The Oxford Classical Dictionary*, edited by Simon Horblower and Antony Spawforth, 632–33. 3rd ed. Oxford: Oxford University Press, 1996.
———. "Strabo." In *The Oxford Classical Dictionary*, edited by Simon Hornblower and Antony Spawforth, 1447. 3rd ed. Oxford: Oxford University Press, 1996.

Quinton, A. "Romanticism, Philosophical." In *The Oxford Companion to Philosophy*, edited by Ted Honderich. Oxford: Oxford University Press, 2005.
Rad, Gerhard von. *Genesis: A Commentary*. Rev. ed. Louisville: Westminster John Knox, 1961.
Rajak, Tessa. *Translation and Survival: The Greek Bible of the Ancient Jewish Diaspora*. Oxford: Oxford University Press, 2009.
Rankin, Jerry A. "International Mission Board Report." In *Annual of the 1998 Southern Baptist Convention*, 169–215. Nashville: Executive Committee of the Southern Baptist Convention, 1998.
———. "International Mission Board Report." In *Annual of the 2010 Southern Baptist Convention*, 174–78. Nashville: Executive Committee of the Southern Baptist Convention, 2010.
———. "Organizing to Reach the Diaspora: A Case Study of the International Mission Board, SBC; Changing Its Overseas Structure from Geographic Components to Global Affinity Groups." In *Diaspora Missiology: Reflections on Reaching the Scattered Peoples of the World*, edited by Michael Pocock and Enoch Wan, 199–213. Evangelical Missiological Society Series 23. Pasadena, CA: William Carey Library, 2015.
Renan, Ernest. *Qu'est-Ce Qu'Une Nation?* Translated by Ethan Rundell. Paris: Presses-Pocket, 1992.
Rengstorf, Karl Heinrich. "Ἀποστέλλω (Πέμπω)." In *TDNT*, 1:398–406. Grand Rapids: Eerdmans, 1964.
Richard, H. L. "Some Observations on William Carey's Bible Translations." *International Bulletin of Mission Research* 42.3 (2018) 241–50.
Robb, John D. *Focus! The Power of People Group Thinking: A Practical Manual for Planning Effective Strategies to Reach the Unreached*. Monrovia, CA: MARC, 1994.
Robinson, George. "Grounding Disciple-Making in God's Creation Order: Filling the Earth with the Image of God." *Global Missiology* 1.13 (2015). http://ojs.globalmissiology.org/index.php/english/article/viewFile/1817/4025.
Rochette, Bruno. "Language Policies in the Roman Republic and Empire." In *A Companion to the Latin Language*, edited by James Clackson, 549–63. Malden, MA: Wiley-Blackwell, 2011.
Roderick, Brad, and Joseph Gordy. "Every People Group, Every Place: Gospel Proclamation and Disciplemaking to the Ends of the Earth." *The Journal* 6 (2019) 71–82.
Rodriguez, Connie. "The Porticus Vipsania and Contemporary Poetry." *Latomus* 51.1 (1992) 79–93.
Rohan-Csermak, Geza de. "European Peoples and Cultures." In *The New Encyclopaedia Britannica*. Chicago: Encyclopaedia Britannica, 1974.
Roller, Duane W. *Eratosthenes' Geography: Fragments Collected and Translated with Commentary and Additional Material*. Princeton, NJ: Princeton University Press, 2010.
———, trans. *The Geography of Strabo*. Cambridge: Cambridge University Press, 2014.
———. "Introduction." In *The Geography of Strabo*, translated by Duane W. Roller, 1–34. Cambridge: Cambridge University Press, 2014.
Romm, James S. *The Edges of the Earth in Ancient Thought: Geography, Exploration, and Fiction*. Princeton, NJ: Princeton University Press, 1992.
Ross, Allen P. *A Commentary on the Psalms*, vol. 1, *1–41*. Grand Rapids: Kregel Academic, 2011.

———. "שֵׁם." In *NIDOTTE*, 4:147–52.
Rost, Leonhard. "Die Bezeichnungen für Land und Volk im Alten Testament." In *Festschrift Otto Procksch*, 125–48. Leipzig: A. Deichert'sche, 1934.
Rubesh, Ted. "Diaspora Distinctives: The Jewish Diaspora Experience in the Old Testament." In *Diaspora Missiology: Theory, Methodology, and Practice*, edited by Enoch Wan, 53–86. 2nd ed. Portland, OR: Western Seminary, 2011.
Rynkiewich, Michael A. "The World in My Parish: Rethinking the Standard Missiological Model." *Missiology* 30.3 (2002) 301–21.
Sack, Robert David. *Homo Geographicus: A Framework for Action, Awareness, and Moral Concern*. Baltimore, MD: Johns Hopkins University Press, 1997.
Sæbø, Magne. "Zur Traditionsgeschichte von Jesaia 8:9–10." *ZAW* 76.2 (1964) 132–44.
Sailhamer, John H. "Genesis." In *Genesis–Leviticus*, edited by Tremper Longman III and David E. Garland, 1:21–332. EBC. Rev. ed. Grand Rapids: Zondervan, 2008.
———. *The Pentateuch as Narrative: A Biblical-Theological Commentary*. Grand Rapids: Zondervan, 1992.
Salway, Benet. "The Nature and Genesis of the Peutinger Map." *Imago Mundi* 57.2 (2005) 119–35.
Sanders, Guy D. R., Jennifer Palinkas, Ioulia Tzonous-Herbst, and James Herbst. *Ancient Corinth: Site Guide*. 7th ed. Princeton, NJ: American School of Classical Studies at Athens, 2018.
Sapir, Edward. *Selected Writings of Edward Sapir in Language, Culture and Personality*. Edited by David G Mandelbaum. Berkeley: University of California Press, 1963.
Sarna, Nahum M. *Exodus*. JPS Torah Commentary. Philadelphia: Jewish Publication Society, 1991.
———. *Genesis*. JPS Torah Commentary. Philadelphia: Jewish Publication Society, 1989.
Šašel Kos, Marjeta. "Illyricum." In *BNP*, 6:732–35.
Schmidt, Karl Ludwig. "Ἔθνος in the NT." In *TDNT*, 2:369–72. Grand Rapids: Eerdmans, 1976.
———. "Ὁρίζω." In *TDNT*, 5:452–56. Grand Rapids: Eerdmans, 1967.
Schnabel, Eckhard J. *Acts*. Zondervan Exegetical Commentary of the New Testament 5. Grand Rapids: Zondervan, 2012.
———. *Der Brief des Paulus an die Römer: Kapital 6–16*. Witten: SCM R. Brockhaus; Giessen; Brunnen, 2016.
———. *Early Christian Mission*. 2 vols. Downers Grove, IL: InterVarsity; Leicester: Apollos, 2004.
———. "Early Christian Mission and Christian Identity in the Context of the Ethnic, Social, and Political Affiliations in Revelation." In *New Testament Theology in Light of the Church's Mission: Essays in Honor of I. Howard Marshall*, edited by Jon C. Laansma, Grant R. Osborne, and Ray F. Van Neste, 369–86. Eugene, OR: Cascade, 2011.
Schoff, Wilfred H., trans. *Parthian Stations by Isidore of Charax*. Philadelphia: Commercial Museum, 1914.
Schreiner, Patrick James. "People and Place: A Spatial Analysis of the Kingdom in Matthew." PhD diss., Southern Baptist Theological Seminary, 2014.
Schreiner, Thomas R. *Galatians*. Exegetical Commentary on the New Testament. Grand Rapids: Zondervan, 2010.
———. *Romans*. 2nd ed. Baker Exegetical Commentary on the New Testament. Grand Rapids: Baker, 2018.

Schreiter, Robert J. *Constructing Local Theologies*. Maryknoll, NY: Orbis, 1985.

———. *The New Catholicity: Theology between the Global and the Local*. Faith and Culture Series. Maryknoll, NY: Orbis, 2004.

Schwartz, Daniel R. "The End of the Gē (Acts 1:8) Beginning or End of the Christian Vision?" *JBL* 105.4 (1986) 669–76.

Scott, James M. "Geographical Perspectives in Late Antiquity." In *Dictionary of New Testament Background*, edited by Craig A. Evans and Stanley E. Porter, 411–14. Downers Grove, IL: InterVarsity, 2000.

———. *Geography in Early Judaism and Christianity: The Book of Jubilees*. Society for New Testament Studies Monograph Series 113. Cambridge: Cambridge University Press, 2002.

———. "Luke's Geographical Horizon." In *The Book of Acts in Its Graeco-Roman Setting*, edited by David W. J. Gill and Conrad H. Gempf, 2:483–544. Grand Rapids: Eerdmans, 1994.

———. *Paul and the Nations: The Old Testament and Jewish Background of Paul's Mission to the Nations with Special Reference to the Destination of Galatians*. WUNT. Tübingen: Mohr Siebeck, 1995.

Seager, Robin. "The Rise of Pompey." In *The Cambridge Ancient History: Volume IX: The Last Age of the Roman Republic, 146–43 B.C.*, edited by J. A. Crook, Andrew Lintott, and Elizabeth Rawson, 208–28. 2nd ed. Cambridge: Cambridge University Press, 1992.

Shank, Nathan. "Generational Mapping: Tracking Elements of Church Formation within CPM's." *Mission Frontiers* (2012) 26–30.

Shils, Edward. "Political Development in the New States." *Comparative Studies in Society and History* 2.3 (1960) 265–92.

Shipley, Frederick W. *Agrippa's Building Activities in Rome*. Eugene, OR: Wipf & Stock, 2008.

Sider, Robert D., ed. *Collected Works of Erasmus*. Translated by John B. Payne, Robert D. Sider, and Warren S. Smith Jr. Vol. 56. Toronto: University of Toronto Press, 1994.

Silva, Moisés, ed. "Διασπορά." In *New International Dictionary of New Testament Theology and Exegesis*, 1:705–7. 2nd ed. Grand Rapids: Zondervan, 2014.

———, ed. "Ἔθνος." In *New International Dictionary of New Testament Theology and Exegesis*, 2nd ed., 2:89–93. Grand Rapids: Zondervan, 2014.

———, ed. "Λαός." In *New International Dictionary of New Testament Theology and Exegesis*, 2nd ed., 3:88–94. Grand Rapids: Zondervan, 2014.

———, ed. "Ὄχλος." In *New International Dictionary of New Testament Theology and Exegesis*, 2nd ed., 3:581–82. Grand Rapids: Zondervan, 2014.

———, ed. "Πέμπω." In *New International Dictionary of New Testament Theology and Exegesis*, 2nd ed., 3:703–4. Grand Rapids: Zondervan, 2014.

———, ed. "Πληρόω." In *New International Dictionary of New Testament Theology and Exegesis*, 2nd ed., 3:784–93. Grand Rapids: Zondervan, 2014.

———, ed. "Σκορπίζω." In *New International Dictionary of New Testament Theology and Exegesis*, 2nd ed., 4:317–19. Grand Rapids: Zondervan, 2014.

———, ed. "Τόπος." In *New International Dictionary of New Testament Theology and Exegesis*, 2nd ed., 4:499–500. Grand Rapids: Zondervan, 2014.

———, ed. "Φυλή." In *New International Dictionary of New Testament Theology and Exegesis*, 2nd ed., 4:626–29. Grand Rapids: Zondervan, 2014.

———, ed. "Χώρα." In *New International Dictionary of New Testament Theology and Exegesis*, 2nd ed., 4:711–13. Grand Rapids: Zondervan, 2014.

Skehan, Patrick W. "A Fragment of the 'Song of Moses' (Deut. 32) from Qumran." *Bulletin of the American Schools of Oriental Research* 136 (1954) 12–15.
Slack, Jim. "A 'Ta Ethne' Ethnolinguistic People Group Focus as Seen in the Scriptures." Paper presented at the 2003 joint ISFM/EFMA meeting, Norfolk, VA, September 15, 2003.
Smith, Anthony D. *Chosen Peoples*. Oxford: Oxford University Press, 2003.
———. *National Identity*. Reno, NV: University of Nevada Press, 1991.
———. *Nationalism: Theory, Ideology, History*. 2nd ed. Cambridge: Polity, 2010.
———. *Nationalism and Modernism: A Critical Survey of Recent Theories of Nations and Nationalism*. London: Routledge, 1998.
Smith, Gary V. *Isaiah 1–39*. NAC. Ebook ed. Nashville: Broadman & Holman, 2007.
Smithers, Gregory D. *The Cherokee Diaspora: An Indigenous History of Migration, Resettlement, and Identity*. New Haven, CT: Yale University Press, 2015.
Snodgrass, J. "To Teach Others Also: An Apostolic Approach to Theological Education in Pioneer Missions." PhD diss., Southeastern Baptist Theological Seminary, 2017.
Speiser, E. A. *Genesis*. AB1. Garden City, NY: Doubleday, 1964.
———. "'People' and 'Nation' of Israel." *JBL* 79.2 (1960) 157–63.
Stahl, William H. "By Their Maps You Shall Know Them." *Archaeology* 8.3 (1955) 146–55.
Stalin, Joseph. *Marxism and the National Question*. Moscow: Foreign Languages Pub., 1945.
Stenschke, Christoph W. "Paul's Jewish Gospel and the Claims of Rome in Paul's Epistle to the Romans." *Neotestamentica* 46.2 (2012) 338–78.
Stetzer, Ed. *Planting Missional Churches*. Nashville: B&H Academic, 2006.
Stevens, David E. "Does Deuteronomy 32:8 Refer to 'Sons of God' or 'Sons of Israel'?" *BSac* 154:614 (April 1997) 131–41.
Strathmann, H., and R. Meyer. "Λαός." In *TDNT*, 4:29–57.
Strauss, Mark L. *Mark*. Exegetical Commentary on the New Testament. Grand Rapids: Zondervan, 2014.
Stuart, Douglas K. *Exodus*. NAC. Nashville: Broadman & Holman, 2006.
Suetonius. *Lives*. Translated by J. C. Rolfe. 2 vols. Londom: Heinemann; New York: Putnam, 1920.
Swanson, James. "Κύκλῳ." In *Dictionary of Biblical Languages with Semantic Domains: Greek (New Testament)*. Oak Harbor, WA: Logos Research Systems, 1997.
Sweeney, Marvin. *Reading Ezekiel: A Literary and Theological Commentary*. Macon, GA: Smyth & Helwys, 2013.
Syme, Ronald. "Military Geography at Rome." *Classical Antiquity* 7.2 (1988) 227–51.
Talbert, Richard. "Geography." In *BNP*, 5:772–76.
———. "The Roman Worldview: Beyond Recovery?" In *Geography and Ethnography: Perceptions of the World in Pre-Modern Societies*, edited by Kurt A. Raaflaub and Richard J. A. Talbert, 252–72. Malden, MA: Wiley-Blackwell, 2010.
———. *Rome's World: The Peutinger Map Reconsidered*. Cambridge: Cambridge University Press, 2010.
Terry, John Mark, and J. D. Payne. *Developing a Strategy for Missions: A Biblical, Historical, and Cultural Introduction*. Grand Rapids: Baker Academic, 2013.
Thesaurus Linguae Gracae. http://stephanus.tlg.uci.edu.
Thornton, T. C. G. "To the End of the Earth: Acts 1:8." *Expository Times* 89.12 (1978) 374–75.

Tierney, J. J. "The Map of Agrippa." *Proceedings of the Royal Irish Academy. Section C: Archaeology, Celtic Studies, History, Linguistics, Literature* 63 (1962) 151–66.
Tucker, Ruth A. *From Jerusalem to Irian Jaya: A Biographical History of Christian Missions*. 2nd ed. Grand Rapids: Zondervan, 2004.
Tuell, Steven S. "טַבּוּר." In *NIDOTTE* 2:333–34.
———. "תָּוֶךְ." In *NIDOTTE*, 4:279–80.
Unger, Eckhard. "From the Cosmos Picture to the World Map." *Imago Mundi* 2 (1937) 1–7.
Unnik, Willem C. van. "Der Ausdruck Ἕως Ἐσχάτου Τῆς Γῆς (Apostelgeschichte I 8) und sein Alttestamentlicher Hintergrund." In *Sparsa Collecta*, 1:386–401. Leiden: Brill, 1973.
———. "Tarsus or Jerusalem: The City of Paul's Youth." In *Sparsa Collecta*, 1:259–320. Leiden: Brill, 1973.
Vaan, Michiel Arnoud Cor de. *Etymological Dictionary of Latin and the Other Italic Languages*. Leiden Indo-European Etymological Dictionary Series 7. Leiden: Brill, 2008.
Van Dam, Cornelis. "אָבַד." In *NIDOTTE*, 1:223–25.
VanderKam, James C. *The Book of Jubilees*. Guides to Apocrypha and Pseudepigrapha. Sheffield: Sheffield Academic, 2001.
———. *Jubilees: A Commentary on the Book of Jubilees*, vol. 1, *1–21*. Edited by Sidnie White Crawford. Hermeneia. Minneapolis: Fortress, 2018.
Velleius Paterculus. *Compendium of Roman History: Res Gestae Divi Augusti*. Translated by Frederick W. Shipley. LCL. Cambridge, MA: Harvard University Press, 1924.
Vilanova, Evangelista. "The Intercession (1963–1964)." In *History of Vatican II: Volume 3: The Mature Council, Second Period and Intercession, September 1963–September 1964*, edited by Giuseppe Alberigo and Joseph A. Komonchak, 347–490. Maryknoll, NY: Orbis, 2000.
Voelz, James W. *Mark 1:1—8:26*. Concordia Commentary. Saint Louis: Concordia, 2013.
Vogelgesang, Jeffrey Marshall. "The Interpretation of Ezekiel in the Book of Revelation." PhD diss., Harvard University, 1985.
Wallace, Richard, and Wynne Williams. *The Three Worlds of Paul of Tarsus*. London: Routledge, 1998.
Wallis Budge, E. A. *The Book of the Dead*. 2nd ed. London: Routledge & Kegan Paul, 1895.
Walvoord, John F. *The Nations, Israel and the Church in Prophecy*. Grand Rapids: Academie, 1967.
Wan, Enoch. *Diaspora Missiology: Theory, Methodology, and Practice*. 2nd ed. Portland, OR: Western Seminary, 2011.
———. "The Importance and Significance of Missiological Research—Christian Stewardship in Leadership." *Global Missiology* 14.2 (2017). http://ojs.globalmissiology.org/index.php/english/article/view/1953.
———. "Inter-Disciplinary and Integrative Missiological Research: The 'What,' 'Why' and 'How.'" *Global Missiology* 14.4 (2017). http://ojs.globalmissiology.org/index.php/english/article/viewFile/2019/4514.
Watts, John D. W. *Isaiah 1–33*. WBC 24. Waco, TX: Word, 1985.
———. *Isaiah 34–66*. Rev ed. WBC 25. Nashville: Thomas Nelson, 2005.
Wazana, Nili. *All the Boundaries of the Land*. Translated by Liat Qeren. Winona Lake, IN: Eisenbrauns, 2013.

Wenham, Gordon J. *Genesis 1–15*. WBC 1. Waco, TX: Word, 1987.

Westermann, Claus. *Genesis 1–11*. Translated by John J. Scullion. A Continental Commentary. Minneapolis: Fortress, 1994.

Wevers, John William. *Notes on the Greek Text of Exodus*. Atlanta: Scholars, 1990.

"What Is a People Group?" Joshua Project, 2019. https://joshuaproject.net/resources/articles/what_is_a_people_group.

Whiston, William, trans. *The Works of Josephus*. Rev. ed. Peabody, MA: Hendrickson, 1987.

Whybray, Roger Norman. *Isaiah 40–66*. New Century Bible Commentary. Grand Rapids: Eerdmans, 1975.

Wieber, Reinhard. "Marinos von Tyros in der Arabischen Überlieferung." In *Historische Interpretationen: Gerold Walser Zum 75. Geburtstag Dargebracht von Freunden, Kollegen und Schülern*, edited by Marlis Weinmann-Walser, 161–90. Stuttgart: Franz Steiner, 1995.

Wilkes, J. J. "The Danubian and Balkan Provinces." In *The Cambridge Ancient History*, edited by Alan K. Bowman, Edward Champlin, and Andrew Lintott, 10:545–85. 2nd ed. Cambridge: Cambridge University Press, 1996.

Williams, Jarvis J., and Trey Moss. "Focus on 'All Nations' as Integral Component of World Mission Strategy." In *World Mission: Theology, Strategy and Current Issues*, edited by Scott N. Callaham and Will Brooks, 131–48. Bellingham, WA: Lexham, 2019.

Williamson, H. G. M. *A Critical and Exegetical Commentary on Isaiah 1–27*, vol. 2, *Isaiah 6–12*. International Critical Commentary. London: Bloomsbury, 2018.

Winter, Ralph D. "Frontier Mission Vision." In *Seeds of Promise: World Consultation on Frontier Missions, Edinburgh '80*, edited by Allan Starling, 45–99. Pasadena, CA: William Carey Library, 1981.

———. "The Highest Priority: Cross-Cultural Evangelism." In *Let the Earth Hear His Voice: Official Reference Volume, Papers, and Response*, edited by James Dixon Douglas, 213–41. Minneapolis: World Wide, 1975.

———. "The New Macedonia: A Revolutionary New Era in Mission Begins." In *Perspectives on the World Christian Movement: A Reader*, edited by Ralph D. Winter and Steven C. Hawthorne, 347–60. 4th ed. Pasadena, CA: William Carey Library, 2009.

———. *Penetrating the Last Frontiers*. Pasadena, CA: William Carey International University Press, 1978.

Winter, Ralph D., and Bruch A. Koch. "Finishing the Task: The Unreached Peoples Challenge." In *Perspectives on the World Christian Movement: A Reader*, edited by Ralph D. Winter and Steven C. Hawthorne, 531–46. 4th ed. Pasadena, CA: William Carey Library, 2009.

Wolters, Al. "יָעַץ." In *NIDOTTE*, 2:490–92.

Woodward, David. "Medieval Mappaemundi." In *The History of Cartography*, edited by J. B. Harley and David Woodward, 1:286–370. Chicago: University of Chicago Press, 1987.

Wright, Christopher J. H. *Knowing Jesus through the Old Testament*. 2nd ed. Downers Grove: IVP Academic, 2014.

———. *The Message of Ezekiel: A New Heart and a New Spirit*. Downers Grove, IL: IVP Academic, 2001.

———. *The Mission of God: Unlocking the Bible's Grand Narrative*. Downers Grove, IL: IVP Academic, 2006.

———. "אֶרֶץ." In *NIDOTTE*, 1:518–24.
———. "נחל." In *NIDOTTE*, 3:77–81.
Wright, N. T. *Paul: In Fresh Perspective*. Minneapolis: Fortress, 2005.
Wrogemann, Henning. *Intercultural Hermeneutics*. Translated by Karl E. Böhmer. Intercultural Theology 1. Downers Grove, IL: IVP Academic, 2016.
———. *Theologies of Mission*. Translated by Karl E. Böhmer. Intercultural Theology 2. Downers Grove, IL: IVP Academic, 2018.
Xenophon. *Anabasis*. Translated by Carleton L. Brownson and John Dillery. LCL. Cambridge, MA: Harvard University Press, 1998.
Yang Hsu, Becky. "Foreword." In *World Christian Encyclopedia*, by Todd M. Johnson and Gina A. Zurlo, xiv–xv. 3rd ed. Edinburgh: Edinburgh University, 2020.
Yonge, C. D., trans. *The Works of Philo: Complete and Unabridged*. Peabody, MA: Hendrickson, 1993.
Young, Edward J. *The Book of Isaiah: The English Text, with Introduction, Exposition, and Notes*. 2 vols. Grand Rapids: Eerdmans, 1965.
Youngblood, R. F. "Gamaliel." In *The International Standard Bible Encyclopedia*, edited by Geoffrey W. Bromiley, 2:393–94. Rev. ed. Grand Rapids: Eerdmans, 1982.
Zimmerli, Walther. *Ezekiel: A Commentary on the Book of the Prophet Ezekiel*, vol. 1, *Chapters 1–24*. Translated by Ronald E. Clements. Hermeneia. Philadelphia: Fortress, 1979.
———. *Ezekiel: A Commentary on the Book of the Prophet Ezekiel*, vol. 2, *Chapters 25–48*. Translated by James D. Martin. Hermeneia. Philadelphia: Fortress, 1983.
Ziogas, Ioannis. "The Topography of Epic Narrative in Ovid's Metamorphoses." In *Geography, Topography, Landscape: Configurations of Space in Greek and Roman Epic*, edited by Marios Skempis and Ioannis Ziogas, 325–48. Trends in Classics, Supplementary Volume 22. Berlin: De Gruyter, 2014.
Zirkle, Conway. "The Death of Gaius Plinius Secundus (23–79 A.D.)." *Isis* 58.4 (1967) 553–59.
Zunz, Leopold. "Essay on the Geographical Literature of the Jews, from the Remotest Times, to the Year 1841." In *The Itinerary of Rabbi Benjamin of Tudela*, edited by Adolph Asher, translated by Adolph Asher, 2:230–317. New York: Hakesheth, 1841.

Subject Index

Abraham, 19, 56, 82, 130
Abram, 18, 21, 55–56
Acton, Lord, 158
Africa, 4, 8, 20, 26, 76, 79, 82, 89, 132, 156, 170–71
agriculture, 17
Agrippa, Marcus, 77, 86–88
Alexander, Philip S., 19, 25–26, 83–85
Alexander, T. Desmond, 59
Alexandria, 81, 94
Allen, Roland, 7, 12
Amasia, 89
Anatolia, 50, 89, 94
Anaximander, 78
Anderson, Benedict, 164–67, 173
Anthes, Rudolf, 34
anthropology, 6, 10, 107, 159, 173, 190, 196
Antony, Marcus, 101
Appian Road, 67
Arabia, 7, 20–21, 45, 51, 82
Aramaeans, 43
Aramaic, 70–71, 94–95
Aristagoras, 78–79
Aristotle, 65–66, 89, 96
Asia, 4, 26, 78–79, 91, 102, 156
Asia Minor, 20, 82–83, 97

Asia, South, 8, 119, 146, 149
Assyria, 21, 42–47
Assyrians, 29, 42, 46–47
Athenians, 27
Athens, 94
Augustus (Octavian), 77, 86–87, 101

Babylon, 45
Bagehot, Walter, 2, 163
Balakrishnan, Gopal, 166
Barrett, C. K., 59
Barrett, David, 110–15, 133
Barth, Fredrick, 167–68
Bauckham, Richard, 127–28
Bavinck, J. H., 9
Bede, 163
Berghe, Pierre van den, 155
Bevans, Stephen, 137–38
biblical theology, 9, 15, 63, 97, 109, 132, 143, 151, 173, 184, 190, 196
Black Sea, 89
blessing, 16, 19, 32, 37, 49, 134
Block, Daniel, 19, 22, 24, 49–51, 53–54, 56, 83, 108, 189
Bock, Darrell L., 58–59
Boehme, Ron, 5, 134–35
Bowers, William, 96

Brechter, Suso, 137
Breuilly, John, 159
Brewer, Raymond, 70
Briggs, Charles and Emilie, 49
Brighton, Louis, 70
Britain, 75
Brodersen, Kai, 76, 86
Bruce, F. F., 70-71, 92-96
Brueggemann, Walter, 20, 55
Bullinger, E. W., 29
Bultmann, Rudolph, 113
Burusho, 192

Cadiz, 60, 75-76
Caligula, emperor, 98
Carey, William, 146, 161
Carlson, Darren, 6, 142
cartography, 66, 77, 80-81
Caspian Sea, 81
caste, 4, 105-6, 115, 119, 136, 149
Childs, Brevard S., 43, 45
Christidis, A. F. A., 64
Chrysostom, John, 101-2
Clark, Elliot, 6, 142
Clarke, Katherine, 90
Claudius, emperor, 93, 98-99
Claudius Ptolemy, 77, 79-81, 89
Clements, Ronald E., 49
Cleomenes, 78
Columns of Hercules, 76
Connor, Walker, 155
Connors, Catherine, 89
contextualization, 7-8, 105, 152, 164, 190
Corduan, Winfried, 123
Corinth, 84, 100
covenant, 16, 36-38, 52, 54, 127
covenant, ark of, 24
covenant curse, 37, 52, 176
Cranfield, C. E. B., 99
creation, 15-18, 23, 25, 27, 61, 82, 154, 173, 184
Crider, Caleb, 11, 176-77, 181
Crook, J. A., 86-87
Crüsemann, Frank, 19
Cyrus, 48

Dayton, Edward, 3, 108-9, 128

Delitzsch, Franz, 46
Delphi, 85
Demosthenes, 99
Dempster, Stephen G., 18
diaspora, 61, 63, 102, 117, 171-72, 193-96
Dibelius, Martin, 28
Diocletian, emperor, 101
Donaldson, Terence L., 82
Dueck, Daniela, 89-90
Dunn, James, 98-99

earth, ix-x, 8, 15-18, 21, 23, 26-28, 30, 32, 34-35, 44, 46, 55, 67, 78, 80, 82, 84, 89-90, 114, 125, 129, 133, 154, 196
earth, all the, 19, 27, 30-31, 42, 44-46, 49, 127
earth, center of the, 23, 50, 85
earth, ends of, xiii, 42, 47-49, 54, 58-61, 92, 102, 126, 197
earth, the inhabited, 67, 90
earth, families of, 55, 130
economic, 3, 20, 106, 136, 159, 168, 173-75
Eden, 16, 18, 26, 85
Edwards, James, 58
Egypt, 20, 22-23, 29-35, 37-38, 41-42, 45, 50, 52, 77, 82-83
emic, 2, 8, 10, 12-14, 21, 29, 33, 102-4, 106, 109, 131-32, 135-36, 143-54, 157, 159, 161, 163, 166-70, 172-75, 178-83, 185-96
Erasmus, 102
Eratosthenes, 60, 67, 80
Ethiopia, 59, 61, 132
ethnic, 3-5, 7, 9, 11, 20, 25, 57-58, 82, 100, 102, 105-6, 111-12, 114-16, 118, 120-30, 132-33, 148, 155, 167-68, 170-73, 185, 186, 193-94, 196-97
ethnic core, 172-73
ethnic culture areas, 114
ethnic solidarity, 104, 131-33, 142, 168, 186
ethnicity, 1, 5, 11, 21, 25, 57, 83, 108-9, 111-12, 115, 122, 131-33, 144,

Subject Index

147, 149, 153, 156, 165, 179, 186, 189, 192, 196
ethnie, 170–73
ethnocentrism, 179
ethnolinguistic, x, 1, 3–6, 108, 110, 112, 115–16, 119–20, 128–29, 133, 141–42, 172, 186, 194
ethno-symbolism, 154, 167–72, 183, 187
etic, 2, 6, 8, 10, 12–14, 105–6, 117, 132, 140, 144–54, 157, 161, 163, 173–76, 178–83, 187, 195
etymology, 17, 63–64
Euclid, 66
Euripides, 95, 99
Europe, 20, 26, 78–79, 82–83, 114, 157–58, 160–61, 163, 165
Eusebius, 98
Evans, Craig, 95, 99–100

Feldman, Louis H., 84
Fitzmyer, Joseph A., 101
Flemming, Dean, 8
Forbes, Greg W., 57
France, R. T., 68–69
Fredriksen, Paula, 91, 97
forgiveness, 37–39, 57

Galilee, 58–59, 69
Gamaliel, 63, 71, 92
garden, 16, 18, 74, 85
Gaul, 60, 76
Geb, 33–34
Geertz, Clifford, 13, 155–57
Gellner, Ernest, 158–60
geography, border, 24, 76, 181
geography, boundary, 2, 6, 11, 15–16, 21, 23–25, 27–29, 31, 36, 38, 57, 60–61, 67–68, 71, 88, 101, 108, 117–19, 132, 135–36, 151–52, 158, 164, 166–69, 172–73, 175–76, 178, 180–84, 186–88, 192–93, 196–97
geography, center, 11, 65–66, 68–70, 79, 91–92, 118, 168–69, 175–78, 180–83, 187–88, 193
geography, contextual, 2, 14, 91, 61–102 151, 153, 180

geography, Jewish, 18–19, 77, 81–85, 96–97, 102, 185
geopolitical, 2–4, 6–8, 103, 105–6, 111, 114–15, 121–22, 130, 152, 161, 171, 176, 181, 186, 190–91, 196
Geyser, Albert S., 92
Goldsworthy, Adrian, 74
Gordy, Joseph, 141
Goshen, 30, 33
Greek (Hellenistic) geography, 28, 64, 77–81, 84–85, 89–90, 100, 102, 185
Greek language, 20, 63–64, 71, 89, 94–95
Greek literature, 28, 59–60, 64, 70, 73, 99, 111, 185
Grudem, Wayne, 57

Hahn, Ferdinand, 101
Halicarnassus, 79
Ham, 20, 26, 82, 84–85, 151
Hamilton, Victor, 17
Harley, J. B., 7, 62
Hart, George, 34
Hastings, Adrian, 161, 163
Headland, Thomas, 173
Hebrew language, 17, 30, 51, 59, 63, 70–72, 112–13, 123
Hecataeus, 78
Heidegger, Martin, 31
Hengel, Martin, 95
Herod Agrippa I, 83–84, 98
Herodotus, 65, 77–80
Herzl, Theodor, 171
Hezekiah, 47
hidden peoples, 4, 136, 152, 193
Hiebert, Paul, 107, 174, 179–80
Hipparchos, 65
Hispania, 60
Hobbs, T. R., 46
Hobsbawm, E. J., 158–61
Homer, 64–65, 74, 78, 83, 95–96, 99
homogeneous unit, 3, 104–7, 131, 133, 141
Hummel, Horace D., 51

Illyricum, 14, 62, 63–64, 73–74, 76, 92, 95–97, 100–102, 124, 185

Subject Index

incorporability, 130
India, 3–4, 26, 60–61, 105–6, 117, 119, 156, 171, 181
inheritance, 5, 22–23, 25, 85, 133
International Mission Board, 5, 115–18, 194
Isidoros of Charax, 80
Islands of the Blessed, 81
Israel, 20, 22–25, 32–33, 35–39, 42–43, 45, 48, 50, 52–59, 70, 73, 82, 93, 112, 114, 127, 133, 155, 161, 171, 176
Italy, 76

Jacob, Christian, 77, 88
Japhet, Sara, 36–37, 39–41
Japheth, 20–21, 26, 82–85, 151
Jenkins, Orville Boyd, 5, 116, 186
Jerusalem, 14, 29, 36, 39, 41, 45, 49–52, 58–63, 73–74, 76, 85, 91–98, 101–2, 124, 141, 176, 185
Johnson, Todd M., 111
Jones, A. H. M., 136
Jordan, James, 120
Josephus, 84
Joshua Project, 118–20
Judah, 34–35, 39–43
Judea, 58–59, 141
Judson, Adoniram, 150
Julius Caesar, 60, 74–75, 100

Kaiser, Otto, 43, 45
Keener, Craig, 28
Kim, Hyun Chul Paul, 43, 45
kingdom, 40–41, 50, 76, 97, 112, 164
Kissinger, Henry, 157
Köstenberger, Andreas J., 59
Knox, John, 92, 97
Koelsch, William A., 89
Kraft, Charles, 174
Kreitzer, Mark, 131–33, 165–67, 186
Kugel, James L, 84, 151

land, arable, 17, 19
land, people of the, 33, 41–42, 113
lands, x, 7, 18, 20, 26, 29, 35–36, 39–44, 46–47, 49–52, 54, 72, 76, 82, 125, 136
lands, all the, 29, 35–36, 46–47, 53
language, x, 1, 4–5, 7, 11, 18–21, 36, 57, 63, 70–71, 75, 83, 89, 94, 105, 108–10, 114–16, 119, 122–23, 126, 128–29, 131, 144–47, 149–50, 153, 156–57, 159, 161–63, 165–67, 174–75, 178–79, 181–82, 186, 189–90, 192, 194–96
Latin language, 63–64, 73, 102
Latin literature, 63
Latourette, Kenneth Scott, 136
Lausanne, 3–4, 10, 103–4, 106–9, 118–19, 121–22, 128, 133, 135, 141, 172, 185–86, 188–91
Lausanne Working Group, 104, 107, 141
Lebo Hamath, 38
Libya, 26, 79
Lindheim, Sara H., 88
Luther, Martin, 163

McGavran, Donald, 3, 104–7, 133
Mabie, Frederick, 38, 40
map, 7–8, 18, 20, 60, 62, 76–81, 85–88, 90, 98, 117–18, 134, 181–83, 188, 193
mapping, 86, 88, 181, 183, 193
Marinos of Tyre, 80
Marlett, Stephen, 174–75, 180
Martin, Ralph, 137
Mediterranean Sea, 21, 76, 90, 97, 102
Menander, 99
Merkle, Benjamin, 58,
Merrill, Eugene, 36
Mesopotamia, 20, 38, 50, 82
metonymy, 15, 24, 29, 31–44, 46–52, 61, 126, 185
Mill, John Stuart, 158
Mishra, Sudesh, 171–72
missions strategy, x, 2, 4–5, 7–9, 11–14, 102–4, 106, 133, 136, 141–42, 144–45, 147, 149, 151–53, 161, 168, 172, 179–80, 184–86, 188–92, 196
modernism, 154, 157–63, 173
Moo, Douglas J., 93
Morris, Leon, 92
Motyer, J. Alec, 43–44
Mounce, Robert, 70

Subject Index

Mount Vesuvius, 67, 75
Moya, Raphael, 139
Murphy-O'Connor, Jerome, 95, 99

Nanning Covenant, 134
nationalism, 123, 157–58, 160, 163
national identity, 8–9, 11, 13, 15, 19, 21, 25, 27, 29, 39, 46, 53–55, 57, 61, 63, 104, 109, 120, 123, 141, 151, 154, 156–57, 163, 167, 172, 183–85, 187–89, 196
nations, all the, ix–x, 12, 21, 27, 36, 42, 44–49, 55, 57–58, 82, 120, 122, 124, 127, 160–61, 163–64, 195–96
Nazareth, 68–69, 98
Neco, King, 35, 41–42
Nel, Philip, 40
Nepal, 135, 170, 181
Nicolet, Claude, 79, 87–88
Northern Kingdom, 42–43

Olivier, J. P. J., 38
Olley, John W., 51
Oppenheimer, Aharon, 42, 113
Osborne, William, 82
Oswalt, John N., 48
Ottosson, Magnus, 24

Pakistan, 4, 157, 181, 192
Paul, Shalom, 48
Pentateuch, 16, 72
people group, x, 1–6, 8–11, 13–14, 104, 108–10, 115–22, 126, 128, 133–34, 140–42, 147, 149–50, 152, 161, 167, 169, 172, 175–78, 180–83, 187–94, 196
perennialism, 154, 161–64, 173
Persia, 78–79, 81, 101, 136
Peters, George, 11–12
Philippines, 169
Philo, 83–84
Philostratus, 60
phonetics, 145, 167, 174–75, 180
phonology, 175, 180
Pike, Kenneth, 10, 12, 145–49, 174–75, 179–82, 187, 195
Piper, John, 120–28

Platt, David, 140–41
Pliny the Elder, 60, 74–76, 80, 87, 89, 100
Plutarch, 67, 89
Pompeii, 75
Pompey the Great, 60
Porter, Stanley, 91, 97
Porticus Vipsania, 86–87
Pratt, Zane, 140
primordialism, 131, 154–57, 164, 166, 173
Proclus, 67
Project 4K, 5–6, 104, 133–36, 186
Propp, William, 30, 32

Rad, Gerhard von, 16, 18
Rajak, Tessa, 63
Rankin, Jerry, 115, 194
Renan, Ernest, 161–63
Robinson, George, xiii, 17
Roderick, Brad, 141
Rohan-Csermak, Geza de, 114
Roller, Duane, 89
Roman Empire, 63, 75, 87–88, 91, 93, 101–2, 136, 140, 185
romanticism, 157, 162
Rome, 58–61, 63, 74, 76, 83, 87–93, 97–99, 102
Ross, Allen, 35, 49
Rost, Leonhard, 20
Rubesh, Ted, 195

Sack, Robert David, 8
Sailhamer, John, 16–17, 56, 83
Samaria, 58–59
Sapir, Edward, 149, 157, 161
Sarna, Nahum M., 17, 19–20, 33
Šašel Kos, Marjeta, 100
Schmidt, Karl Ludwig, 111, 127
Schnabel, Eckhard, 7, 58, 60, 92–93, 98
Schwartz, Daniel R., 59
Scott, James, 20, 23, 27, 61, 79, 81, 84–85, 95–97, 151
Septuagint (LXX), 22–23, 27–28, 30–31, 43, 46–47, 51–52, 67, 70–73, 95–96, 112, 124, 153
Shem, 20, 26, 82, 84–85, 151
Sherpa, 109, 170

Shipley, Frederick W., 86
Siéyès, Abbé, 154
Silva, Moisés, 112–14
Slack, Jim, 5
Smith, Anthony D., 11, 154–55, 168–73, 183, 187
Smith, Gary V., 44
Smithers, Gregory, 123
Snodgrass, J., 125
social constructionism, 131, 162, 164–67, 173
sociobiology, 155
socioeconomic, 109, 149, 167, 179, 192
sociology, 3, 9–10, 14, 104–5, 107–9, 128, 131, 141, 144, 154, 172–73, 183–85, 187–90, 196
Solinus, Gaius Julius, 76
Spain, 60–61, 64, 76, 89, 91–92, 94, 125
Sparta, 79
Speiser, E. A., 55
Sri Lanka, 76
Stahl, William H., 77, 85
Stalin, Joseph, 159
Stetzer, Ed, 122
Stevens, Daniel, 21
Strabo, 60, 65, 67–68, 75, 77, 80, 86, 89–91, 94–95, 96
Stuart, Douglas, 30

tabernacle, 72–73
Table of Nations, 17–18, 20, 22, 23, 25, 27, 61, 81–84, 95, 97, 124, 131, 151–52, 184
territory, 19–21, 23–26, 28, 31–32, 38, 41, 47, 54, 56–57, 76–77, 85–86, 88, 96, 100, 102, 114, 123, 135, 151–52, 159, 161, 166, 168, 170–72, 175–77, 192

Talbert, Richard, 88
Tarsus, 88, 94–95
temple, 24, 35–36, 38–39, 67, 72–73, 176
Tippett, Allen, 107
Titus, emperor, 84
Thucydides, 78
topography, 11, 24, 77, 114, 176, 178, 183, 187

unimax, 4, 104, 122, 128–30, 142, 186
Unnik, Willem van, 94–95
unreached people groups, x, 5, 9, 14, 140–42

VanderKam, James C., 26–27
Vatican II, 133–34, 136–39
Vespasian, emperor, 84
Voelz, James W., 68–69

Wagner, C. Peter, 128, 133
Walvoord, John, 151–52
Wan, Enoch, 13, 108, 110
Watts, John D., 48
Wazana, Nili, 24, 56
Wenham, Gordon, 16, 21
Westphalia, Treaty of, 157, 161
Williamson, H. G. M., 43
Winter, Ralph, 4, 122, 128–30, 133, 136, 152, 186, 191
Wolters, Al, 44
World Christian Database, 6, 134
Wright, Christopher, 9, 24, 50–52, 55

Young, Edward J., 43, 45, 47

Zunz, Leopold, 18–19

Ancient Document Index

ANCIENT NEAR EASTERN DOCUMENTS

Jubilees

8–9	22, 25–27, 84–85
8:12	26, 85
8:13	26
8:14	26
8:15	26
8:16	26
8:19	23
8:21	26
8:22–23	26
8:25	27
8:26	26
8:27	26
8:29	26
8:30	26
9:2	26
9:3	27
9:4–5	26–27
9:6	26
9:8	26
9:11–12	26
9:14–15	151
9:14	23
9:18	26

OLD TESTAMENT

Genesis

1–11	82
1–10	27
1:1	19–20
1:26	18, 32
1:27	16
1:28	32
2	18, 28
2:4–17	15–19, 184
2:4	13, 27–28
2:7	16–18, 27–28
2:19–20	32
3:19	17
3:23	17
6:2	29
9:2	32
10–11	28
10	18, 22, 25, 28, 77, 81–82, 97, 124
10:1–32	1, 20, 23, 82, 131

Genesis (cont.)

10:1–31	16
10:2–5	20, 82
10:6–20	20, 82
10:10–12	21
10:4	28
10:5	6, 14, 49, 124, 184
10:19	21
10:20	6, 14, 28, 46, 49, 124, 184
10:21–31	20, 82
10:30	21
10:31	6, 14, 28, 49, 124, 184
10:32	28, 82
11:1–9	22
11:1	29
11:9	21
12:1–3	14, 18, 55–57
12:1	19, 21
12:2	55
12:3	49, 123–24, 130
12:6	56
12:8	56
12:9	56
13:14–17	56
15:9–20	54
18:18	124
22:18	124
26:2–5	21
26:4	124
28:13	21
28:14	49, 123
28:25	29
34–35	56
41:30	29
41:48	72
41:57	29
46:26–27	22–23
47:15	29

Exodus

1:5	22–23
7–11	14, 29–34, 37, 185
7:2	30
7:3	30
7:4	30
7:19	30, 32
7:21	30, 32
7:24	32
8:2	31
8:3–4	32
8:5–7	30
8:5–6	31–32
8:13	32
8:14	30
8:16–17	30, 32
8:18	32
8:22	30, 33, 112
8:24–25	30
8:24	32
8:31	32
9:5	30
9:9	30, 32
9:11	32
9:14–16	30
9:22–25	30
9:22	32
9:23–24	32
9:25	32
9:26	30
9:29	30
9:33	30
10:4	31
10:5	30–31
10:12–14	30
10:14	31–32
10:15	30
10:19	31
10:21–22	30, 33
10:23	33
11:3	30
11:4–5	33
11:5–6	30
11:9	30
11:10	30
12:29–30	33
12:30	34
16:13	72
17:6	112
19:5–6	127
19:6	57
20:24	17
21:2–5	36
21:22	42
23:10–11	31
25:10	73

25:23–24		3:37	73
27:17	73	4:32	73
28:28	73	11:31–32	72
28:29–30	73	16:24	72
29:16	73	16:27	72
29:21	73	16:34	72
30:3	73	16:46	36
34:13	54	32:3	72
36:31	73	35:2	72
36:33–34	73	34:4	72
37:18	73	35:26	24
39:9	73		
40:6	73		
40:27	73		

Deuteronomy

2:25	35
4:6	129
9:1	29

Leviticus

1:5	73	12:10	72
1:11	73	12:29	54
3:2	73	17:14	72
3:8	73	19:1–2	14
3:13	73	19:1	54–55
6:32	73	19:13	24
8:15	73	19:14	25, 176
8:19	73	22:19	42
8:24	73	24:2	36
9:12	73	25:19	72
9:18	73	26:19	45
16:18	73	28:17	129
17:6	73	29:12	54
17:10	54	29:14	54
25:1–7	32	30:3–5	52
25:31	72	32	23
25:44	72	32:8–9	24, 133
25:54	36	32:8	1, 14, 16, 21–25, 28, 131, 184
26	32		
26:1–6	32		
26:16	32		

Joshua

26:20	32	8:6	29
26:30	54	13–21	56
26:33–45	52	13–19	176
29:3	54	15:3	71
29:5–6	54	15:10	71
		15:12	72
		16:5	24

Numbers

1:50	72	16:6	71
1:53	72	18:1	176
2:2	72	18:11	24

Joshua (cont.)

18:14	71
19:8	72
19:10	24
20:1–9	176
21:11	72
21:42	72
24:29–33	176
24:33	72

Judges

2:9	24–25
5:7	29
7:18	72
7:21	72
7:29	72
9:48	54
18:31	176

1 Samuel/1 Kingdoms (LXX)

1:3	176
2:33	54
14:21	72
14:29	29
14:47	72
20:31	40
22:19	29
26:5	72

2 Samuel/2 Kingdoms (LXX)

5:9	72
6	176
7:1	72
7:3	72
8:2	29
25:23	29

1 Kings/3 Kingdoms (LXX)

2:12–15	40
2:35	72
6–8	176
9:7	54
15:13	54

2 Kings/4 Kingdoms (LXX)

19:17	46–47
23:35	42
25:1	72
25:4	72

1 Chronicles

1	61
1:10	35
1:19	35
1:43	34
4:33	72
6:55	35, 72
10:9	35
11:8	72
12:24	40
14:17	1, 14, 29, 35–36, 40, 45, 185
16:14	35
16:23	35
16:30	35
16:31	35
16:33	35
17:8	35
17:21	35
17:11	41
21:12	35
21:16	35
29:11	35
29:15	35
29:30	40

2 Chronicles

1:9	35
2:12	35
6	36
6:3–42	38
6:14	35
6:18	35
6:26–28	37
6:33	35
7:8	38
7:13–16	37
7:13	37
7:14	14, 35–39, 112, 185

Ancient Document Index

7:15–16	38
7:17–22	38
9:11	35
9:26	35
11:23	35
14:14	72
15:8	35
16:9	35
17:1	40
17:2	35, 39
17:3	40
17:5	39–40
17:6	39
17:7	39
17:9	39
17:10	35, 39–41, 185
17:11	40
17:12	39–40
17:13	39
17:14	39
17:19	39
17:20	14, 29
19:5	35
20	40
20:3	39
20:4	39
20:5	39
20:13	39
20:15	39
20:17	39
20:18	39
20:22	39
20:24	39
20:27	39
20:29	14, 29, 35, 39–41, 185
20:31	40
20:35	40
32:39	35
34:6	72
36:1	41
36:2–3	41
36:3	14, 29, 35, 41–42, 185

Esther

1:4	40

Job

8:10	36
10:8	72
12:23	29, 151
15:13	36
18:11	72

Psalms

1:24	45
9:8	29
17:12 (LXX)	72
22:27	29, 48–49, 124
22:28	49
25:11–18	38
29:8	29
32:10	71
43:14 (LXX)	72
47:3	45
49:3 (LXX)	72
49:6	71
55:11	71
57:6	45
66:1	29
66:4	29
68:31	29
77:28 (LXX)	72
78:3 (LXX)	72
79:7	29
81:11	112
83:19	45
97:2 (LXX)	72
97:9	45
101:8	54
105:38	29
109:13	54
109:15	54
124:2 (LXX)	72

Proverbs

17:26	42
21:11	42
22:3	42
22:28	176
27:12	42
28:2	29
29:4	131

Isaiah

5:25	44
5:26	48
6	70
6:2	70
6:10	37
8:9	14, 29, 42–44, 185
9:12	44
9:17	44
9:20	44
10:4	44
14	45
14:3–23	45
14:24–27	44
14:24–25	45
14:24	44
14:25	44
14:26–27	44
14:26	14, 29, 42, 44–46, 185
14:28–32	45
14:31	29
15:1—16:12	45
17:1–3	45
17:4–11	45
17:12–14	46
18:1–6	45
19:1–24	45
19:18	20
19:20	47
21:1–10	45
21:11–12	45
21:13–15	45
22:1–14	45
22:15–25	45
23:1–18	45
23:1	29
23:17	48
24–25	46
24:16	48
25:17	45
28:22	45
31:3	45
34:2	45
37:18	1, 14, 29, 42, 46–47, 185
41:1	29
41:9	48
42:10	48
43:3	29
43:6	48
45:1–13	48
45:18–25	48
45:18	48–49
45:22–25	48
45:22	14, 29, 42, 47–49, 185
48:20	36, 48
49:6	48
60:5	93
62:11	48
66:20	93

Jeremiah

1:15	72
1:18	45
3:23	29
4:29	29
5:22	25
6:3	72
9:3	36
11:11	36
12:17	1, 14, 54–55
15:6	45
25:9	72
25:13	45
26:14	72
27:14	72
27:32	72
30:5	72
30:17	37
39:44	72
40:13	72
48:8	29
49:23	29
49:34	40
51:62	54
52:4	72
52:7	72
52:14	72

Ezekiel

1	70
2	125
4:2	72

5:2	72	36:36	72
5:5–7	72	36:19	14, 29, 50, 52–53, 185
5:5–6	14, 29, 49–51, 185		
5:5	50–51, 61	36:24	14, 29, 50, 52–53, 185
5:6	1, 51		
5:7	51	37:24	51
5:14–15	72	38:12	50
6:14	45	40–48	24
8:10	72	40:5	73
11:20	51	40:14	73
12:15	14, 29, 50, 52–53, 185	40:16–17	73
		40:29	73
14:8	54	40:33	73
14:9	45	40:36	73
14:13	45	40:43	73
14:17	54	41:6–8	73
14:19	54	41:10	73
14:21	54	41:16–17	73
16:57	72	42:17	72
18:9	51	42:20	73
18:17	51	43:20	73
18:21	51	44:24	51
20:11	51	46:23	73
20:13	51	47:15	24
20:16	51	47:17	24
20:19	51	48:1	24
20:21	51		
20:23	14, 29, 50, 52–53, 185	**Daniel**	
		5:25–30	29
20:24	51	7:7	72
22:15	14, 29, 50, 52–53, 185	7:12	72
		9:19	38
23:24	72		
25:7	45	**Hosea**	
25:13	45	4:6	112
25:16	45	5:10	176
27:11	72	5:13	37
29:7	54	6:1	37
29:12	14, 29, 50, 52–53, 185		
29:13	54	**Amos**	
30:26	14, 29, 50, 52–53, 185	2:3	54
31:4	72	**Obadiah**	
35:3	45	1:15	45
36:3	72		

Micah

1:4	29
2:8	112
6:9	30

Zephaniah

1:4	45
2:13	45

Zechariah

7:14	45
12:2	72
14:9	45

Malachi

2:12	54

APOCRYPHA

2 Esdras

15:17	72
16:16	72

Judith

1:2	72
15:3	72

Baruch

2:4	72

1 Maccabees

1:4	47
1:11	72
1:31	72
1:54	72
3:23	72
5:10	72
5:38	72
5:57	72
7:17	72
10:84	72
12:13	72
12:53	72
14:36	72

2 Maccabees

4:32	72

Psalms of Solomon

8:16	60

NEW TESTAMENT

Matthew

3:5	30
4:23	112
5:13	30
11:21	30
11:23	30
	21:43
23:37	30
24:14	129
26:5	112
27:64	112
28:18–20	58, 126–27
28:19	105, 121, 124, 127

Mark

1:5	30
1:33	30
3:31	68
3:32	68
3:34	68
6:6	68–69
6:36	68–69

Luke

5:29	113
9:12	68
9:51	59
10:2	17
13:33	59
18:31	59
24:1–11	59
24:36–49	59
24:47	1, 14, 57–61

John

1:10	30
3:16–17	30
6:33	30
7:7	30
7:49	113
11:52	125
18:33–36	111–12
19:17	30
19:31	30
20:21	58
27:21	30

Acts

1:7	164
1:8	1, 14, 28, 54, 57–61, 92, 126, 141
2:5–11	28
2:10	98
6:7	113
7:2–53	28
8:9	153
8:25	30
8:26–39	59
9:26	92
13:14	93
14:1	93
15:4	92
16:37–38	77
17:2	93
17:10	93
17:26–27	133
17:26	14, 16, 27–29, 131, 185
18:4	93
18:22	92
19:21	58–59
21:15–18	92
21:39	94
22:2–3	63
22:3	63
22:25–29	77
23:11	58–59
23:26	77
27	59
28	59

Romans

1:8	94
1:11	94
1:16	7, 100
10:14–15	134
13:1	29
15:9–12	97
15:18–24	125
15:18–21	124–25
15:19	1, 7, 14, 58, 62–64, 66, 68, 70, 73, 75, 77, 91–98, 100–102, 124, 153, 185
15:22–24	94
15:23–24	125
15:23	125
15:24	91
15:28	91
15:26	30

1 Corinthians

9:22	91
11:32	30
12:2	123, 153
16:1	7, 62
16:2	62

2 Corinthians

1:1	62
2:2	7
5:19	30
9:2	7, 62
11:9	7, 62

Galatians

1:6	94
1:14	71
4:21–31	96
4:25	7, 62
4:26	96

Ephesians

1:1	7, 62

Philippians

1:1	7, 62
3:15	70
4:14	7, 62

Colossians

1:1	7, 62
4:15	7, 62

1 Thessalonians

1:7–8	7, 62
2:1	7, 62
3:1	7, 62

1 Timothy

1:3	7, 62

2 Timothy

1:15	7, 62
1:17–18	7, 62
3:11	7, 62
4:10	7, 62
4:12	7, 62
4:20	7, 62

Titus

1:5	7, 62
3:12	7, 62

1 Peter

2:9	54, 57–61

1 John

2:2	30
3:1	30
5:19	30

Revelation

4:6	68–70
5:9–10	127
5:9	110, 126–27, 130
5:11	68–70
7:4–8	114
7:9	110, 114
7:11	68, 70
10:11	110, 130
13:7	110
14:6	110
17:15	110, 113
19:16	57
21–22	1
22:2	127

DEAD SEA SCROLLS

4QDeut	22
1QIsaa	46

RABBINIC WRITINGS

Tg. Ps.-J.	22–23

GRECO-ROMAN WRITINGS

Appian, *Bell. civ.*

5.65	101

Appian, *Mithrid.*

101	96

Aritstotle, *Cael.*

268b	66

Aristotle, *Hist. an.*

572b	66
621a	66

Aristotle, *Pol.*

1324b10	111

Caesar, *Bell. gal.*

1.21	75
1.41	74
2.29	75
2.30	75

5:13	75
5.42	75
7.45–46	74
7.69	75
7.83	75

Caesar, *Bell. civ.*

1.59	74
1.61	74
1.63–64	74
1.68	74
2.24	74
3.30	74
3.41	74
3.44–45	75
3.63	75

Columella, *Rust.*

5.6.15	74
8.15.3–4	74

Diogenes Laertius, *Vit.*

2.1.1–2	78

Frontinus, *Stratagems*

1.1.16	74

Herodotus, *Hist.*

2.53	65
3.159–60	79
4.37–58	79
4.42	78
4.45	79
5.49–51	78
5.52–54	78

Homer, *Il.*

18.395–409	78
18.505	65

Homer, *Od.*

8.279	65
20.65	78

Josephus, *Ant.*

1.121–47	84

Lucan, *Pharsalia*

3.454	60

Philo, *Legat.*

250	96
281	84

Philostratus, *Vit. Appol.*

6.1	

Pliny the Elder, *Nat.*

P.13	75
2.167	60, 76
3.17	86–87
6.81	76
9.106	76

Plutarch, *Num.*

16.1	28

Seneca the Younger, *De remediis Fortuitorum*

1.3	74

Strabo, *Geog.*

1.1.1	90
1.1.2	65, 89
1.1.16	90
1.1.23	89
1.4.6	89
2.1.1	60
2.3.5	66
2.5.17	86
3.1.4	60, 90
3.1.8	60
5.3.7	68
5.3.12	66
5.4.8	68
6.2.6	90
6.2.7	68

Strabo, *Geog.* (cont.)

7.1.4	90
7.5.2–3	100
8.6.23	100
10.5.3	90
12.6.2	90
13.1.7	96
14.5.13–15	70
14.5.13	94
17.1.5	68
17.1.19	96
17.1.44	90
17.3.1–23	90
17.3.24	90

Suetonius, *Claud.*

25.3–4	98

Xenophon, *Anab.*

7.1.14	96

Res gest. divi Aug.

30	101

EARLY CHRISTIAN WRITINGS

Clement of Alexandria, *Stromata*

7.2	23

Eusebius, *Eusebi Chronicorum Liber Prior*

	98

Orosius, *Historiarum adversum paganos*

7.6	98

Pseudo-Dionysus, *On the Heavenly Hierarchy*

9.3	22

NPNF1

11.544	102